Hermann Jacobi

The Ayaramga Sutta of the Cvetambara Jains

Vol. I

Hermann Jacobi

The Ayaramga Sutta of the Cvetambara Jains
Vol. I

ISBN/EAN: 9783348014687

Printed in Europe, USA, Canada, Australia, Japan

Cover: Foto ©Lupo / pixelio.de

More available books at **www.hansebooks.com**

THE

ÂYÂRAṂGA SUTTA

OF

THE ÇVETÂMBARA JAINS.

EDITED BY

HERMANN JACOBI.

PART I.—TEXT.

LONDON:
PUBLISHED FOR THE PALI TEXT SOCIETY,
BY HENRY FROWDE,
OXFORD UNIVERSITY PRESS WAREHOUSE, 7, PATERNOSTER ROW.

1882.

HERTFORD:

PRINTED BY STEPHEN AUSTIN AND SONS.

PREFACE.

THE insertion of a Jaina text in the publications of the Pâli Text Society will require no justification in the eyes of European scholars. For them all Jaina documents would have an interest of their own, even if they did not throw a light on the times, or the moral and intellectual world, in which Buddha lived. But it is possible that Buddhist subscribers, who aid our labours by their accession to the Pâli Text Society, and by the interest they show in it, might take umbrage at the intrusion, as it were, of an heretical guest into the company of their sacred Suttas. Yet if they look him attentively in the face, they will find there many traces that will interest them strongly, though they may not come to like them. The Nigaṇṭha Nâtaputta was, it is true, an opponent, if not an enemy, of Gotama the Buddha. Still he was one of his contemporaries; and in the writings handed down amongst his successors and followers there are treated many of those questions and topics for which the superior genius of Buddha found the solutions which still form the tenets of the Buddhist Saṃgha in Burma, Siam, and Ceylon. Besides this, though the Piṭakas frequently mention the Nigaṇṭhas, yet they do not clearly describe the institutes and tenets of that sect, which played so conspicuous a part during the times of the early rise of Buddhism. A Buddhist

Bhikkhu therefore will gladly avail himself of an opportunity of studying them in one of their own books. For it is generally and justly considered incumbent on an enlightened divine to make himself acquainted with the dogmas and writings of a hostile sect, while we pity and disdain the narrow-minded fanatic who ignores, yet despises, the works of his opponents. I hope, therefore, that our subscribers in Ceylon will not think this edition of the Âcârâṅga Sûtra an unwelcome gift, but rather look upon it, as indeed it really is, as a thing of which they will be able to make good use.

I now proceed to give an outline of the Grammar of Jaina Prâkṛit by comparing it with Pâli. My remarks are only intended to assist Pâli students in their first attempt to read a Jaina book, and they have no claim to any other merit beyond their practical usefulness.

The Jaina Prâkṛit is an old Indian dialect nearly related to, but decidedly more modern than, Pâli. The vowels are, on the whole, the same in both languages. They are: *a â i î u û e o;* there are no real diphthongs, but each vowel forms a syllable, thus *vayai* is pronounced *va-ya-i.* Note the following differences: 1) The Prâkṛit has frequently *i* for Pâli *a* when derived from Sanskṛit *ṛi,* e.g. *giha=gaha, giṇhati ganhati, alaṃkiya alaṃkata, ukkiṭṭha ukkaṭṭha, kapaṇa kivaṇa, hidaya hadaya,* etc. 2) In final syllables *o* is frequently represented by *e* in Prâkṛit; *dhamme=dhammo, ne no, ahe adho;* in the middle of words: *kareti=karoti, suṇeti sunoti.* 3) Final vowels are sometimes lengthened or nasalized: *teṇaṃ=tena, tehiṃ tehi, vayaî vadati, gacchejjâ gaccheyya*; in the latter case the short vowel is retained when disjunctive *vâ* follows, e.g. *nikkhamejja vâ pavisejja vâ;* and the anusvâra is dropped before the same particle and before *ya=ca*: *devehi ya devîhi ya.* 4) The law of position that a short vowel before two consonants is equivalent to a long one before one consonant, and that a long vowel cannot be followed by more than one consonant, is observed in both languages, the latter clause even more strictly in Prâkṛit than in Pâli, where *âkhyâta, brâhmaṇa* occur, which in Prâkṛit become *akkhâta, bamhaṇa.* The former part of our rule occasions different spellings of the same word in both languages, e.g. *âtâ=attâ, pâta=patta*, or even in Prâkṛit itself: *âtâ*, but acc. *attâṇaṃ*.

The consonants in Prâkṛit differ more widely from those of the sister idiom, especially if single between two vowels. In that position *k g c j t d p* (*b*) *v* are most frequently dropped or, before *a â*, replaced by euphonic *y*; witness *loo=loko, miya miga, loyaṇa locaṇa, gae gajo, kayaṃ kataṃ, hiyaya hadaya, niuṇa nipuṇa, niyattai nivattati. y* is retained only before *a â*. The surds *k kh t th* are rarely replaced by the corresponding mediae *g gh d dh*, while *ṭ ṭh p* are generally changed into *ḍ ḍh v*, e.g. *ege=eke, âghâti akkhâti, pâda* (*pâta*) *patta, tadhâ tathâ, mauḍa makuṭa, paḍhama paṭhama, lavai lapati. ḷ* is replaced by *l*, and *ḷh* by *ḍh*: *talâga=taḷâka, daḍha daḷha; n* by *ṇ, maṇo=mano. kh gh th dh* (*ph*) *bh* are generally changed to *h*: *sâhâ sâkhâ, dîha dîgha, tahâ tathâ, vaha vadha; loha lobha*; but *bh* is not unfrequently retained: *lâbha*.

As regards compound consonants, Prâkṛit avoids even more than Pâli to join two consonants of different classes, except *n ṇ m* with *h, brâhmaṇa* becomes *bamhaṇa* or *mâhaṇa, vyâkaraṇa vâgaraṇa, mayhaṃ majjhaṃ, âkhyâta akkhâta*, etc. It substitutes *nn* for *ññ, vv* for *bb, jj* for *yy*: *anna añña, savva sabba, kajjati kayyati*. Initial *ñ* is changed to *n, y* to *j*: *nâta ñâta, jahâ yathâ*.

Prâkṛit has lost little or nothing of the copiousness and variety of declensional forms preserved in Pâli. I subjoin the paradigms of the principal declensions in both languages.

	Prâkṛit.	Pâli.
	SINGULAR.	
Nom.	*dhamme*,[1] *dhammo*	*dhammo*
Voc.	*dhammâ*	*dhamma*, °*â*
Acc.	*dhammaṃ*	*dhammaṃ*
Inst.	*dhammeṇaṃ*, °*eṇa*	*dhammena*
Dat.	*dhammâya*, °*âe*	*dhammâya*
Abl.	*dhammâ*, °*âo* (*ato*)	*dhammâ*, °*asmâ*, °*amhâ*
Gen.	*dhammassa*	*dhammassa*
Loc.	*dhamme*, °*aṃsi*, °*ammi*	*dhamme*, °*asmiṃ*, °*amhi*.

	Prâkṛit.	Pâli.
	PLURAL.	
Nom. Voc.	*dhammâ*	*dhammâ*
Acc.	*dhamme*	*dhamme*
Instr.	*dhammehiṃ, °ehi*	*dhammebhi, °ehi*
Abl.	*dhammehiṃto*	„
Gen. (Dat.)	*dhammâṇaṃ*	*dhammânaṃ*
Loc.	*dhammesu*	*dhammesu*

Neuter nouns make in Nom. Voc. Acc.:

Sing.	*phalaṃ, phale*	*phalaṃ*
Plur.	*phalâṇi, phalâiṃ, phalâ*	*phalâni, phalâ*

Feminine nouns in *â î û*.

	Prâkṛit.	Pâli.		Prâkṛit.	Pâli.
	SINGULAR.			PLURAL.	
Nom.	*kannâ*	*kaññâ*		*kannâo, °â*	*kaññâ, °âo*
Voc.	*kanne*	*kaññe*		„	„
Acc.	*kannaṃ*	*kaññam*		„	„
Inst. Gen. Dat. Loc.	*kannâe*	*kaññâya*	I. Ab.	*kannâhiṃ, °hi*	*kaññabhi, °hi*
Loc.	„	*kaññâyam*	G. D.	*kannâṇaṃ, °ṇa*	*kaññânaṃ*
Abl.	*kannâto*	*kaññâya*	Loc.	*kannâsu*	*kaññâsu*
Nom. Voc.	*devî, râî*	*devî, ratti*		*devîo, °î*	*deviyo devî*
Acc.	*deviṃ*	*deviṃ*		„	„
I. D. G. L.	*devîe*	*deviyâ*	I. Ab.	*devîhiṃ, °hi*	*devîbhi, °hi*
Loc.	„	*deviyaṃ*	D. G.	*devîṇaṃ, °ṇa*	*devînaṃ*
Abl.	*devîto*	—	L.	*devîsu*	*devîsu.*

Masculine nouns in *i u*.

	Prâkṛit.		Pâli.	
	SINGULAR.			
N.V.	*aggî*	*bhikkhû*	*aggi*	*bhikkhu*
A.	*aggiṃ*	*bhikkhuṃ*	*aggiṃ*	*bhikkhuṃ*
I.	*aggiṇâ*	*bhikkhuṇâ*	*aggiṇâ*	*bhikkhunâ*
Gen.	*aggiṇo, °issa*	*bhikkhuṇo, °ussa*	*aggino, °issa*	*bhikkhuno, °ussa*
L.	*aggiṃsi, °mhi,* *bhikkhuṃsi, °mhi*		*aggismiṃ, °mhi* *bhikkhusmiṃ, °mhi*	

PLURAL.

N. V. A.	*aggî* / *aggiṇo*	*bhikkhû* / *bhikkharo*, °*are*	*aggî* / *aggayo*	*bhikkhû* / *bhikkharo*
I. Ab.	*aggîhiṃ*, °*hi*	*bhikkhûhiṃ*, °*hi*	*aggîbhi*, °*hi*	*bhikkhûbhi*, °*hi*
G. D.	*aggîṇaṃ*, °*ṇa*	*bhikkhûṇaṃ*, °*ṇa*	*aggînaṃ*	*bhikkhûnaṃ*
L.	*aggîsu*	*bhikkhûsu*	*aggîsu*	*bhikkhûsu*.

NEUTER.

Sing. N.V.A.	*sappiṃ*	*madhuṃ*	*sappi*	*madhu*
Plur. ,,	*sappîṇi*, °*îiṃ*	*madhûṇi*, °*ûiṃ*	*sappî*, °*îni*	*madhû*, °*ûni*.

Bases ending in Sanskṛit in consonants have retained only some of the original forms, the rest being formed from bases ending in vowels, e.g. *râyâ* = *râjâ*, Acc. *râyaṃ*, Instr. *rannâ*, Gen. *ranno*. Plur. *râyâṇo*, Inst. *râîhiṃ*, Gen. *râîṇaṃ*.

âyâ = *attâ*, Acc. *âyâṇaṃ*, *attâṇaṃ*, *appâṇaṃ*, Inst. *appaṇâ*, *appâṇeṇaṃ*, Gen. *appaṇo*.

bhagavaṃ = *bhagavâ*, Acc. *bhagavaṃ*, *bhagavaṃtaṃ*, Inst. *bhagavatâ*, Gen. *bhagavato*, Inst. *bhagavati*. Pl. Nom. *bhagavaṃto*. The other forms from base *bhagavaṃta*. Notice the Voc. *âuso* and *âusaṃto*.

pitâ, *mâtâ*, Acc. *pitaraṃ*, *mâtaraṃ*. Pl. *pitaro*, *mâtaro*. The other forms from *piu*, *mâû* (or in Inst. Plur. from *piî*, *mâî*).

Pronouns and Adjectives are declined like nouns in *a*, *â*, except in the following cases: Sing. Abl. masc. *tamhâ* (Gen. fem. *tîse*). Plur. Nom. masc. *te*, Gen. masc. *tesiṃ* (fem. *tâsiṃ*).

Of the personal pronoun I have found the following forms:

ahaṃ, Acc. *mamaṃ*, Inst. *mae*, *me*, Gen. Dat. *mama*, *mamaṃ*, *mahaṃ*, *me*, Loc. *maî*.

tumaṃ, Acc. *tumaṃ*, Inst. *tume*, *te*, Gen. Dat. *tava*, *tubbhaṃ*, *te*, Loc. *tumaṃsi*.

amhe, *vayaṃ*, Inst. *amhehiṃ*, Gen. Dat. *amhâṇaṃ*, *amhaṃ*, *ne*.

tumhe, *tubbhe*, Inst. *tubbhehiṃ*, Gen. Dat. *tumhaṃ bhe*.

The numerals are: 1 *ege ekke*, 2 *duve donni*, 3 *tao tinni*, 4 *cattâri*, 5 *paṃca*, 6 *cha*, 7 *satta*, 8 *aṭṭha*, 9 *nava*, 10 *dasa*, 11 *ekârasa*, 12 *duvâlasa*, *bâraha*, 13 *terasa*, 14 *cauddasa*, *coddasa* etc., 20 *vîsaṃ* °*â*, 30 *tîsaṃ* °*â*, 40 *cattâlîsaṃ* °*â*, 50 *pannâsaṃ*, 60 *saṭṭhi*, 70 *sattari*, 80 *asîti*, 90 *nauya*, 100 *saya*, 1000 *sahassa*, 100,000 *lakkha*, 100 *lakkha* = *koḍi*, *koḍi* + *koḍi* = *koḍâkoḍi*.

The numerals 2–19 make the Inst. Gen. Loc. by adding *hi(ṃ)*, *ṇha(ṃ)*, *su* to the bases *do*, *ti*, *cau*, *paṃca*, etc. 20, etc. have in Inst. Gen. Loc. *vîsâe*, etc.

The ordinals: 1 *paḍhama*, 2 *docca bitiya bîya*, 3 *tacca tatiya*, 4 *cauttha*, 5 *paṃcama*, 6 *chaṭṭha*, 7 *sattama*, 8 *aṭṭhama*, 9 *navama*, 10 *dasama etc.*, 20 *vîsaima*, 30 *tîsaima tîsa* etc.

The conjugational forms in Prâkṛit have been considerably reduced, even if compared with those in Pâli. In some tenses the third persons of the singular and plural only seem to be used.

As regards the verbal bases, little difference exists between Prâkṛit and Pâli except those occasioned by the above phonetical laws of the former. Observe that verbs of the 5th class (*svâdi*) and *kar* take *e* instead of *o*: *suṇeti*, *kareti*, and that the *â* of the 9th class (*kiyâdi*) is generally shortened, *jâṇati*.

The Attanopadam is nearly disused, rests are: *seve*, *sevate*, *sevaṃte*. The Parassapadam is also used in the Passive (*bhâve*).

The Present (vattamânâ).

gacchâmi	*gacchâmo* (Pâli *gacchâma*)
gacchasi	*gacchaha* (Pâli *gacchatha*)
gacchati, °*aî*	*gacchaṃti*.

Thus *suṇemi*, *kahemi*, etc.

Imperative (pañcamî).

gacchâmi	*gacchâmo*
gaccha, *gacchâhi*, °*ahi*	*gacchaha*, °*hâ*
gacchatu	*gacchaṃtu*

The regular form of the Optative (sattamî) ends in *ejjâ*, and properly belongs to the 3rd person sing. *gacchejjâ*; 2nd person *gacchejjâsi* (?). Another frequent form of the 3rd person ends in *e*, *gacche*, etc., while that in *iyâ* is used of a few verbs: *jâṇiya*, *haṇiyâ*, *siyâ*. Notice also *hŏjjâ*, *kujjâ*, *bûyâ*.

The three persons of the Imperfect (hîyattanî) or Aorist (ajjattanî) end in *itthâ* and *iṃsu*: Sing. *gacchitthâ*, Plur. *gacchiṃsu* (*karĕtthâ*, *kareṃsu*). Notice *hotthâ*, *âhu*, *âhaṃsu*. Irregular are the following forms: 1st person Sing. *akarissaṃ*, *akâsî*; 3rd person Sing. *âsî*, *âsi*, *bhuvi*, *kare*, *pucche*; *akâsî*, *acârî*, *addakkhu*, *ahesî*, *vadâsî*.

The Future (bhavissantî), as in Pâli, usually takes *issa* and conjugates like the present, *gacchissâmi, gacchissâmo* etc. Other forms are: *bokkhâmi, vocchâmi, dâsâmi; dâhâmi, dâhisi, dâhiti; kâhisi, kâhiti* (*kar*), *pajâhisi, pajâhiti.* All these forms occur in Pâli too.

The Perfect (parokkhâ) and Conditional (kâlâtipatti) are lost in Prâkṛit.

The Passive is formed by *ijja* and conjugated like the present, e.g. *bujjhijjati.* Other forms of the Passive add *ya* to the root, and assimilate the two consonants as in Pâli: *vuccati, dissati, dajjati, katthati, hammati* (= *haññate*), *chijjati, tappati, kîrati* and *kajjati, gheppati,* etc.

The Causative (kârita) is formed by adding to the root,

1. *aya*, e.g. *padisaṃvedayati, dalayati.*
2. *e*, e.g. *kâreti, khâmeti, vedeti.*
3. *âve*, e.g. *kârâveti, khamâveti, kiṇâveti, dâveti, ṭhaveti, ṭhâveti.*

The present and future participles are formed as in Pâli by adding *aṃt* resp. *aṃta* or *mâṇa* to the bases of those tenses: *gacchaṃ*, Acc. *gacchaṃtaṃ*; *gacchissaṃ*; *gacchamâṇa, gacchissamâṇa.* Notice *samâṇa* and *saṃta* from root *as.*

The past passive participle is formed by adding *ta, na* or *ita* to the root: *diṭṭha mutta litta* etc., *bhinna juṇṇa* (=*jiṇṇa*), *kârita.* All these forms are almost identical with the same in Pâli.

The future passive participles are formed by adding *tavva* (*itavva*), *aṇijja, ya* to the root, just as *tabba, anîya, ya* in Pâli: *vattava, karaṇijja, vacca.*

The indeclinable past participle has a great variety of forms. The root is compounded with (1) *tâ* or *tâ ṇaṃ*: *maṃtâ* or *mattâ, chittâ,* etc. To this (?) formation belong: *naccâ*=*ñatvâ, soccâ* = *sutvâ, hiccâ* = *hitvâ.* (2) *ittâ* or *ittâ ṇaṃ*: *gacchittâ, uvagacchittâ* (*ṇaṃ*). (3) *tu*: *kaṭṭu âhaṭṭu, nimakkhu*; *tuṃ*: *laddhuṃ,* and *tûṇa*: *viyattûṇa* from *vat.* (4) *ittu*: *jâṇittu, vijahittu.* (5) *ya* or *e*: *âdâya, âdâe*; *nisamma, sammuddissa, samârabbha, âsajja, parigijjha* (*samecca atiyacca*). (6) *iya*: *dâliya, chiṃdiya, pâsiya, vigiṃciya, visohiya. Aṇuvîi* from *aṇu vi ciṃtiya* (?).

The infinitive takes *tuṃ, uṃ, ituṃ* or *tae, ittae* after the root *khaṃtuṃ, pâuṃ, jîvituṃ*; *bhattae, pâyae, gacchittae.*

To illustrate the above remarks on the Prâkṛit language I subjoin a Pâli translation of the beginning of the Âcârâṅga Sûtra: sutaṃ mayâ âvuso tena bhagavatâ evaṃ akkhâtaṃ: iha ekesaṃ no saññâ bhavati, taṃ yathâ: puratthimâya disâya âgato ahaṃ asmi, dakkhiṇâya vâ disâya âgato ahaṃ asmi pacchimâya vâ disâya âgato ahaṃ asmi, uttarâya vâ disâya âgato ahaṃ asmi, uddhâya vâ disâya âgato ahaṃ asmi, adhodisâya vâ âgato ahaṃ asmi, aññatarâya vâ disâya anudisâya vâ âgato ahaṃ asmi; evaṃ ekesaṃ no ñâtaṃ bhavati: atthi me attâ opapâtiko, natthi me attâ opapâtiko, ko ahaṃ âsiṃ, ko vâ ito cuto peccâ bhavissâmi, aduṃ yaṃ puna jâneyya sahasammutiyâ paravyâkaraṇena vâ aññesaṃ vâ antike sutvâ, taṃ yathâ, etc.

This edition of the Âcârâṅga Sûtra is based on two very good and old MSS.

A a MS. on palm-leaves containing the text and the Commentary of Çîlâṅka. It has been fully described in Dr. Bühler's Report on Sanskrit MSS., 1872–73, p. 4. The date at the end is Saṃvat 1348, being equal to 1292 A.D.

B a MS. on paper, 37 leaves, 15 lines, Saṃvat 1498 or 1442 A.D. It is accordingly just 150 years younger than A. Berlin Collection MSS. or. fol. 643. Besides these MSS. I have inspected, and occasionally consulted, three MSS. of my collection and some more of that of Berlin, all of which are considerably younger than AB. As all MSS. contain the same text, viz. that on which Çîlâṅka commented (Çaka 798 or 876 A.D.), and which can be almost verbally reconstructed from his commentary, and as the difference between them relates only to spelling and abbreviations, not to mention clerical mistakes, I thought myself justified to dispense with comparing these MSS. throughout and noting their irrelevant various readings.

As regards the orthographical questions I can briefly refer the reader to my remarks on that point in the "Zeitschrift der Deutschen Morgenländischen Gesellschaft," v. 34, 180 ffl.

There is little hope to find a self-consistent system of orthography even in the oldest MSS.; for inconsistency in spelling is probably as old as Jaina writing. The differences between our two MSS. are chiefly the following:—

1) A more generally retains the original consonant between two vowels, while B prefers a substitute (resp. a *luk* or blank) allowed by the laws of Jaina Prâkṛit. Not to extend unduly the various readings by noting every single case of difference, yet to show as much as possible the actual state of the MSS., the consonants which are retained only in one MS. are printed in italics, *e.g.* vadati is printed 'vadati' if both MSS. read thus, but 'va*d*a*t*i,' if A or B has vayai. An italicized *h* indicates that B has *dh*.

2) B has in the greater part of the work no *yaçruti* after *i*, *î*, *u*, *û*, *e*, *o*. We have, in this regard, followed the not quite uniform practice of A.

3) B prefers *i* and *u* before two consonants, while A has *e* and *o*. Where both MSS. differ, a semicircle is added to *e* and *o*, viz. *ĕ*, *ŏ*.

It must be mentioned that both MSS. are equally inconsistent in the choice between the lingual and dental nasals when initial or doubled. We have adopted the lingual only where the Sanskrit prototype has it.

Another help for my labours was the Calcutta edition of the Âcârâṅga, together with Pârçvacandra's Bâlâvabodha or Guzerati Gloss, Jinahaṃsasûri's Dîpikâ, Çîlâṅka's Ṭîkâ and Bhadrabâhu's Niryukti (Calcutta Saṃ. 1935). This edition is of the ordinary stamp of native publications, which generally have about the same value as a corrected MS. In the present instance, the practice of not separating the Prâkṛit words, nor visibly marking the end of sentences, even of lessons and lectures, renders the book rather inconvenient for our use. Nevertheless this edition is more convenient than MSS.; I have therefore constantly used it. Occasionally noted various readings from the text of this edition, which nearly agrees with that of A, even in minor details, are marked C.

The division of my text into paragraphs is partly my own

work. In the first Çrutaskandha a paragraph generally represents the parts into which the author of the Dîpikâ has divided his texts, while in the second Çrutaskandha I have deviated from Jinahaṃsasûri's practice in order not to introduce paragraphs of too great or unequal length.

The numbers on the margin refer to the pages of the Calcutta edition. They will make it easier to identify passages and to find out where they are treated in the commentaries. The spaced passages in the first Çrutaskandha are fragments of trishṭubh and anushṭubh verses. A great number of passages which might have been single pâdas of a çloka are not made visible to the eye, because they may only accidentally resemble a pâda. The very loose metrical laws of the çloka make it unsafe to recognize smaller parts than half a çloka. Sometimes half a çloka or a trishṭubh are printed in a separate line. In all these cases the commentators treat these passages as prose, as they also sometimes do regarding whole verses.

The second part of this work will contain a glossary of the more important and difficult words together with their Sanskrit prototypes and the explanations or definitions of the commentators.

My thanks are due to Dr. Rost, Librarian of the India Office Library; K. M. Chatfield, Director of Public Instruction, Bombay; and Professor Dr. Lepsius, Chief Librarian of the Royal Library at Berlin; who have most liberally and readily provided me with the materials necessary for preparing the text of this edition and the translation of it which will shortly appear in the "Sacred Books of the East."

H. Jacobi.

Münster, Westphalia,
December, 1882.

PAḌHAME SUYAKKHAṂDHE.

PAḌHAMAṂ AJJHAYAṆAṂ.

SATTHAPARINNÂ.

Suyaṃ me, âusaṃ! teṇa bhagavayâ evam akkhâyaṃ: iham egesiṃ no sannâ bhavati; ||1|| taṃ jahâ: puratthimâo vâ disâo âgao aham aṃsi, dâhiṇâo vâ disâo âgao aham aṃsi, paccatthimâo vâ disâo âgao aham aṃsi, uttarâo vâ disâo âgao aham aṃsi, uḍḍhâo vâ disâo âgao aham aṃsi, ahedisâo vâ âgao aham aṃsi, anna*t*arîo vâ disâo vâ aṇudisâo vâ âgao aham aṃsi. evam egesiṃ[1] no nâ*t*aṃ bhava*t*i: ||2|| atthi me âyâ ovavâie, n' atthi me âyâ ovavâie,[2] ke aham[3] âsî, ke vâ io cue[4] pĕccâ bhavissâmi?[4] ||3|| se jaṃ puṇa jâṇĕjjâ saha-sammudiyâe[5] paravâgaraṇeṇaṃ annesiṃ[6] vâ aṃtie[6] sŏccâ, taṃ jahâ: puratthimâo vâ disâo âgao aham aṃsi *jâva*[8] anna-tarîo[6] vâ disâo vâ aṇudisâo vâ âgao aham aṃsi; evam egesiṃ[1] nâ*t*aṃ bhavati: atthi me âyâ ovavâie, jo imâo disâo aṇudisâo aṇusaṃcarai, savvâo disâo, savvâo aṇudisâo,[9] so 'haṃ. ||4|| se âyâvâî loyâvâî[10] kammâvâî[11] kiriyâvâî: akarissaṃ[12] c' ahaṃ, kârâvissaṃ[13] c' ahaṃ karao yâvi samaṇunne bhavissâmi;[4] eyâvaṃti[14] savvâvaṃti[14] logaṃsi kammasamârambhâ parijâ-ṇiyavvâ bhavaṃti. ||5|| aparinnâyakammo khalu ayaṃ purise, jo imâo disâo aṇudisâo vâ aṇusaṃcarai, savvâo disâo aṇudisâo sahe*t*i, aṇegarûvâo joṇîo saṃdhei, virûvarûve phâse ya paḍi-saṃveei.[15] ||6|| tattha khalu bhagava*t*â parinnâ[6] paveiyâ: imassa c' eva jîviyassa parivaṃdaṇamâṇaṇapûyaṇâe jâi-[16] maraṇamoyaṇâe dukkhaparighâyaheuṃ eyâvaṃti[14] savvâ-vaṃti[14] logaṃsi[10] kammasamârambhâ parijâṇiyavvâ bha-

[1] A ekesiṃ. [2] A from n' i. marg. [3] B ṃ. [4] A °o. [5] B sahasammaie. [6] A ṇṇ. [7] A om. [8] B evaṃ dâhiṇâo vâ puratthimâo vâ, etc. [9] B adds vâ. [10] A lok. [11] B kaṃma. [12] B °uṃ. [13] B °ravesuṃ. [14] B °î. [15] A °vetai. [16] A jâî.

vaṃti. jass' e*t*e kammasamâraṃbhâ parinnâyâ[6] bhavaṃti, se hu muṇî parinnâya[6]-kamme[17] tti[18] bemi. || 7 || **1** ||

padhamo uddesao.

aṭṭe loe parijuṇṇe[1] dussaṃbohe avi*j*âṇae, assiṃ loe pavvahie
29 tattha tattha puḍho pâsa[2] âturâ pari*t*âvĕṃti. || 1 || saṃti pâṇâ puḍho siyâ, lajjamâṇâ puḍho pâsa; aṇagârâ 'mŏ tti ege pavayamâṇâ, jam iṇaṃ virûvarûvehiṃ satthehiṃ puḍhavikammasamâraṃbheṇaṃ[3] puḍhavisatthaṃ samâraṃbhamâṇe[4] aṇegarûve pâṇe vihiṃsai. || 2 || tattha khalu bhagavayâ parinnâ[1] paveiyâ: imassa c' eva jîviyassa parivaṃdaṇamâṇaṇapûyaṇâe jâimaraṇamoyaṇâe[5] dukkhaparighâyaheuṃ se sayam eva puḍhavisatthaṃ samâraṃbha*t*i, annehiṃ[1] vâ samâraṃbhâvei,
31 anne[6] vâ puḍhavisatthaṃ samâraṃbhaṃte[7] samaṇujâṇai. || 3 || taṃ se ahiyâe, taṃ abohîe; se taṃ saṃbujjhamâṇe âyâṇîyaṃ samuṭṭhâe[8] soccâ[9] khalu[10] bhagavao aṇagârâṇaṃ (vâ aṃtie),[7] iham egesiṃ nâyaṃ[11] bhavati: esa khalu gaṃthe, esa khalu mohe, esa khalu mâre, esa khalu narae, icc atthaṃ gaḍhie loe, jam iṇaṃ virûvarûvehiṃ[12] satthehiṃ[12] puḍhavikammasamâraṃbheṇaṃ puḍhavisatthaṃ samâraṃbhamâṇe anne[1] aṇegarûve pâṇe vihiṃsai. se bemi. || 4 ||

app ege aṃdham[13] abbhe, app ege aṃdham[13] acche; app ege pâyam abbhe, app ege pâyam acche; app ege guppham[14]
33 abbhe, (app ege guppham acche);[15] app ege jaṃgham abbhe 2; app ege jâṇum abbhe 2; app ege ûrum abbhe 2; app ege kaḍim abbhe 2; app ege nâbhim[11] abbhe 2; app ege udaram[16] abbhe 2; app[17] ege piṭṭhim abbhe 2; app ege pâsam abbhe 2; app ege uram abbhe 2; app ege hiyam abbhe 2; app ege thaṇam abbhe 2; app ege khaṃdham abbhe 2; app ege bâhum abbhe 2; app ege hattham abbhe 2; app ege aṃgulim abbhe 2; app ege naham[11] abbhe 2; app ege gîvam abbhe 2; app ege haṇum[18] abbhe 2; app ege huṭṭham[19] abbhe 2; app ege daṃtam abbhe 2; app ege jibbham abbhe 2; app ege tâlum abbhe 2; app ege galam

[17] B kaṃmi. [18] A ti.

[1] A ṇṇ, B nn. [2] A pâse. [3] B ṃm. [4] A °bhe mâṇâ. [5] A jâî. [6] A °siṃ, cf. 1. [7] A om. [8] B âya. [9] B su°. [10] B om. [11] A n. [12] A °esu. [13] A andham. [14] A gupphagam. [15] B 2. [16] B uy°. [17] A after the following phrase. [18] B °uam. [19] A ha°.

abbhe 2; app ege gaṃḍam abbhe 2; app ege kaṇṇam[1] abbhe 2; app ege nâsam[11] abbhe 2; app ege acchim abbhe 2; app ege bhamuham[20] abbhe 2; app ege nilâḍam abbhe 2; app ege 34
sîsam abbhe 2; app ege saṃpamârae, app ege uddavae. ‖5‖ ĕttha satthaṃ samâraṃbhamâṇassa icc ete samâraṃbhâ aparinnâyâ[1] bhavaṃti. ĕttha[21] satthaṃ asamâraṃbhamâṇassa icc ete samâraṃbhâ parinnâyâ[1] bhavaṃti. taṃ parinnâya[1] mehâvî n[11] eva sayaṃ puḍhavisatthaṃ samâraṃbhĕjjâ, n[11] eva annehiṃ[1] puḍhavisatthaṃ samâraṃbhâvĕjjâ,[22] anne[1] puḍhavisatthaṃ samâraṃbhaṃte na samaṇujâṇĕjjâ. jass' ete puḍhavikammasamâraṃbhâ parinnâyâ[1] bhavaṃti, se hu muṇî parinnâyakamme[1] tti[23] bemi. ‖6‖**2**‖

biio uddesao.

se bemi,[1] jahâ: aṇagâre ujjukaḍe niyâga[2]-paḍivanne[3] amâ- 36
yaṃ kuvvamâṇe viyâhie. ‖1‖ jâe saddhâe nikkhaṃto, tâm eva aṇupâlijjâ[4] viyahittu[5] visŏttiyaṃ [puvvasaṃjogaṃ[6] pâṭhântaraṃ] paṇayâ vîrâ mahâvîhiṃ logaṃ ca âṇâe ahisamĕcca[7] akutobhayaṃ se bemi. ‖2‖ n[8] eva sayaṃ logaṃ abbhâikkhĕjjâ, n[8] eva attâṇaṃ abbhâikkhĕjjâ; je logaṃ[9] abbhâikkhai, se attâṇaṃ abbhâikkhai; je attâṇaṃ abbhâikkhai, se logaṃ[9] abbhâikkhai. ‖3‖ lajjamâṇâ puḍho pâsa, aṇagârâ 'mu tti ege[10] pavayamâṇâ, jam iṇaṃ virûvarû- 42
vehiṃ satthehiṃ udayakammasamâraṃbheṇa udayasatthaṃ samâraṃbhamâṇâ[11] anne[12] aṇegarûve pâṇe vihiṃsaṃti. ‖4‖ tattha khalu bhagavayâ parinnâ[12] paveiyâ: imassa c' eva jîviyassa parivaṃdaṇamâṇaṇapûyaṇâe jâimaraṇamoyaṇâe[13] dukkhaparighâyaheuṃ se sayam eva udayasatthaṃ samâraṃbhati, annehiṃ[12] vâ udayasatthaṃ samâraṃbhâveti, anne[12] vâ udayasatthaṃ samâraṃbhaṃte samaṇujâṇati. ‖5‖ taṃ se ahiyâe[13] se abohîe se taṃ saṃbujjhamâṇe etc. [*all* 43
down to: vihiṃsai. se bemi **2**, 4: *substitute only* udaya *for* puḍhavi]. ‖6‖ saṃti pâṇâ udayanissiyâ jîvâ aṇege,[14] ihaṃ ca khalu bho aṇagârâṇaṃ udayaṃ jîvâ viyâhiyâ. satthaṃ

[20] B °him. [21] B itthaṃ. [22] A adds ṇeva. [23] A ti.

[1] B adds se. [2] A °ya; pâṭhântara nikâya = moksha (niyâga = yajña). [3] A pari, cf. **2.** [1]. [4] A °liyâ. [5] B vijahittâ. [6] A °yo°. [7] B abhi°. [8] cf. **2.** [11]. [9] A loy°. [10] A eke. [11] AB °ṇe. [12] cf. **2.** [1]. [13] cf. **2**, [5]. [13] B *om. all down to* virûva. [41] B °yâ.

46 c' ettha aṇuvîi pâsa puḍho[15] sattham paveiyaṃ.[16] aduvâ
adinnâdâṇaṃ.[12] kappai ṇo[17] kappai no[17] pâuṃ aduvâ[18] vibhûsâe.
puḍho satthehiṃ viuṭṭaṃti. ĕttha vi tesiṃ no[8] nikaraṇâe.[8]
ĕttha satthaṃ samâraṃbhamâṇassa icc ee âraṃbhâ aparinnâyâ[12] bhavaṃti. ĕttha satthaṃ asamâraṃbhamâṇassa
icc ee âraṃbhâ parinnâyâ[12] bhavaṃti. ‖7‖ taṃ parinnâya[12]
mehâvî n[8] eva sayaṃ udayasatthaṃ samâraṃbhĕjjâ, n[8] ev'
49 annehiṃ[12] udayasatthaṃ samâraṃbhâvĕjjâ etc. [*all as in* **2**, 6
down to the end; substitute only udaya *for* puḍhavi]. ‖8‖**3**‖

taio uddesao.

se bemi: n' eva sayaṃ logaṃ[1] abbhâikkhĕjjâ, n' eva attâṇaṃ abbhâikkhĕjjâ: je logaṃ[1] abbhâikkhai, se attâṇaṃ abbhâikkhai; je attâṇaṃ abbhâikkhai, se logaṃ abbhâikkhai.[2] ‖1‖
je dîhalogasatthassa kheyanne, se asatthassa kheyanne; je
asatthassa kheyanne,[3] se dîhalogasatthassa kheyanne. ‖2‖
vîrehiṃ eyaṃ abhibhûya diṭṭhaṃ saṃjatehiṃ sayâ
55 jaehiṃ sayâ appamattehiṃ. je pamatte guṇaṭṭhî,[4] se daṃḍe
pavuccai. taṃ parinnâya[3] mehâvî: iyâṇiṃ no,[5] jam ahaṃ
puvvam akâsî pamâeṇaṃ. ‖3‖ lajjamâṇâ puḍho pâsa [*all as
in* **2**, 2–4 *down to* vihiṃsai ti bemi, *substitute only* agaṇi *for*
57 puḍhavi]. ‖4 and 5‖ saṃti pâṇâ puḍhavinissiyâ[5] taṇanissiyâ[8]
pattanissiyâ[5] kaṭṭhanissiyâ[8] gomayanissiyâ[5] kayavaranissiyâ,[5]
saṃti saṃpâtimâ pâṇâ âhacca saṃpayaṃti, agaṇiṃ ca khalu
puṭṭhâ ege saṃghâyam âvajjaṃti. je taṭṭha saṃghâyam
âvajjaṃti, te tattha pariyâvajjaṃti;[6] je tattha pariyâvajjaṃti,[6]
te tattha uddâyanti.[7] ‖6‖ ĕttha satthaṃ[8] samâraṃbhamâṇassa icc ee âraṃbhâ aparinnâyâ[3] bhavaṃti; ĕttha satthaṃ
asamâraṃbhamâṇassa icc ee âraṃbhâ parinnâyâ bhavaṃti.
59 taṃ parinnâya mehâvî n' eva sayaṃ [*all as in* **2**, 6 *down to
the end.* agaṇi *for* puḍhavi]. ‖7‖**4**‖

cauttho uddesao.

tan[1] no karissâmi samuṭṭhâe[2] mattâ maimaṃ abhayaṃ

[15] pâṭhântaraṃ: puḍho 'pâsaṃ paveditaṃ. [16] A °veti°. [17] A ṇe, B ṇo. [18] B ahavâ.

[1] A loy°. [2] B adds ti. [3] cf. **2**. [1]. [4] B °ṭṭhie. [5] cf. **2**. [11]. [6] A °vi°. [7] B °ṃti. C ḍḍ. [8] A om.

[1] B taṃ. [2] B °âya.

viditâ. taṃ je no karae, eso 'varae; ĕttho[3] 'varae, esa
aṇagâre tti pavuccati. ‖1‖ je guṇe, se âvaṭṭe; je âvaṭṭe, se
guṇe. uḍḍhaṃ adhaṃ tiriyaṃ pâîṇaṃ pâsamâṇe rûvâiṃ
pâsati, suṇamâṇe saddâiṃ suṇeti.[4] ‖2‖ uḍḍhaṃ adhaṃ tiri- 68
yaṃ pâîṇaṃ mucchamâṇe rûvesu mucchati saddesu yâvi.[5]
esa loe[6] viyâhie, ĕttha agutte aṇâṇâe puṇo puṇo guṇâsâe
vaṃkasamâyâre matte agâram[7] âvase. ‖3‖

lajjamâṇâ puḍho pâsa aṇagârâ 'mŏ tti ege pavayamâṇâ,
jam iṇaṃ virûvarûvehiṃ satthehiṃ vaṇassaikammasamâraṃ-
bheṇaṃ vaṇassaisatthaṃ samârambhamâṇe anne[8] aṇega[9]-
pâṇe vihiṃsati. ‖4‖ tattha khalu etc. (*all as in* **2**, 3, 4 70
down to vihiṃsati se bemi. vaṇassai *for* puḍhavi). ‖5‖

imaṃ pi jâidhammayaṃ,[10] eyaṃ pi jâidhammayaṃ;[10]
imaṃ pi vuḍḍhidhammayaṃ, eyaṃ pi vuḍḍhidhammayaṃ;
imaṃ pi cittamaṃtayaṃ, eyaṃ pi cittamaṃtayaṃ; imaṃ pi
chinnaṃ milâi, eyaṃ pi chinnaṃ milâi; imaṃ pi âhâragaṃ,
eyaṃ pi âhâragaṃ; imaṃ pi aṇiccayaṃ, (eyaṃ pi aṇiccayaṃ; imaṃ pi asâsayaṃ),[11] eyaṃ pi asâsayaṃ; imaṃ pi
cayâvacaiyaṃ, eyaṃ pi cayâvacaiyaṃ; imaṃ pi vipariṇâmadhammayaṃ, eyaṃ pi vipariṇâmadhammayaṃ. ‖6‖

ĕttha satthaṃ samârambhamâṇassa etc. [*all as in* **2**, 6 73
down to the end. vaṇassai *for* puḍhavi]. ‖7‖**5**‖

paṃcamo uddesao.

se bemi. saṃt' ime tasâ pâṇâ; taṃ jahâ: aṃḍayâ, poyayâ,
jarâuyâ, rasayâ, saṃseyayâ, sammucchimâ,[1] ubbhiyâ, ovavâiyâ. 78
esa saṃsâre tti pavuccati ‖1‖ maṃdassa[2] aviyâṇao. nijjhâ-
ittâ paḍilehittâ patteyaṃ parinivvâṇaṃ savvesiṃ pâṇâṇaṃ,
savvesiṃ bhûyâṇaṃ, savvesiṃ jîvâṇaṃ, savvesiṃ sattâṇaṃ,
asâyaṃ[3] aparinivvâṇaṃ[4] mahabbhayaṃ dukkhaṃ ti bemi
tasaṃti pâṇâ padiso disâsu ya. tattha tattha puḍho
pâsa âurâ pariyâveṃti.[5] ‖2‖ saṃti pâṇâ puḍho siyâ, lajjamâṇâ puḍho pâsa aṇagârâ mŏ tti ege pavayamâṇâ, jam iṇaṃ
virûvarûvehiṃ satthehiṃ tasakâyasamârambheṇaṃ tasakâya- 81
satthaṃ samârambhamâṇe anne aṇegarûve pâṇe vihiṃsati. ‖3‖

[3] B itth. [4] B °ai. [5] AB âvi. [6] B loge. [7] gâram. [8] cf. **2**. [1]. [9] A vaṇ° or caṇ. [10] B ṇım. [11] A om (—).

[1] B °iyâ. [3] B maṃdassâvi°. [3] A ass. [4] A °nevv. [5] B aṃti.

[*all as in* **2**, 3, 4 *down to* vihiṃsati. se bemi. tasakâya *for*
puḍhavi]. ‖4‖
app ege accâe haṇaṃti, app ege ajiṇâe vahaṃti, app[6] ege[6]
maṃsâe vahaṃti, app[6] ege[6] soṇiyâe vahaṃti,[7] evaṃ hidayâe[8]
pittâe vasâe picchâe pucchâe vâlâe siṃgâe visâṇâe daṃtâe
dâḍhâe nahâe ṇhâruṇîe aṭṭhîe[9] aṭṭhimiṃjâe[10] aṭṭhâe[11]
82 aṇaṭṭhâe. app ege hiṃsiṃsu me tti vâ, app ege hiṃsaṃti
me[7] tti vâ, app ege hiṃsissaṃti me[7] tti vâ vahaṃti. ‖5‖
ĕttha satthaṃ samârambhamâṇassa icc *ete* ârambhâ etc.
[*all as in* **2**, 6 *down to the end.* tasakâya *for* puḍhavi]. ‖6‖**6**‖
chaṭṭho uddesao.

83 pahû ejassa[1] duguṃchaṇâe[2] âyaṃkadaṃsî[3] ahiyaṃ ti
naccâ. je ajjhatthaṃ jâṇai, se bahiyâ jâṇai; je bahiyâ
jâṇai, se ajjhatthaṃ jâṇai. *etaṃ* tulam annesiṃ. saṃtigayâ
daviyâ nâ[4] 'vakaṃkhaṃti jîvituṃ. ‖1‖ lajjamâṇâ puḍho pâsa
aṇagârâ mŏ tti ege pavayamâṇâ, jam iṇaṃ virûvarûvehiṃ
satthehiṃ vâukammasamârambheṇa vâusatthaṃ samârambha-
mâṇâ anne aṇegarûve[5] pâṇe vihiṃsaṃti ‖2‖ etc. [*all as in*
88 **2**, 3, 4 *down to* vihiṃsati. se bemi. vâukâya *for* puḍhavi]. ‖3‖
saṃti saṃpâimâ pâṇâ âhacca saṃpayaṃti ya pharisaṃ[6] ca
khalu puṭṭhâ ege saṃghâyam âvajjaṃti; je tattha saṃghâyam âvajjaṃti, te tattha pariyâvajjaṃti;[7] je tattha pariyâvajjaṃti,[8] te tattha uddâyaṃti. ‖4‖
ĕttha[9] satthaṃ samârambhamâṇassa icc *ete* ârambhâ etc.
89 [*all as in* **2**, 6 *down to the end.* vâukâya *for* puḍhavi.] ‖5‖
itthaṃ[10] pi jâṇa uvâdîyamâṇâ, je âyâre na[4] ramaṃti;
ârambhamâṇâ viṇayaṃ vayaṃti chaṃdovaṇîyâ[12] ajjhovavannâ[13] ârambhasattâ pakareṃti saṃgaṃ. se vasumaṃ savvasamannâgayapannâṇeṇaṃ[13] appâṇeṇaṃ karaṇijjaṃ
91 pâvaṃ kammaṃ tan[14] no annesiṃ. ‖6‖ taṃ parinnâya[13] mehâvî n' eva sayaṃ chajjîvanikâyasatthaṃ samârambhejjâ etc. [*all
as in* **2**, 6 *down to the end.* chajjîvanikâya *for* puḍhavi]. ‖7‖**7**‖
sattamo uddesao.

padhamam ajjhayaṇaṃ.

satthaparinnâ samattâ.

[6] B evaṃ. [7] B om. [8] B hiyâe. [9] B °ie. [10] A aṭṭhamimjjhâe. [11] A om.
[1] pâṭhântaram: pahuya egassa. [2] A °gaṃ°. [3] B dîsaṃ. [4] A ṇ, B n.
[5] A v'aṇ. [6] A par°. [7] A corr °vijj°. [8] B °vijj°. [9] B ittha. [10] A e°. [11] A °e.
[12] A viṇîyâ. [13] cf. **2**.[1]. [14] B om.

BIIYAM AJJHAYAṆAṂ.

LOGAVIJAO.

je guṇe, se mûlaṭṭhâṇe; je mûlaṭṭhâṇe, se guṇe. iya[1] se
guṇaṭṭhî mahayâ pariyâveṇa vase[2] pamatte; taṃ jahâ:
mâyâ me, pi*t*â me, bhâyâ me, bha*g*iṇî me, bhajjâ me, puttâ
me, dhû*t*â me, suṇhâ me, sahisayaṇasaṃgaṃthasaṃthuyâ[3]
me, vicittovagaraṇa[4]-pariyaṭṭaṇabhoyaṇacchâyaṇaṃ[5] me—icc 108
atthaṃ gaḍhie loe vase pamatte aho ya râo paritappamâṇe
kâlâkâlasamuṭṭhâî saṃjogaṭṭhî aṭṭhâlobhî âlumpe sahasâkâre
viṇiviṭṭhacitte ĕttha satthe puṇo puṇo. ‖1‖ appaṃ ca khalu
âuṃ iham egesiṃ mâṇavâṇaṃ; taṃ jahâ: soyaparinnâṇehiṃ
parihâyamâṇehiṃ, cakkhuparinnâṇehiṃ parihâyamâṇehiṃ,
ghâṇaparinnâṇehiṃ parihâyamâṇehiṃ, rasa[6]-parinnâṇehiṃ
parihâyamâṇehiṃ, phâsaparinnâṇehiṃ parihâyamâṇehiṃ 112
abhikkaṃtaṃ vayaṃ sa pehâe, ta*t*o se egayâ mûḍhabhâvaṃ
jaṇayaṃti; jehiṃ vâ saddhiṃ saṃvasa*t*i, te vâ[7] ṇaṃ egadâ
niyagâ[8] puvviṃ parivayaṃti, so vâ te niyage[9] pacchâ parivaĕjjâ. nâ[8] 'laṃ te tava tâṇâe vâ saraṇâe vâ, tumaṃ pi
tesiṃ nâ 'laṃ tâṇâe vâ saraṇâe vâ. ‖2‖ se na[8] hassâe,[10] na[8]
kiḍḍâe, na ra*t*îe, na vibhûsâe.[11] icc evaṃ samuṭṭhie aho
vihârâe aṃtaraṃ ca khalu imaṃ sa pehâe dhîre muhuttam
avi no pamâyae. vao acce*t*i, jovvaṇaṃ ca jîvi*t*e. iha je[12] pa- 117
mattâ, se haṃtâ, chĕttâ, bhĕttâ, lumpittâ, uddavittâ, uttâsaittâ,
akaḍaṃ karissâmi tti mannamâṇe; jehiṃ vâ saddhiṃ saṃvasa*t*i, te vâ[7] ṇaṃ egayâ niyagâ puvviṃ posaṃti, so vâ te
niyage pacchâ posĕjjâ. nâ'lam te tava tâṇâe vâ saraṇâe vâ,
tumaṃ pi tesiṃ nâ'laṃ tâṇâe vâ saraṇâe vâ. ‖3‖ uvâ*d*î*t*a[13]-
seseṇa vâ saṃnihi[8]-saṃnicao kajjai[14] iham egesiṃ asaṃjayâ-
ṇaṃ[15] bhoyaṇâe. ta*t*o se egayâ rogasamuppâyâ samuppa-

[1] A iti. [2] A saṃvase. [3] A om. sahi. [4] A pak°. [5] B °ṇaach°. [6] B rasaṇa.
[7] A vă. [8] A ṇ, B n. [9] A ṇigae. [10] B hâsâe. [11] A vihûs°. [12] B je ihaṃ.
[13] B uvâiya. [14] A kk. [15] B mâṇavâṇaṃ.

jjaṃti; jehiṃ[16] vâ saddhiṃ saṃvasa*t*i, te vâ[7] ṇaṃ egayâ
119 niyagâ puvviṃ pariharaṃti, so vâ te niyage[9] pacchâ pariharĕjjâ. nâ'laṃ te tava tâṇâe vâ saraṇâe vâ, tumaṃ pi tesiṃ
nâ 'laṃ tâṇâe vâ saraṇâe vâ. ||4|| jâṇittu dukkhaṃ patte-
yaṃ[17] sâyaṃ, aṇabhikkaṃtaṃ[18] ca khalu vayaṃ sa pehâe,
khaṇaṃ jâṇâhi paṃḍie jâva soya[19]-parinnâṇehiṃ[20] aparihâyamâṇehiṃ,[20] jâva[3] nĕttaparinnâṇehiṃ[20] aparihâyamâṇehiṃ,[20] jâva[3] ghâṇaparinnâṇehiṃ[20] aparihâyamâṇehiṃ,[20] jâva[3]
rasa[21]-parinnâṇehiṃ[20] aparihâyamâṇehiṃ,[20] jâva[3] phâsa[22]-
121 parinnâṇehiṃ[20] aparihâyamâṇehiṃ:[20] icc e*t*ehiṃ virûvarûvehiṃ parinnâṇehiṃ aparihâyamâṇehiṃ[23] âyaṭṭhaṃ sammaṃ
samaṇuvâsĕjjâ si tti bemi. ||5||**1**||

padhamo uddesao.

ara*t*iṃ âuṭṭe se mehâvî, khaṇaṃsi mukke. aṇâṇâe puṭṭhâ
vi ege niyaṭṭaṃti maṃdâ moheṇa pâuḍâ. 'apariggahâ bhavissâmo' samuṭṭhâe[1] laddhe kâme abhigâha*t*i. aṇâṇâe muṇiṇo paḍilehaṃti; ettha[2] mohe puṇo puṇo sannâ no havvâe no
pârâe. vimukkâ hu te jaṇâ, je jaṇâ pâragâmiṇo. lobhaṃ
126 alobheṇa duguṃchamâṇâ laddhe kâme nâ[3] 'bhigâha*t*i. viṇâ
vi[4] lobhaṃ nikkhamma esa akamme jâṇai pâsai, paḍilehâe
nâ 'vakaṃkha*t*i, esa aṇâgârĕ tti pavucca*t*i. ||1|| aho ya râo
paritappamâṇe kâlâkâlasamuṭṭhâî aṭṭhâlobhî âlumpe sahasâkâre viṇiviṭṭhacitte ĕttha satthe puṇo puṇo. se âyabale, se[5]
nâibale,[5] se[6] mittabale, se pĕccabale, se devabale, se râyabale, se
corabale, se atihibale, se kivaṇabale,[7] se samaṇabale. ||2|| icc
128 e*t*ehiṃ virûvarûvehiṃ kajjehiṃ daṃḍasamâ*d*âṇaṃ saṃpehâe
bhayâ kajjai pâvamŏkkhŏ tti mannamâṇe, aduvâ âsaṃsâe.
taṃ parinnâya mehâvî n' eva sayaṃ e*t*ehiṃ kajjehiṃ daṃḍaṃ
samâraṃbhĕjjâ, n' ev' annaṃ[8] e*t*ehiṃ kajjehiṃ daṃḍaṃ samâraṃbhâvĕjjâ,[9] n' ev' annaṃ eehiṃ kajjehiṃ daṃḍaṃ samâ-
raṃbhaṃtaṃ samaṇujâṇĕjjâ. esa magge âriehiṃ pave*d*ie,
jah' ĕttha kusale no 'valiṃpijjâ[10] si tti bemi. ||3||**2**||

biio uddesao.

[16] A. jesiṃ. [17] A patteya. [18] A aṇati°, B °ika°. [19] A sotta, B soa.
[20] B °ṇâparihîṇâ. [21] B jîha. [22] B phâsu. [23] B aparihîṇehiṃ.

[1] B °âya. [2] AB ittha. [3] A ṇo. [4] pâṭhântaram: viṇaittu, AC. [5] A om.
[6] B adds se sayaṇabale. [7] A kip. [8] B anne. [9] B eehiṃ k. d. samâraṃbhaṃte
anne vi na s. [10] A vi°.

se asaiṃ[1] uccâgoe, asaiṃ[2] nîyâgoe, no hîṇe, no airitte, no pîhae.[3] iya[4] saṃkhâe[5] ke goyâvâî, ke mâṇâvâî, kaṃsi vâ 132
ege gijjhe? ‖1‖

tamhâ paṃḍie no harise, no kujjhe.[6] bhû*t*ehiṃ jâṇa paḍileha sâyaṃ samie[7] eyâṇupassî; taṃ jahâ: aṃdhattaṃ, bahirattaṃ, mûyattaṃ, kâṇattaṃ, kuṃṭattaṃ, khujjattaṃ, vaḍabhattaṃ, samattaṃ, sabalattaṃ saha pamâeṇaṃ aṇegarûvâo joṇîo saṃdhei,[8] virûvarûve phâse parisaṃvedei.[9] ‖2‖

se abujjhamâṇe ha*t*ovaha*t*e jâi[10]-maraṇaṃ aṇupariyaṭṭamâṇe; jîviyaṃ puḍho piyaṃ iham egesiṃ mâṇavâṇaṃ khĕttavatthu mamâyamâṇâṇaṃ ârattaṃ virattaṃ maṇiṃ kuṃḍalaṃ 135
saha hiraṇṇeṇaṃ itthiyâo parigijjha[11] tatth' eva rattâ 'na ĕttha tavo vâ damo vâ niyamo vâ dissai' saṃpuṇṇaṃ jîviukâme lâlappamâṇe mûḍhe vippariyâsam uve*t*i.[12] ‖3‖

iṇam eva nâ 'vakaṃkhaṃti, je jaṇâ dhuvacâriṇo. |
jâi[10]-maraṇaṃ parinnâya[13] care saṃkamaṇe daḍhe. ‖

n' atthi kâlassa n' âgamo. savve pâṇâ piyâuyâ,[14] suhasâyâ, dukkhapaḍikûlâ, appiyavahâ, piyajîviṇo, jîviukâmâ, savvesiṃ jîviyaṃ piyaṃ. ‖4‖

taṃ parigijjha dupayaṃ cauppayaṃ abhijuṃjiyâṇaṃ 138
saṃsaṃciyâṇaṃ[15] tiviheṇa, jâ vi se tattha mattâ bhava*t*i appâ vâ bahugâ vâ, se tattha gaḍhie ciṭṭha*t*i bhoyaṇâe. ta*t*o se ega*d*â vivihaṃ[16] parisiṭṭhaṃ saṃbhû*t*aṃ mahovagaraṇaṃ[17] bhava*t*i. taṃ pi se egayâ dâyadâ[18] vibhayaṃti, adattâhâro vâ se avaharati, râyâṇo vâ se vilumpaṃti, nassai[19] vâ se, viṇassai vâ se, agâraḍâheṇa vâ se ḍajjhai. iya[20] se parass' aṭṭhâe kûrâiṃ kammâiṃ bâle pakuvvamâṇe teṇa dukkheṇa[21] mûḍhe vippariyâsam uve*t*i. ‖5‖

muṇiṇâ hu e*t*aṃ pave*d*i*t*aṃ: aṇohaṃtarâ ee, no ya ohaṃ 140
tarittae; atîraṃgamâ ee, no ya tîraṃ gamittae; apâraṃgamâ ee, no ya pâraṃ gamittae;

âyâṇijjaṃ ca â*d*âya tammi ṭhâṇe na ciṭṭhai; |
avitahaṃ pappa kheyanne taṃmi ṭhâṇaṃmi[22] ciṭṭhai. ‖

[1] A °yaṃ. [2] A °tiṃ. [3] Nâgârjunîyâs tu paṭhanti: evaṃ ege khalu jîve atîyaddhâe asaiṃ uccagoe asaiṃ nîyâgoe kaṃḍaṭṭhayâe no hîṇe no airitte. [4] A iti. [5] B °âya. [6] B kuppe. [7] Nâgârjunîyâs tu paṭhanti: purise ṇaṃ dukkhuvveyasuhesae. [8] A saṃdhâeti. [9] A paḍi°, B °veai. [10] A jâî. [11] A adds ti. [12] B ei. [13] cf. 1, 2. 1. [14] pâṭhântaram: piyâyayâ. [15] B saṃsiṃ°. [16] A vi. [17] B °karaṇaṃ. [18] A °ya. [19] B nâsai. [20] B ai, A iti. [21] A adds saṃ. [22] A °mmi.

uddeso pâsagassa n' atthi. bâle puṇa nihe kâmasamaṇunne asami*t*adukkhe dukkhî dukkhâṇam eva âvaṭṭaṃ aṇupariyaṭṭai tti bemi. ‖6‖**3**‖

taio uddesao.

tao se egayâ rogasamuppâyâ samuppajjaṃti; jehiṃ vâ
143 saddhiṃ saṃvasa*t*i, te vâ [1] ṇaṃ egayâ niyagâ puvviṃ parivayaṃti, so vâ te niyae pacchâ parivaĕjjâ: [2] nâ 'laṃ te tava tâṇâe vâ saraṇâe vâ, tumaṃ pi tesiṃ nâ 'laṃ tâṇâe vâ saraṇâe vâ. ‖1‖

jâṇittu dukkhaṃ patteyaṃ sâyaṃ bhogâm eva aṇusoyaṃti. iham egesiṃ mâṇavâṇaṃ tiviheṇa, jâ vi se tattha mattâ bhava*t*i appâ vâ bahuyâ vâ, bhoyaṇâe se tattha gaḍhie ciṭṭhati. ta*t*o se egayâ viparisiṭṭhaṃ saṃbhû*t*aṃ mahovagaraṇaṃ bhava*t*i. taṃ pi se egayâ dâyâ*d*â vibhayaṃti, adattâhâro vâ se avaha-
144 rati,[3] râyâṇo vâ se vilumpanti,[4] nassai vâ se, viṇassai vâ se, agâraḍâheṇa vâ se ḍajjhai. iya [5] parassa aṭṭhâe kûrâiṃ [6] kammâiṃ [6] bâle pakuvvamâṇe teṇa dukkheṇa [7] mûḍhe vippariyâsam uve*t*i. ‖2‖

âsaṃ ca chaṃdaṃ ca vigiṃca dhîre, tumaṃ c' eva taṃ sallam âhaṭṭu.[8] jeṇa siyâ, teṇa no siyâ, iṇam eva nâ 'vabujjhaṃti. je jaṇâ mohapâuḍâ thîbhi loe pavvahie, te bho va*d*aṃti: eyâiṃ âya*t*aṇâiṃ. se dukkhâe, mohâe, mârâe, naragâe, naragatirikkhâe; sa*t*a*t*aṃ mûḍhe dhammaṃ nâ 'bhijâṇa*t*i. ‖3‖

147 u*d*âhu vîre; [9] appamâ*d*o mahâmohe; alaṃ kusalassa pamâeṇaṃ saṃtimaraṇaṃ saṃpehâe [10] bheuradhammaṃ saṃpehâe, nâ'laṃ pâsa alaṃ te eehiṃ. eyaṃ pâsa muṇî mahabbhayaṃ, nâ '*t*ivâĕjjâ kaṃcaṇa. esa vîre pasaṃsi*t*e, je na nivijja*t*e [11] â*d*âṇâe; na me de*t*i, na kuppĕjjâ; thovaṃ laddhuṃ, na khiṃsai; paḍisehio pariṇamĕjjâ. eyaṃ moṇaṃ samaṇuvâsijjâ si tti bemi. ‖4‖**4**‖

cauttho uddesao.

jam iṇaṃ virûvarûvehiṃ satthehiṃ logassa kammasamâraṃbhâ kajjaṃti, taṃ jahâ: appaṇo se puttâṇaṃ dhûyâṇaṃ

[1] A va. [2] A vv. [3] B harati. [4] B °ṃti. [5] cf. 3. 20. [6] B °âṇi. [7] A adds saṃ°. [8] A tt. [9] MSS. dhîre. [16] MSS. sapehâe. [11] B niva°. C niya°.

suṇhâṇaṃ,[1] nâîṇaṃ, dhâîṇaṃ, râîṇaṃ, dâsâṇaṃ, dâsîṇaṃ 150
kammakarâṇaṃ, kammakarîṇaṃ â*d*esâe puḍho paheṇâe sâ-
mâsâe pâ*t*arâsâe saṃnihisaṃnicao kajjai. ‖1‖

iham egesiṃ mâṇavâṇaṃ bhoyaṇâe. samuṭṭhie aṇagâre ârie
âriyapanne[2] âriyadaṃsî, ayaṃ saṃdhî ti adakkhu,[3] se nâ''*d*ie,
nâ''*d*iyâvae, na samaṇujâṇa*t*i,[4] savvâmagaṃdhaṃ parinnâya
nirâmagaṃdhe parivvae. ‖2‖

adissamâṇe kayavikkaesu se na kiṇe, na kiṇâvae,
kiṇaṃtaṃ na samaṇujâṇai.[5] se bhikkhû kâlanne, bâlanne,
mâyanne, kheyanne, khaṇayanne, viṇayanne, samayanne, 153
bhâvanne, pariggahaṃ amamâyamâṇe, kâle[6] 'ṇuṭṭhâî, apaḍinne, duhao chittâ niyâi. vatthaṃ, paḍiggahaṃ, kaṃbalaṃ,
pâyapuṃchaṇaṃ, ŏggahaṃ ca kaḍâsaṇaṃ: eesu c' eva jâṇejjâ;
laddhe âhâre aṇagâro mâyaṃ jâṇĕjjâ. se jah' eyaṃ bhagava*t*â
pave*d*i*t*aṃ: lâbhŏ tti na majjĕjjâ, alâbhŏ tti na soĕjjâ, bahuṃ
pi laddhuṃ na nihe, pariggahâo appâṇaṃ avasakkĕjjâ, annahâ
ṇaṃ pâsae pariharĕjjâ. esa magge âriehiṃ pave*d*i*t*e, jah'
ĕttha kusale no 'valiṃpijjâ si tti bemi. ‖3‖ 157

kâmâ duratikkamâ, jîviyaṃ duppaḍivûhaṇaṃ,[7] kâmakâmî
khalu ayaṃ purise se soyati, jûra*t*i,[8] tippa*t*i, piḍḍa*t*i, paritappa*t*i.
âyacakkhû logavipassî logassa ahe[9] bhâgaṃ jâṇai, uḍḍhaṃ
bhâgaṃ jâṇa*t*i, tiriyaṃ bhâgaṃ jâṇai. gaḍḍhie loe pari-
yaṭṭamâṇe, saṃdhiṃ vi*d*ittâ iha macciehiṃ esa vîre
pasaṃsite, je baddhe paḍimoyae. ‖4‖

jahâ aṃto, tahâ bâhiṃ; jahâ bâhiṃ, tahâ aṃto. aṃto
aṃto pûi[10]-dehaṃtarâṇi pâsa*t*i puḍho vi savaṃtâiṃ[11] paṃḍie 161
paḍilehâe. se maimaṃ parinnâya:[2] mâ ya hu lâlaṃ paccâsî,
mâ tesu tiriccham appâṇam âvâyae, kâsaṃkase 'yaṃ[12] khalu
purise,[13] bahumâî kaḍeṇa mûḍhe puṇo taṃ karei lobhaṃ,
veraṃ vaḍḍhei appaṇo. jam iṇaṃ parikahijjai, imassa
c' eva paḍivûhaṇaṭṭhâe.[14] amarâyai mahâsaḍḍhî; aṭṭam eyaṃ
tu pehâe aparinnâe kaṃda*t*i. · se taṃ jâṇaha, jam ahaṃ
bemi. ‖5‖

teicchaṃ paṃḍie pavayamâṇe, se haṃtâ, chĕttâ, bhĕttâ,
luṃpittâ, viluṃpittâ, uddavaittâ, akaḍaṃ karissâmi tti manna-

[1] B nh. [2] A ṇṇ, B nn. [3] pâṭhântaraṃ vâ: ayaṃ saṃdhiṃ adakkhu. [4] A °âti. [5] B ae. [6] B kâlâ. [7] B °hagaṃ. [8] Calc. jhûrai. [9] A aho. [10] A pûî. [11] A °tâî. [12] B om. [13] B adds ayaṃ. [14] B °ṇayâe.

164 mâṇe; jassa vi ya ṇaṃ kare*t*i, alaṃ bâlassa saṃgeṇa; je vâ se kârei, bâle; na evaṃ aṇagârassa jâyai tti bemi. ||6||**5**||

pamcamo uddesao.

se taṃ saṃbujjhamâṇe âyâṇîyaṃ samuṭṭhâe[1] tamhâ pâvaṃ kammaṃ n' eva kujjâ, na kârave; siyâ tatth' egayaraṃ viparâmusa*t*i, chasu annayaraṃsi[2] kappa*t*i. suhaṭṭhî lâlappamâṇe saeṇa[3] dukkheṇa mûḍhe vippariyâsam uve*t*i, ||1|| saeṇa[3] vippamâeṇaṃ puḍho vayaṃ pakuvvai, jaṃs' ime pâṇâ pavvahi*t*â. paḍilehâe no nikaraṇâe. esâ parinnâ pa-
169 vucca*t*i. kammovasaṃtî je mamâi*t*aṃ[4] ma*t*iṃ jahâ*t*i, se jahâi[5] mamâiyaṃ.[4]

se hu diṭṭhapahe[6] muṇî, jassa n' atthi mamâiyaṃ.
taṃ parinnâya mehâvî vidittâ logaṃ,[7] vaṃtâ loga[7]-sannaṃ se maimaṃ parakkamĕjjâ si[8] tti bemi. ||2||

nâ 'ra*t*iṃ sahaî[9] vîre[10] vîre[10] no sahaî ra*t*iṃ |
jamhâ avimaṇe vîre[10] tamhâ vîre na rajjai ||

sadde phâse ahiyâsamâṇe nivviṃda[11] naṃdî[12] iha jîviyassa.
muṇî moṇaṃ samâ*d*âya dhuṇe kammasarîragaṃ.
paṃtaṃ [ca] lûhaṃ sevanti[13] vîrâ[10] sammattadaṃsiṇo.
es' ohaṃtare muṇî tiṇṇe mutte vira*t*e viyâhie tti bemi. ||3||
172 duvvasu muṇî aṇâṇâe tucchae gilâi vattae. esa vîre pasaṃsie, acce*t*i logasaṃjogaṃ, esa nâe pavuccati. jaṃ dukkhaṃ pave*d*iyaṃ iha mâṇavâṇaṃ, tassa dukkhassa kusalâ parinnaṃ[14] udâharaṃti. ||4||

iya[15] kammaṃ parinnâya savvaso, je aṇannadaṃsî, se aṇannârâme; je aṇannârâme, se aṇannadaṃsî. jahâ puṇṇassa kattha*t*i, tahâ tucchassa kattha*t*i; jahâ tucchassa kattha*t*i, tahâ puṇṇassa kattha*t*i. avi ya haṇe aṇâiyamâṇe. itthaṃ[16] pi jâṇa: seyaṃ ti n'atthi. ke 'yaṃ purise kaṃ ca nae?[11] esa
177 vîre pasaṃsie, je baddhe paḍimoyae uḍḍhaṃ ahaṃ tiriyaṃ disâsu. se savvao savvaparinnâcârî; na lippaî chaṇapa*d*eṇa[17] vîre. se mehâvî, je aṇugghâyaṇassa kheyanne,[18] je ya baṃdhapamukkham[19] annesî. kusale no[11]

[1] B °âya. [2] BC °ṃmi. [3] A se teṇa. [4] B °iam. [5] B cayai. [6] A bhae. [7] A loy°. [8] A pari°. [9] A sahate. [10] A dhîre. [11] A ṇ. [12] B naṃdiṃ, A ṇ. [13] B °ṃti, cf. 5. 3. § 5. [14] A °ṇṇâ. [15] A iti. [16] A ettham. [17] B chaṇaṇa. [18] cf. 5. [2]. [19] B pp. [20] B jaṃ.

baddhe, no [11] mukke, se jjaṃ [20] ca ârabhe, jaṃ ca n [11] ârabhe, aṇâraddhaṃ ca n [11] ârabhe :

chaṇaṃ chaṇaṃ parinnâya [18] logasannaṃ ca savvaso.

uddeso pâsagassa n' atthi; bâle puṇa nihe kâmasamaṇunne asamitadukkhe dukkhî dukkhâṇam eva âvaṭṭaṃ aṇupariyaṭṭai tti bemi. ‖ 5 ‖ **6** ‖

chaṭṭho uddesao.

biiyam ajjhayaṇaṃ.

logavijao samatto.

TAIYAM AJJHAYAṆAṂ.

SÎOSAṆIJJAṂ.

182 suttâ amuṇî,[1] muṇiṇo sayayaṃ[2] jâgaraṃti. lo*g*aṃsi jâṇa ahiyâya dukkhaṃ. samayaṃ logassa jâṇittâ ĕttha satthovarae. jass' ime saddâ ya rûvâ ya gaṃdhâ ya rasâ ya phâsâ ya abhisamannâgayâ bhavaṃti, ‖1‖ se âyavaṃ nâṇavaṃ[3] dhammavaṃ baṃbhavaṃ pannâṇehiṃ pari*j*âṇa*t*i logaṃ muṇî ti vacce, dhammavi*d*u tti ujû.[4] âvaṭṭasoe saṃgam abhijâṇa*t*i; sî*t*osiṇaccâgî se niggaṃthe ara*t*ira*t*isahe pharusiyaṃ[5] no vedeti jâgaraverovarae dhîre[6] evaṃ dukkhâ pamokkhasi. ‖2‖

186 jarâmaccuvasovaṇîe[7] nare sayayaṃ[8] mûḍhe dhammaṃ nâ 'bhijâṇati. pâsiya[9] â*t*ure[10] pâṇe appamatto parivvae. maṃtâ eyaṃ ma*t*imaṃ pâsa:

> ârambhajaṃ dukkham iṇaṃ ti naccâ
> mâî[11] pamâî puṇar e*t*i gabbhaṃ |
> uvehamâṇo saddarûvesu ujjû[12]
> mârâbhisaṃkî maraṇâ pamucca*t*i ‖

appamatto kâmehiṃ uvarao pâvakammehiṃ vîre âyagutte, je kheyanne. ‖3‖

je pajjavajâyasatthassa kheyanne, se asatthassa kheyanne; je asatthassa kheyanne, se pajjavajâyasatthassa kheyanne.

189 akammassa vavahâro na vijjai,[13] kammaṇâ uvâhî jâyai.[14] kammaṃ ca paḍilehâe kammamûlaṃ ca[15] jaṃ chaṇaṃ. paḍilehiya savvaṃ samâ*d*âya dohiṃ aṃtehiṃ adissamâṇe. taṃ parinnâya mehâvî vi*d*ittâ logaṃ, vaṃtâ logasaṇnaṃ se ma*t*imaṃ parakkamejjâ si tti bemi. ‖ 4‖**1**‖

paḍhamo uddesao.

> jâ*t*iṃ ca vuḍḍhiṃ ca ih' ajja pâsa
> bhûehiṃ sâtaṃ paḍileha jâṇe,|[1]

[1] B adds sayâ. [2] B sayâ. [3] pâṭhântaraṃ vâ: se âyavî ṇâṇavî. [4] A ajû. [5] B °sa°. [6] B vîre. [7] B maccû. [8] B °tat°. [9] A pâsitaṃ. [10] A ra. [11] AC mâyî. [12] A ujû. [13] A vijíatti. [14] A jâyayati. [15] pâṭhântaraṃ vâ: kammâhûya jaṃ chaṇaṃ.

[1] BC order: bh. j. p. s.; B jâṇa.

tamhâ 'tivijjo paramaṃ ti naccâ[2]
saṃmattadaṃsî na karei pâvaṃ. ||i||
ummucca pâsaṃ iha macciehiṃ
ârambhajîvî ubhayâṇupassî |
kâmesu giddhâ nicayaṃ[2] karemti,
saṃsiccamâṇâ puṇar eṃti gabbhaṃ. ||ii||
avi se hâsam âsajja haṃtâ naṃdî ti manna*t*i | 192
alaṃ bâlassa saṃgeṇa veraṃ vaḍḍha*t*i appaṇo. ||iii||
tamhâ '*t*ivijjo paramaṃ ti naccâ[2]
âyaṃkadaṃsî na karei pâvaṃ |
aggaṃ ca mûlaṃ ca vigiṃca dhîre
palicchiṃdiyâ ṇaṃ nikkammadaṃsî. ||iv||

esa maraṇâ pamucca*t*i, se hu diṭṭhabhae muṇî
logaṃsi paramadaṃsî vivittajîvî uvasaṃte[3] samie sahi*t*e sayâ
ja*t*e kâlâkaṃkhî[4] parivvae. bahuṃ ca khalu pâvaṃ
kammaṃ pagaḍaṃ; saccaṃsi[5] dhi*t*iṃ kuvvahâ. ettho 'varae
mehâvî savvaṃ kammaṃ jhosei. ||1|| aṇegacitte khalu 196
ayaṃ purise; se keyaṇaṃ arihai[6] pûraittae se annavahâe
annapariyâvâe annapariggahâe jaṇavayavahâe jaṇavayapari-
vâyâe jaṇavayapariggahâe. âsevittâ eyam aṭṭhaṃ icc ev'
ege samuṭṭhiyâ. ||2|| tamhâ taṃ biiyaṃ[7] no sevate,[8]
nissâraṃ pâsiya nâṇî uvavâyaṃ cavaṇaṃ naccâ
aṇannaṃ cara mâ haṇe. se na chaṇe, na chaṇâvae cha-
ṇaṃtaṃ nâ 'ṇujâṇai. nivviṃda naṃdî[2] arae payâsu
aṇomadaṃsî nisanno pâvehiṃ kammehiṃ. ||3||

kohâ*d*imâṇaṃ haṇiyâ ya vîre
lobhassa pâse nirayaṃ[2] mahaṃtaṃ,| 198
tamhâ hi[9] vîre virao vahâo
chiṃdejja soyaṃ lahubhûyagâmî. ||v||
gaṃthaṃ parinnâya ih' ajja vîre
soyaṃ parinnâya carejja daṃte |
ummugga[10] laddhuṃ iha mâṇavehiṃ
no pâṇiṇaṃ pâṇe samârabhĕjjâ ||vi||**2**||
si tti bemi.

biio uddesao.

[2] A ṇ. [3] upa. [4] A kâla. [5] B °ṃmi. [6] B arahai. [7] B bîyaṃ. [8] B seve.
[9] B ti. [10] B ummajja.

saṃdhiṃ logassa jâṇittâ, â*t*ato bahiyâ pâsa, tamhâ na haṃtâ na vighâ*t*ae. jam iṇaṃ annamannavitigiṃchâe[1] paḍilehâe na karei pâvaṃ kammaṃ. kiṃ tattha muṇîkâraṇaṃ siyâ?

samayaṃ tatth'[2] uvehâe appâṇaṃ vippasâ*d*ae. ||1||

aṇannaparamaṃ nâṇî no pamâe[3] kayâi vi |
202 âyagutte sayâ dhîre[4] jâyâmâyâĕ jâvae. ||i||

virâgaṃ[5] rûvesu gacchejjâ mahayâ khuḍḍaehi vâ; âga*t*iṃ ga*t*iṃ ca parinnâya dohiṃ aṃtehiṃ adissamâṇehiṃ se na chijja*t*i, na bhijja*t*i, na ḍajjha*t*i, na hamma*t*i ||2|| kaṃcaṇaṃ savvaloe. avareṇa puvvaṃ na saraṃti ege: kim ass' a*t*î*t*aṃ kiṃ vâ''gamissaṃ. bhâsaṃti ege iha mâṇavâo: jam ass' a*t*îtaṃ taṃ vâ''gamissaṃ.[6]

nâ 'î*y*am aṭṭhaṃ na ya âgamissaṃ
aṭṭhaṃ niyacchaṃti tahâgayâo |

vidhûtakappe[7] eyâṇupassî vijjhosaittâ

205 kâ ara*t*î ke y 'âṇaṃde ĕtthaṃ pi aggahe care |
savvaṃ hâsaṃ pariccajja âlîṇagutto parivvae. ||ii|| ||3||

purisâ! tumam eva tumaṃ mittaṃ; kiṃ bahiyâ mittam icchasi? jaṃ jâṇĕjja uccâlaiyaṃ, taṃ jâṇĕjjâ dûrâlaiyaṃ; jaṃ jâṇĕjjâ dûrâlaiyaṃ, taṃ jâṇĕjjâ uccâlaiyaṃ. purisâ! attâṇam eva abhiṇigijjha evaṃ dukkhâ pamŏkkhasi. purisâ! saccam eva samabhiyâṇahi![8] saccassa[9] âṇâe[10] uvaṭṭhi*t*e me*dh*âvî mâraṃ tarati. ||4||

sahie dhammam â*d*âe[11] seyaṃ samaṇupassa*t*i |

208 duhao jîviyassa parivaṃdaṇamâṇaṇapûyaṇâe jaṃsi ege pamâyaṃti. sahie dukkhamattâe puṭṭho na jhaṃjhâe, pâs' imaṃ davie loe loâloyapavaṃcâo pamucca*t*i tti bemi. ||5||**3**||

taio uddesao.

[1] A °gaṃch°, B °gicch°. [2] A tattha. [3] B pamâyae. [4] B vîre. [5] Nâgârjunîyâs tu paṭhanti: visayaṃmi paṃcayaṃ vi duvihaṃmi tiyaṃ tiyaṃ | bhâvao suṭṭhu jâṇitthâ se na lippai dosu vi || [6] apare tu paṭhanti: avareṇa puvvaṃ kiha se tîtaṃ kiha âgamissaṃ na samaraṃti ege bhâsaṃti ege iha mâṇavâo jaha se aîyaṃ taha âgamissaṃ. [7] B vihûa°. [8] B °ṇâhi. [9] B saccass. [10] B adds se. [11] B âyâya.

se 'vaṃtâ kohaṃ ca mâṇaṃ ca mâyaṃ ca lo*bh*aṃ ca, eyaṃ pâsagassa daṃsaṇaṃ uvarayasatthassa paliyaṃtakaḍassa[1] âyâṇaṃ sakaḍabbhi. je egaṃ jâṇa*t*i, se savvaṃ jâṇa*t*i; je savvaṃ jâṇa*t*i, se egaṃ jâṇa*t*i. savva*t*o pamattassa bhayaṃ, savvato appamattassa n'atthi bhayaṃ. ‖ 1 ‖

je ega[2] nâme, se bahu[2] nâme; je bahu[2] nâme, se ega nâme.
dukkhaṃ logassa jâṇittâ, vaṃtâ logasaṃjogaṃ, jaṃti 213
vîrâ mahâjâṇaṃ, pareṇa paraṃ jaṃti, nâ 'vakaṃkhaṃti jîvi*t*aṃ. ‖ 2 ‖

egaṃ vigiṃcamâṇe puḍho vigiṃca*t*i, puḍho vigiṃcamâṇe egaṃ vigiṃca*t*i. saḍḍhî âṇâe mehâvî logaṃ ca âṇâe abhisameccâ aku*t*obhayaṃ. atthi satthaṃ pareṇa paraṃ, n'atthi asatthaṃ pareṇa paraṃ. ‖ 3 ‖

je kohadaṃsî, se mâṇadaṃsî; je mâṇadaṃsî, se mâyadaṃsî; je mâyadaṃsî, se lo*bh*adaṃsî; je lo*bh*adaṃsî, se pĕjjadaṃsî; je pĕjjadaṃsî, se dosadaṃsî; je dosadaṃsî, se mohadaṃsî; je mohadaṃsî, se gabbhadaṃsî; je gabbhadaṃsî, se 215
jammadaṃsî; je jammadaṃsî, se mâradaṃsî; je mâradaṃsî,
se narayadaṃsî; je narayadaṃsî,[3] se tiriyadaṃsî; je tiriyadaṃsî, se dukkhadaṃsî.

se mehâvî abhinivaṭṭĕjjâ kohaṃ ca mâṇaṃ ca mâyaṃ ca lo*bh*aṃ ca pĕjjaṃ ca dosaṃ ca mohaṃ ca gabbhaṃ ca jammaṃ ca mâraṃ ca[4] narayaṃ[3] ca tiriyaṃ ca dukkhaṃ ca.

eyaṃ pâsagassa daṃsaṇaṃ uvarayasatthassa paliyaṃtakaḍassa,[5] âyâṇaṃ nisiddhâ sagaḍabbhi. kim atthi uvâ*dh*î[6] pâsagassa? na vijjati, n'atthi tti bemi. ‖ 4 ‖ ‖ **4** ‖

cauttho uddesao.

taiyam ajjhayaṇaṃ.

sîosaṇijjaṃ samattaṃ.

[1] B karassa. [2] B °ṃ. [3] B nir°. [4] A adds maraṇaṃ ca. [5] A °gaḍ°, B °kar°. [6] A uva°, B °hî.

CAUTTHAM AJJHAYAṆAṂ.

SAMMATTAṂ.

219 se bemi: je ya[1] aîyâ, je ya paḍuppannâ, je ya[2] âgamissâ arahaṃtâ bhagavaṃto, savve te evam âikkhaṃti, evaṃ bhâsaṃti, evaṃ pannavemti,[3] evaṃ parûveṃti: savve pâṇâ savve bhûyâ savve jîvâ savve sattâ na haṃtavvâ na ajjâveyavvâ[4] na parighĕttavâ na paritâveyavvâ na uddaveyavvâ. ‖1‖

esa dhamme suddhe nitie sâsae samecca loyaṃ kheyannehiṃ pave*dit*e, taṃ jahâ: uṭṭhiesu vâ aṇuṭṭhiesu vâ, uvaṭṭhiesu vâ aṇuvaṭṭhiesu vâ, uvarayadaṃḍesu vâ aṇuvarayadaṃḍesu
222 vâ, sovahiesu[5] vâ aṇuvahiesu vâ, saṃjogaraesu vâ asaṃjogaraesu vâ:

taccaṃ c'eyaṃ tahâ c'eyaṃ assiṃ c'eyaṃ pavucca*t*i. ‖2‖

taṃ âittu[6] na nihe na nikkhive. jâṇittu dhammaṃ jahâ tahâ diṭṭhehiṃ nivveyaṃ gacchĕjjâ, no lo*g*ass' esaṇaṃ çare.

jassa n'atthi imâ nâ*t*î[7] annâ tassa kao siyâ?

diṭṭhaṃ suyaṃ mayaṃ vinnâyaṃ, jaṃ eyaṃ parikahijja*t*i. samemâṇâ palemâṇâ puṇo puṇo jâ*t*iṃ pakappĕṃti.[8] aho ya râo[9] ja*t*amâṇe dhîre[10] sayâ âgayapannâṇe. pamatte bahiyâ pâsa; appamatte sayâ parakkamĕjjâ si tti bemi. ‖3‖**1**‖

padhamo uddesao.

224 je âsavâ, se parissavâ; je parissavâ, se âsavâ. je aṇâsavâ se aparissavâ; je aparissavâ, se aṇâsavâ. e*t*e pae saṃbujjhamâṇe lo*g*aṃ ca âṇâe abhisamĕccâ puḍho pave*d*i*t*aṃ. âghâti[1] nâṇî iha mâṇavâṇaṃ saṃsârapaḍivannâṇaṃ saṃbujjhamâṇâṇaṃ vinnâṇapattâṇam. ‖1‖

[1] A om. [2] B om [3] B °vaṃti. [4] B âṇâveavvâ. [5] A dh. [6] A âti°, B âii°. [7] A jâti. [8] A °ku°. [9] A ahotarâto. [10] A vîre.

[1] B akkhâi. Nâgârjunîyâs tu paṭhanti: dhammaṃ khalu se jîvâṇaṃ taṃ jahâ: saṃsârapaḍivaṇṇâṇaṃ maṇussabhavaṭṭhâṇaṃ ârambhavinaeṇaṃ dukkhayasuhesagâṇaṃ dhammassavaṇagavesayâṇaṃ sussûsamâṇâṇaṃ paḍipucchamâṇâṇaṃ viṇṇâṇapattâṇaṃ.

aṭṭâ vi saṃtâ aduvâ pamattâ ahâsaccam iṇaṃ ti
bemi. nâ 'ṇâgamo maccumuhassa atthi icchâpaṇî*t*â
vaṃkanikeyâ kâlaggahî*t*â[1] nicae niviṭṭhâ puḍho puḍho jâiṃ
pakappeṃti.[2]

[pâṭhântaraṃ vâ: ĕttha mohe puṇo puṇo iham egesiṃ 228
tattha tattha saṃthavo bhava*t*i, ahovavâie phâse paḍisaṃve-
*d*ayaṃti.

ciṭṭhaṃ kûrehiṃ kammehiṃ ciṭṭhaṃ pariviciṭṭha*t*i.

aciṭṭham akûrehiṃ kammehiṃ no ciṭṭhaṃ pariviciṭṭha*t*i.] ‖2‖

ege va*d*aṃti aduvâ vi nâṇî, nâṇî va*d*aṃti aduvâ
vi ege. âvaṃtî ke yâ "vaṃtî lo*g*aṃsi samaṇâ ya mâhaṇâ
ya puḍho puḍho vivâ*d*aṃ va*d*aṃti: se diṭṭhaṃ ca ṇe, suyaṃ
ca ṇe, mayaṃ ca ṇe, vinnâyaṃ ca ṇe, uḍḍhaṃ ahaṃ tiriyaṃ
disâsu savva*t*o supaḍilehiyaṃ ca ṇe: savve pâṇâ savve bhûyâ
savve jîvâ savve sattâ haṃtavvâ ajjâveyavvâ[3] pari*t*âveyavvâ 230
parighĕttavvâ uddaveyavvâ;[4] itthaṃ pi[5] jâṇaha: n'atth'
ĕttha doso. ‖3‖ aṇâriyavayaṇam eyaṃ. tattha je te âyariyâ,[6]
te evaṃ vayâsî: se dudditthaṃ ca bhe, dussuyaṃ ca bhe,
dummayaṃ ca bhe, duvvinnâyaṃ ca bhe, uḍḍhaṃ ahaṃ
tiriyaṃ disâsu savva*t*o duppaḍilehiyaṃ, jaṇ ṇaṃ[7] tubbhe
evam âikkhaha, evaṃ bhâsaha, evaṃ pannaveha: savve pâṇâ
savve bhûyâ savve jîvâ savve[3] sattâ haṃtavvâ ajjâveyavvâ
pari*t*âveyavvâ parighĕttavvâ uddaveyavvâ; itthaṃ pi[8] jâṇaha
n'atth' ĕttha doso. aṇâriyavayaṇam eyaṃ. ‖4‖ vayaṃ puṇa 231
evam âikkhâmo, evaṃ bhâsâmo, evaṃ pannavemo: savve pâṇâ
savve bhûyâ savve jîvâ savve sattâ na haṃtavvâ na ajjâveyavvâ na pari*t*âveyavvâ na parighĕttavvâ na uddaveyavvâ;
itthaṃ pi[8] jâṇaha: n'atth' ĕttha doso. âriyavayaṇam
eyaṃ. ‖5‖ puvvaṃ nikâya samayaṃ patteyaṃ patteyaṃ
pucchissâmo: haṃbho pâvâuyâ! kiṃ bhe sâyaṃ dukkhaṃ,
uyâhu asâyaṃ? samiyâ paḍivanne[9] yâvi bûyâ: savvesiṃ
pâṇâṇaṃ savvesiṃ bhûyâṇaṃ savvesiṃ jîvâṇaṃ savvesiṃ 232
sattâṇaṃ asâyaṃ aparinivvâṇaṃ mahabbhayaṃ dukkhaṃ ti
bemi. ‖6‖**2**‖

bîo uddesao.

[1] B kâlaga°. [2] B pakappayaṃti. [3] A om. [4] A ud°, par°. [5] A ittha vi.
[6] B âriyâ. [7] B jannaṃ. [8] A ettha vi. [9] B paḍivanni.

uvehi[1] eṇaṃ bahiyâ[2] ya loyaṃ;[3]
se savvaloyaṃsi[3] je kei vinnû.
aṇuvîi[4] pâsa nikkhittadaṃḍâ je kei sattâ paliyaṃ cayaṃti
narâ muyaccâ dhammavidu tti aṃjû
ârambhajaṃ dukkham iṇaṃ ti naccâ
evam âhu sammattadaṃsiṇo. ‖ 1 ‖

te savve pâvâ*d*iyâ dukkhassa kusalâ parinnam udâharaṃti. iya[5] kamma parinnâya savvaso iha âṇâkaṃkhî paṃḍi*t*e
237 aṇihe egam appâṇaṃ saṃpehâe dhuṇe sarîraṃ[6] kasehi appâṇaṃ jarehi appâṇaṃ.

jahâ juṇṇâiṃ[7] kaṭṭhâiṃ havvavâho pamattha*t*i.

evam *attasamâhie* aṇihe vigiṃca kohaṃ avikaṃpamâṇe *imaṃ viruddhâuyaṃ* sa pehâe dukkhaṃ ca jâṇa aduvâ "gamĕssaṃ puḍho phâsâiṃ ca phâsae logaṃ ca pâsa viphaṃdamâṇaṃ.[8] ‖ 2 ‖ je nivvuḍâ pâvehiṃ kammehiṃ aṇiyâṇâ te viyâhiyâ. tamhâ 'tivijjo no paḍisaṃjâlijjâ si tti bemi. ‖ 3 ‖ 3 ‖

taio uddesao.

âvîlae pavîlae nippîlae[1] caittâ puvvasaṃjogaṃ hiccâ uvasamaṃ; tamhâ avimaṇe vîre sârae samie sahite sayâ
240 jae. duraṇucaro maggo vîrâṇaṃ aṇiyaṭṭagâmîṇaṃ. vigiṃca maṃsasoṇiyaṃ. ‖ 1 ‖

esa purise davie vîre âyâṇijje viyâhie, je dhuṇâi samussayaṃ vasittâ baṃbhaceraṃsi nĕttehiṃ palicchinnehiṃ.[2] âyâṇasoyagaḍhie bâle avvŏcchinnabaṃdhaṇe[3] aṇabhikkaṃtasaṃjoe; tamaṃsi avi*j*âṇao âṇâe laṃbho[4] n'atthi tti bemi. ‖ 2 ‖

jassa n'atthi purâ pacchâ, majjhe tassa kuo siyâ.
se hu pannâṇamaṃte buddhe âraṃbhovarae samam eyaṃ ti pâsaha.
jeṇa baṃdhaṃ vahaṃ ghoraṃ paritâvaṃ ca dâruṇaṃ,
242 palicchiṃdiya vâhiragaṃ ca soyaṃ nikkammadaṃsî iha macciehiṃ.

[1] B uveh'. [2] A vahetâ. [3] B log. [4] B aṇuvitiya. [5] A iti. [6] B sarîragaṃ. [7] MSS. nn. [8] B vipph°.

[1] A nipîlae. [2] A °cha°. [3] A âvvoch°. [4] B lâbho.

kammâṇi[5] saphalaṃ daṭṭhuṃ ta*t*o nijjâi ve*d*avî. ||3||
je khalu bho vîrâ sami*t*â sahi*t*â sayâ jayâ saṃghaḍadaṃsiṇo âovarayâ ahâtahâ logaṃ uvehamâṇâ pâîṇaṃ paḍîṇaṃ dâhiṇaṃ udîṇaṃ iti saccaṃsi pariviciṭṭhiṃsu : sâhissâmo[6] nâṇaṃ vîrâṇaṃ sami*t*âṇaṃ sahi*t*âṇaṃ sa*d*â ja*t*âṇaṃ saṃghaḍadaṃsîṇaṃ ahovarayâṇaṃ ahâtahâ lo*g*aṃ samuppehamâṇâṇaṃ.[7] kim atthi uvâhî[8] pâsagassa? na vijjai, n'atthi tti 244
bemi. ||4||**4**||

cauttho uddesao.

cauttham ajjhayaṇaṃ.

sammattaṃ samattaṃ.

[5] MSS. kammuṇâ. [6] A appâh°. [7] B uvveh°. [8] A uvahî.

PAṂCAMAM AJJHAYAṆAṂ.

LOGASÂRO.

Âvaṃtî keyâ "vaṃtî[1] loyaṃsi vipparâmusaṃti aṭṭhâe
aṇaṭṭhâe vâ, e*t*esu vipparâmusaṃti, gurû se kâmâ, tao se
mârassa aṃto; *j*ao se mârassa aṃto, tao se dûre; n' eva se
aṃto,[2] n' eva se dûre, se pâsa*t*i phusitam iva kusagge pa-
ṇunnaṃ nivai*t*aṃ vâ*t*eriyaṃ evaṃ bâlassa jîvitaṃ maṃdassa avijâṇa*t*o. kûrâiṃ kammâiṃ bâle pakuvvamâṇe
teṇa dukkheṇa mûḍhe vippariyâsam uve*t*i[3] moheṇa gabbhaṃ maraṇâi ei. ĕttha mohe puṇo puṇo saṃsayaṃ pari*j*â-
249 ṇao saṃsâre parinnâ*t*e bhava*t*i; saṃsayaṃ apari*j*âṇao saṃsâre
aparinnâ*t*e bhava*t*i. je chee, sâgâriyaṃ na se[4] sevae;[5] kaṭṭu
evam avi*j*âṇao bîyâ[6] maṃdassa bâlayâ.[7] laddhâ huratthâ
paḍilehâe âgamĕttâ âṇavĕjjâ âṇâsevaṇâe tti bemi. || 1 ||
pâsaha ege rûvesu giddhe parinijjamâṇe;[8] ĕttha phâse[9]
puṇo puṇo.[10] âvaṃtî keyâ "vaṃtî loyaṃsi ârambhajîvî, e*t*esu
c'eva ârambhajîvî. ittha vi bâle paripaccamâṇe[11] rama*t*i
251 pâvehiṃ kammehiṃ asaraṇaṃ saraṇaṃ ti mannamâṇe; iham
egesiṃ egacariyâ bhava*t*i. || 2 || se bahukohe bahumâṇe
bahumâe bahulobhe bahura*t*e bahunaḍe bahusaḍhe bahu-
saṃkappe âsavasakkî paliŏcchinne uṭṭhi*t*avâ*d*aṃ pavayamâṇe.
"mâ me kei addakkhû!" annâṇapamâyadoseṇaṃ sayayaṃ
mûḍhe dhammaṃ nâ 'bhijâṇa*t*i; aṭṭâ payâ, mâṇava! kamma-
koviyâ je aṇuvarayâ avijjâe parimokkham[12] âhû:[13] âvaṭṭam
evam aṇupariyaṭṭaṃti tti bemi. || 3 || **1** ||

paḍhamo uddesao.

âvaṃtî keyâ "vaṃtî logaṃsi[1] aṇârambhajîvî, e*t*esu[2] c' eva
254 aṇârambhajîvî. ĕttho 'varae taṃ jhosamâṇe ayaṃ saṃdhî
ti[3] addakkhû,[4] je imassa viggahassa ayaṃ khaṇe tti annesî;

[1] A ke tâvaṃtî. [2] A aṃte. [3] A eti, cf. II. 4. [3]. [4] B om. [5] A seve. [6] B biiyâ. [7] Nâgârjunîyâs tu paṭhanti: je khalu visae sevai sevittâ vâ nâ "loiei pareṇa vâ puṭṭho ninhavai ahavâ taṃ paraṃ saeṇa vâ dâseṇa (!) pâviṭṭhiyareṇa vâ doseṇa vâ uvalimpijji. [8] B pariṇi°. [9] pâṭhântaraṃ: mohe. [10] A adds saṃsayaṃ parijâṇao. [11] B parivaçca°. [12] B pali°. [13] B âhu.

[1] A logammi. [2] A tesu. [3] B saṃdhi tti. [4] B ada°.

esa magge âriehiṃ pave*di*t*e*. ‖1‖ uṭṭhite na pamâyae jâṇittu
dukkhaṃ patteyaṃ sâyaṃ. puḍhochaṃdâ iha mâṇavâ;
puḍho dukkhaṃ pave*d*i*t*aṃ. se avihiṃsamâṇe[5] aṇavayamâṇe
puṭṭho phâse vipaṇollae.[6] esa samiyâ pariyâe viyâhi*t*e. ‖2‖
je asattâ pâvehiṃ kammehiṃ udâhu, te âyaṃkâ phusaṃti iti
udâhu, dhîre[7] te phâse puṭṭho 'hiyâsae. se puvvaṃ p' eyaṃ
pacchâ p' eyaṃ. bheuradhammaṃ viddhaṃsaṇadhammaṃ
adhuvaṃ aṇitiyaṃ[8] asâsayaṃ cayâvacaiyaṃ[9] vipariṇâma- 257
dhammaṃ; pâsaha evaṃ rûvasaṃdhiṃ. samuvehamâṇassa
ekâyataṇarayassa iha vippamukkassa n' atthi magge vira*t*assa
tti bemi. ‖3‖ âvaṃtî keyâ "vaṃtî logaṃsi[1] pariggahâvaṃtî
—se appaṃ vâ bahuṃ vâ aṇuṃ vâ thûlaṃ vâ cittamaṃtaṃ
vâ acittamaṃtaṃ vâ—e*t*esu c' eva pariggahâvaṃtî. evam
ev' egesiṃ mahabbhayaṃ bhavati. logavittaṃ ca ṇaṃ
uvehâe e*t*e saṃge avi*j*âṇao: se suppaḍibuddhaṃ[10] sûvaṇî-
yaṃ ti naccâ purisâ paramacakkhû vipparakkamma! e*t*esu
c'eva baṃbhaceraṃ ti bemi. ‖4‖ 260

se suyaṃ ca me ajjhatthaṃ ca me: baṃdhapamŏkkho tujjha
ajjhatthe 'va, ĕttha vira*t*e aṇagâre dîharâyaṃ titikkhae.
pamatte bahiyâ[11] pâsa appamatte[12] parivvae.
e*t*aṃ moṇaṃ sammaṃ aṇuvâsijjâ si tti bemi. ‖5‖**2**‖

bîo uddesao.

âvaṃtî[1] keyâ "vaṃtî logaṃsi apariggahâvaṃtî, e*t*esu c' eva
apariggahâvaṃtî. sŏccâ vaî[2] mehâvî paṃḍiyâṇa nisâmiya.
sami*t*âe dhamme âriehiṃ pave*dit*e: jah' ĕttha mae saṃdhî
jhosie, evam annattha saṃdhî[3] dujjhosae bhava*t*i. tamhâ
bemi: no niṇhavejja[4] vîriyaṃ. ‖1‖ je puvvuṭṭhâî, no pacchâ 262
nivâ*t*î; je puvvuṭṭhâî, pacchâ nivâ*t*î,[5] je no puvvuṭṭhâî, no
pacchâ nivâ*t*î. se vi târisae siyâ, je parinnâya logam annesitâ.[6] eyaṃ niyâya muṇiṇâ pave*d*i*t*aṃ. iha âṇâkaṃkhî
paṃḍie aṇihe puvvâvararâyaṃ jayamâṇe sayâ sîlaṃ saṃpehâe
suṇiyâ bhave[7] akâme ajhaṃjhe. imeṇa c'eva jujjhâhi!
kiṃ te jujjheṇa bajjhao? juddhârihaṃ khalu dulla*bh*aṃ.

[5] A avah°. [6] B °ṇunnae. [7] A vîre. [8] B aṇiayaṃ [9] A cayo°. [10] A supa°. [11] A vahitâ. [12] B °tto.

[1] A âvaṃti. [2] A vatiṃ Com.: vai tti sup-vyatyayena dvitîyârthe prathamâ. [3] A saṃdhi. [4] B nihaṇijja. [5] B om. the last five words. [6] A aṇusiyâ, B annesaṃti. Calc.: annesitâ. Com.: mat'â śritâ anveshati vâ. [7] A bhâve.

266 jah' ĕttha kusalehiṃ parinnâvivege bhâsie. cue hu bâle gabbhâisu rajja*t*i. ‖2‖ assiṃ c'eyaṃ pavucca*t*i rûvaṃsi vâ chaṇaṃsi vâ. se hu ege[9] saṃviddhapahe muṇî annahâ logaṃ uvehamâṇe iti kammaṃ parinnâya savvaso se na hiṃsa*t*i; saṃjama*t*i, no pagabbha*t*î. ‖3‖ uvehamâṇo patteyaṃ sâtaṃ vaṇṇâ*d*esî nâ "rabhe kaṃcaṇaṃ savvaloe: egappamuhe vidisappaiṇṇe nivvinnacârî ara*t*e payâsu. se vasumaṃ savvasamannâga*t*apannâṇeṇaṃ appâṇeṇaṃ akaraṇijjaṃ pâvaṃ kammaṃ taṃ no annesî. jaṃ sammaṃ ti
268 pâsahâ, taṃ moṇaṃ ti pâsahâ; jaṃ moṇaṃ ti pâsahâ, taṃ sammaṃ ti pâsahâ. na imaṃ sakkaṃ siḍhilehiṃ âdijjamâṇehiṃ guṇâsâehiṃ[10] vaṃkasamâyârehiṃ gâram âvasaṃtehiṃ. ‖4‖ muṇî moṇaṃ samâyâe dhuṇe sarîragaṃ; paṃtaṃ lûhaṃ[11] sevaṃti vîrâ samattadaṃsiṇo. esa ohaṃtare muṇî tiṇṇe mutte virae viyâhie tti bemi. ‖5‖**3**‖

taio uddesao.

gâmâṇugâmaṃ dûijjamâṇassa dujjâ*t*aṃ dupparakkaṃtaṃ bhavati aviyattassa bhikkhuṇo. vayasâ[1] vi ege coiyâ[2] ku-
272 ppaṃti mâṇavâ, unnayamâṇe ya nare maha*t*â moheṇa mujjha*t*i. ‖1‖ saṃbâhâ bahave bhujjo duraikkammâ ajâṇao apâsao. eyaṃ te mâ hou. eyaṃ kusalassa[2] daṃsaṇaṃ. tadditthîe tammŏttîe tappurakkâre tassannî tannivesaṇe[3] jayavihârî cittanivâî paṃthanijjhâî balibâhire pâsiya pâṇe gacchĕjjâ. ‖2‖ se abhikkamamâṇe paḍikkamamâṇe[4] saṃkucamâṇe[5] pasâremâṇe viṇiyaṭṭamâṇe[6] saṃpalimajjamâṇe.[7] egayâ guṇasami*t*assa rîya*t*o kâyasaṃphâsam aṇuciṇṇâ ega*t*iyâ pâṇâ
276 uddâyaṃti: ihalogave*d*aṇavejjâvaḍiyaṃ; jaṃ âuṭṭikammaṃ,[8] taṃ parinnâya vivegam eti. evaṃ se appamâeṇa vivegaṃ kiṭṭa*t*i veyavî. ‖3‖ se pabhû*t*adaṃsî pabhû*t*aparinnâṇe uvasaṃte sami*t*e sahi*t*e sayâ jae daṭṭhuṃ vippaḍive*d*e*t*i appâṇaṃ: kim esa jaṇo karissa*t*i? esa se paramârâme, jâo logaṃsi[9] itthîo.[10] muṇiṇâ eyaṃ pave*d*i*t*aṃ. ‖4‖ ubbâhijjamâṇe gâmadhammehiṃ avi nibbalâsae, avi omoyariyaṃ kujjâ, avi uḍḍhaṃ ṭhâṇaṃ ṭhâĕjjâ, avi gâmâṇugâmaṃ dûijjâ, avi âhâraṃ vŏcchiṃ-

[8] B °ai. [9] B adds muṇî. [10] A sâtehiṃ. [11] C adds ca, cf. 2. 5. § 3.

[1] B vaisâ. [2] A puiyâ. [3] A ṭaṃṇi°. [4] A pari°. [5] B °kuce°. [6] A om. [7] A saṃpaliv°. [8] B âuṭṭikayaṃ. [9] B logaṃmi. [10] B itthio (çloka !?).

dĕjjâ, avi cae itthîsu maṇaṃ. puvvaṃ daṃḍâ, pacchâ phâsâ; 278
puvvaṃ phâsâ, pacchâ daṃḍâ: icc e*t*e kalahâsaṃgakarâ bhavaṃti. paḍilehâe âgamittâ âṇâvĕjjâ aṇâsevaṇâe[11] tti bemi.
se no[12] kâhie, no pâsaṇie, no saṃpasârae,[13] no mamâe,[14] no
ka*t*akirie. vaigutte ajjhappasaṃvuḍe[15] parivajjae sayâ pâ-
vaṃ. eyaṃ moṇaṃ samaṇuvâsĕjjâ si tti bemi. ||5||**4**||

cauttho uddesao.

se bemi,[1] taṃ jahâ: avi hara*d*e paḍipuṇṇe ciṭṭha*t*i samaṃsi
bhome[1] uvasaṃtarae sârakkhamâṇe se ciṭṭha*t*i. so*t*amajjhaga*t*e 281
se pâsa savvato gutte, pâsa loe mahesiṇo, je ya pannâṇamaṃtâ
pabuddhâ ârambhovara*t*â sammam eyaṃ ti pâsaha: kâlassa
kaṃkhâe parivvayaṃti[2] tti bemi. ||1||

vitigiṃchasamâvanneṇaṃ appâṇeṇaṃ no la*bh*a*t*i samâhiṃ.
siyâ v' ege aṇugacchaṃti, asiyâ v' ege aṇugacchaṃti aṇu-
gacchamâṇehiṃ aṇaṇugacchamâṇe[3] kahaṃ na nivijje?[4] tam
eva saccaṃ nîsaṃkaṃ, jaṃ jiṇehiṃ pave*dit*aṃ. ||2||

saḍḍhissa ṇaṃ samaṇunnassa saṃpavvayamâṇassa[5] samiyaṃ[6] ti mannamâṇassa ega*d*â samiyâ ho*t*i, samiyaṃ ti 284
mannamâṇassa ega*d*â asamiyâ ho*t*i; asamiyaṃ ti mannamâṇassa ega*d*â samiyâ ho*t*i, asamiyaṃ ti mannamâṇassa ega*d*â
asamiyâ ho*t*i.[7] samiyaṃ ti mannamâṇassa samiyâ vâ asamiyâ
vâ samiyâ ho*t*i uvehâe. asamiyaṃ ti mannamâṇassa samiyâ
va asamiyâ vâ asamiyâ ho*t*i uvehâe. uvehamâṇe aṇuveha-
mâṇaṃ bûyâ: uvehâhi samiyâe! icc eva tattha saṃdhî jhosie
bhava*t*i. ||3||

se uṭṭhiyassa ṭhiyassa ga*t*iṃ samaṇupassaha,[8] ĕttha vi 287
bâlabhâve appâṇaṃ no uvadaṃsejjâ. tumaṃsi nâma
sacceva jaṃ haṃtavvaṃ ti mannasi; tumaṃsi nâma
sacc eva jaṃ ajjâve*t*avvaṃ ti mannasi; tumaṃsi nâma sacc
eva jaṃ pari*t*âve*t*avvaṃ ti mannasi; evaṃ taṃ ceva jaṃ
parighĕttavvaṃ ti mannasi;[9] evaṃ taṃ ceva jaṃ uddave-
yavvaṃ ti mannasi; aṃjû c' eyappaḍibuddhajîvî[10] tamhâ na
haṃtâ na vi ghâyae. aṇusaṃve*d*aṇam appâṇeṇaṃ jaṃ

[11] A °ṇayâe. [12] A always ṇo. [13] A °raṇie. [14] B mamâae, A mamâte.
[15] A saṃp°.

[1] AB adds ciṭṭhai. [2] A parijjayaṃti, B pariva°, C parivajjayaṃti. [3] A °ṇâ.
[4] B vv, A °va°, C vijjati. [5] B °pava°. [6] A om. [7] A eva bhavati. [8] B °pâsaha.
[9] A om. this clause. [10] A eyaṃpa°.

haṃtavvaṃ ti nâ 'bhipatthae. ‖4‖ je âyâ, se vinnâyâ; je
289 vinnâyâ, se âyâ; jeṇa vijâṇa*ti*, se âyâ, taṃ paḍucca paḍisaṃkhâe. esa[11] âyâvâ*dî* samiyâe pariyâe viyâhie tti bemi. ‖5‖**5**‖

pamcamo uddesao.

aṇâṇâe ege sovaṭṭhâṇâ, âṇâe ege niruvaṭṭhâṇâ: eyaṃ te mâ hou! eyaṃ kusalassa daṃsaṇaṃ. taddiṭṭhîe tammŏttîe tappurakkâre tassannî tannivesaṇe abhibhûya addakkhû,[1] aṇabhibhû*te* pahû[2] nirâlaṃbaṇa*t*âe. je mahaṃ avahîmaṇe pavâeṇaṃ pavâdaṃ jâṇejjâ sahasammaiyâe paravâgaraṇeṇaṃ annesiṃ vâ aṃtie[3] sŏccâ niddesaṃ nâ '*t*ivattĕjjâ[4] mehâvî.
292 supaḍilehiya[5] savva*to* savvayâe sammam eva samabhijâṇiyâ.

ihâ "râmaṃ parinnâya allîṇagutto parivvae.

niṭṭhiyaṭṭhî vîre âgameṇaṃ sadâ parakkamejjâ si tti bemi. ‖1‖

uḍḍhaṃ soyâ ahe soyâ tiriyaṃ soyâ viyâhiyâ |
e*te* soyâ viyakkhâ*t*â jehiṃ saṃgaṃ ti pâsahâ ‖

âvaṭṭaṃ tu[6] uvehâe ettha viramejja ve*d*avî; viṇaĕttu soyaṃ, nikkhamma, esa maham akammâ jâṇa*ti* pâsa*ti*, paḍilehâe nâ 'vakaṃkha*ti*. ‖2‖
295 iha âga*ti*ṃ ga*ti*ṃ parinnâya acce*ti* jâimaraṇassa vaṭṭamaggaṃ[7] vikkhâ*t*arate savve sarâ niyaṭṭaṃti takkâ jattha na vijja*t*î[9] ma*t*î tattha na gâhiyâ. oe appa*t*iṭṭhâṇassa kheyanne. ‖3‖ se na[8] dîhe na[8] hasse na vaṭṭe na taṃse na cauraṃse na parimaṃḍale na kiṇhe[10] na nîle na lohie na halidde na sukkile na surabhigaṃdhe na durabhigaṃdhe na titte na kaḍue na kasâe[11] na aṃbile na mahure[12] na kakkhaḍe na maue na garue[13] na lahue na sîe na uṇhe[10] na niddhe na lukkhe na kâû na ruhe na saṃge na itthî na[8]
297 purise na[8] annahâ. parinne sanne uvamâ na[8] vijjai arûvî sattâ apayassa payaṃ n'atthi. se na[8] sadde na rûve na gaṃdhe na rase na phâse icc e*t*âvaṃti tti bemi. ‖4‖**6**‖

chaṭṭho uddesao.

paṃcamam ajjhayaṇaṃ.

logasâro samatto.

[11] B es.

[1] B ada°. [2] B pabhû. [3] B om°. [4] B °jja°. [5] A °iyâ. [6] AB âvaṭṭam eyaṃ t'. [7] AB °magam. [8] A°ṇ°. [9] B vijjai. [10] B nh. [11] A kasâyae. [12] B adds va lavaṇe. [13] B gurue.

CHAṬṬHAM AJJHAYAṆAṂ.

DHUTAṂ.

obujjhamâṇe iha mâṇavesu agghâ*t*i[1] se nare[2] jass' imâo jâ*t*îo savvâo[3] supaḍilehiyâo[4] bhavaṃti, agghâ*t*i se nâṇam[2] aṇelisaṃ. se kiṭṭa*t*i tesiṃ samuṭṭhi*t*âṇaṃ nikkhittadaṃḍâṇaṃ samâhiyâṇaṃ pannâṇamaṃtâṇaṃ iha[5] muttimaggaṃ. evaṃ p[6] ege mahâvîrâ vipparikkamaṃti;[7] pâsaha ege visîyamâṇe[8] aṇattapanne se bemi. ‖1‖ se jahâ nâmae[9] vi kumme harae viṇiviṭṭhacitte pacchannapalâse ummuggaṃ[10] se na[2] la*bh*a*t*i, bhaṃjagâ iva saṃnivesaṃ[2] no[2] cayaṃti: evaṃ p' ege aṇegarûvehiṃ kulehiṃ[9] jâyâ vi[11] rûvehiṃ sattâ kaluṇaṃ thaṇaṃti; ni*d*âṇa*t*o te na[2] labhaṃti mŏkkhaṃ. ‖2‖ aha pâsa tehiṃ kulehiṃ âyattâe jâyâ:

gaṃḍî aduvâ koṭṭhî râyaṃsî avamâriyaṃ |
kâṇiyaṃ jhimmiyaṃ c'eva kuṇiyaṃ khujjiyaṃ tahâ ‖i‖
udariṃ ca pâsa mûyaṃ[12] ca sûṇiyaṃ ca gilâsiṇî[13] |
vevaiṃ pîḍhasappiṃ ca silavayaṃ[14] ma*dh*umehaṇiṃ ‖ii‖
solasa e*t*e rogâ akkhâyâ aṇupuvvaso |
aha ṇaṃ phusaṃti âyaṃkâ phâsâ ya asamaṃjasâ ‖iii‖
maraṇaṃ tesiṃ sapehâe uvavâyaṃ cavaṇaṃ ca naccâ |
paripâgaṃ[15] ca sapehâe taṃ suṇeha jahâ tahâ ‖iv‖

saṃti pâṇâ aṃdhâ tamasi viyâhiyâ, tâm eva saiṃ asaiṃ[16] aiyacca uccâvace[17] phâse paḍisaṃve*d*e*t*i; buddhehiṃ eyaṃ pave*d*i*t*aṃ. ‖3‖ saṃti pâṇâ vâsagâ rasagâ udae udayacarâ âgâsagâmiṇo pâṇâ pâṇe kilesaṃti. pâsa loe mahabbhayaṃ; bahudukkhâ hu jaṃtavo. sattâ kâmehiṃ mâṇavâ abaleṇa va*dh*aṃ gacchaṃti sarîreṇa pabhaṃgureṇa. aṭṭe se bahudukkhe iti bâle pakuvva*t*i. ee roge[18] bahû naccâ âurâ pari*t*âvae? nâ'laṃ pâsa, alaṃ tav[19] e*t*ehiṃ! eyaṃ

[1] B akkhâi. [2] A ṇ. [3] A °âto. [4] B °hiâ. [5] A iham. [6] A pp. [7] B vipa°.
[8] B avasî°. [9] A om. [10] A umu°, B umma°. [11] B om. [12] A muttiṃ. [13] B °ṇiṃ.
[14] B sile°, A °vaiṃ. [15] A pariyâgaṃ. [16] A asayaṃ. [17] A uccâvae. [18] A roe.
[16] B tava.

pâsa muṇî mahabbhayaṃ! nâ 'ivâ*d*ĕjja kaṃcaṇaṃ, âyâṇa bho! sussûsa bho! dhûyavâyaṃ pave*d*issâmi.[20] ||4|| iha khalu attattâe tehiṃ tehiṃ kulehiṃ a*bh*iseeṇa abhisaṃbhûtâ abhisaṃjâ*t*â abhinivvaṭṭâ abhisaṃvuḍḍhâ[21] abhisaṃbuddhâ[9] abhinikkhaṃtâ aṇupuvveṇa mahâmuṇî. taṃ parikkamaṃtaṃ
310 paridevamâṇâ mâ ne[2] cayâhi iti[22] te va*d*aṃti. ||5|| chaṃdovaṇîyâ ajjhovavannâ akkaṃdakârî jaṇagâ ru*d*aṃti. atârise muṇî ohaṃtarae, jaṇagâ jeṇa vippajaḍhâ. saraṇaṃ tattha no[2] same*t*i. kiha nâma se tattha rama*t*i? eyaṃ nâṇaṃ sayâ samaṇuvâsĕjjâ si tti bemi. ||6||**1**||

padhamo uddesao.

âuraṃ lo*g*am âyâe caittâ puvvasaṃjogaṃ hiccâ uvasamaṃ vasittâ baṃbhaceraṃsi vasu vâ aṇuvasu vâ jâṇittu dhammaṃ ahâtahâ ah' ege tam acâ*t*i. kusîlâ vatthaṃ paḍiggahaṃ
312 kaṃbalaṃ pâyapuṃchaṇaṃ viusijjâ aṇupuvveṇa[1] aṇahiyâsemâṇâ parîsahe durahiyâsae. kâme mamâyamâṇassa i*d*âṇiṃ vâ muhutteṇa vâ aparimâṇâe bhe*d*o.[2] evaṃ se aṃtarâiehiṃ kâmehiṃ âkevaliehiṃ avitiṇṇâ[3] c' e*t*e. ||1|| ah' ege dhammam âyâe âdâṇapabhi*t*isu[4] ppaṇihie care apalîyamâṇe[4] daḍhe,[5] savvaṃ gehiṃ[6] parinnâya esa paṇae mahâmuṇî a*t*iyacca savva*t*o saṃgaṃ, na mahaṃ atthî 'ti.[7] iya[8] ego aham aṃsi jayamâṇe ĕttha vira*t*e aṇagâre savva*t*o muṃḍe rîyaṃte. je acele parivusi*t*e saṃcikkhai omoyariyâe, se
314 akkuṭṭhe va[9] hae va[9] lûsie va.[9] paliyaṃ pakaṃtha aduvâ pakaṃtha atahehiṃ saddaphâsehiṃ. iya[8] saṃkhâe ega*t*are anna*t*are abhinnâya titikkhamâṇe parivvae[10] je ya[11] hirî, je u[12] ahirîmâṇe. cĕccâ savvaṃ visŏttiyaṃ saṃphâse phâse samiyadaṃsaṇe. ||3|| ee bho nagiṇâ vuttâ, je logaṃsi aṇâgamaṇadhammiṇo âṇâe mâmagaṃ dhammaṃ. esa uttaravâe iha[13] mâṇavâṇaṃ viyâhie. ĕttho 'varae taṃ jhosamâṇe âyâṇijjaṃ parinnâya pariyâeṇaṃ vigiṃca*t*i. iham egesiṃ egacariyâ
317 tatth' i*t*arâ iyarehiṃ kulehiṃ suddhesaṇâe savvesaṇâe se mehâvî parivvae; subbhiṃ vâ aduvâ[14] dubbhiṃ, aduvâ

[20] A pavedayissâmi. [21] A abhisaṃtuḍḍhâ. [22] B ia.
[1] B °ṇaṃ. [2] B bhee. [3] B avaitinnâ, A nn. [4] B app°. [5] A daḍhâ. [6] B giddhiṃ. [7] B atthi tti. [8] A iti. [9] B vâ. [10] A cc. [11] AB a. [12] B om. [13] A idha. [14] A ahavâ.

tattha bheravâ pâṇâ pâṇe kilesaṃti te phâse puṭṭho
vîre ahiyâsĕjjâ[15] si tti bemi. ||4||**2**||

biio uddesao.

eyaṃ khu muṇî âyâṇaṃ sayâ suakkhâyadhamme *vidhûta*-
kappe nijjhosaittâ.[1] je acele parivusie, tassa ṇaṃ bhikkhussa
no evaṃ bhavai: parijuṇṇe me vatthe, vatthaṃ jâissâmi,
suttaṃ jâissâmi, sûiṃ jâissâmi, saṃdhissâmi, sivvissâmi,[2]
vukkasissâmi, parihissâmi, pâuṇissâmi. ||1|| aduvâ tattha 319
parakkamaṃtaṃ bhujjo acelaṃ taṇaphâsâ phusaṃti, sîyaphâsâ phusaṃti, teophâsâ phusaṃti, daṃsamasagaphâsâ phusaṃti; egayare annayare virûvarûve phâse ahiyâse*ti* acele
lâghavam âgamamîṇe.[3] tave se abhisamannâga*t*e bhava*ti*.
jah' eyaṃ bhagava*t*â pave*ditaṃ*, tam eva abhisamĕccâ
savva*t*o savvattâe[4] saṃmattam eva samabhijâṇiyâ. evaṃ
tesiṃ mahâvîrâṇaṃ cirarâtaṃ[5] puvvâiṃ vâsâiṃ rîyamâṇâ-
ṇaṃ daviyâṇaṃ pâsa ahiyâsiyaṃ;[6] âga*t*apannâṇâṇaṃ kisâ bâhâ
bhavaṃti payaṇue ya maṃsasoṇie. visseṇiṃ[7] kaṭṭu parinnâ- 321
ya esa tinne mutte virae viyâhie tti bemi. ||2|| virayaṃ bhi-
kkhuṃ rîyaṃtaṃ cirarâ*t*osiyaṃ ara*t*î tattha kiṃ vidhârae?
saṃdhemâṇe samuṭṭhi*t*e. jahâ se dîve asaṃdîṇe, evaṃ se
dhamme âriyapadesie.[8] te aṇavakaṃkhamâṇâ pâṇâ aṇativâe-
mâṇâ daiyâ[9] me*dh*âviṇo paṃḍiyâ. evaṃ tesiṃ bhagava*t*o
aṇuṭṭhâṇe; jahâ se diyâ poe, evaṃ te sissâ diyâ ya râo ya
aṇupuvveṇaṃ vâiya tti bemi. ||3||**3**|| 325

taio uddesao.

evaṃ te sissâ diyâ ya râo ya aṇupuvveṇaṃ vâi*t*â tehiṃ mahâvîrehiṃ pannâṇamaṃtehiṃ[1] tesiṃ 'tie pannâṇam uvalabbha. [2]hiccâ uvasamaṃ phârusiyaṃ[3] samâ*d*iyaṃti. vasittâ baṃbhaceraṃsi âṇaṃ taṃ no tti mannamâṇâ âghâyaṃ tu sŏccâ nisamma samaṇunnâ jîvissâmo ege nikkhamma te asaṃbhavaṃtâ viḍajjhamâṇâ kâmehiṃ giddhâ ajjhovavannâ

[15] A biyâsaejjâ.

[1] A ṇ. [2] B sîv. [3] Nâgârjunîyâs tu paṭhanti: evaṃ khalu se uvagaraṇalâghaviyaṃ tavaṃ kammakkhayakâraṇaṃ kareti. [4] A savvatâe. [5] B °râiṃ. [6] A hiy°. [7] A ṇî. [8] A âriyadesie. [9] A datiyâ.

[1] A tesaṃ. [2] pâthântaraṃ vâ: heccâ uvasamamaṃthâ h' ege phârusiyaṃ samâruhaṃti. [3] A pharusiyaṃ.

samâhim âghâ*t*am ajhosayaṃtâ[3] satthâram evaṃ pharuṣaṃ va*d*aṃti. sîlamaṃtâ uvasaṃtâ saṃkhâe rîyamâṇâ, asîlâ aṇuvayamâṇassa bi*t*iyâ maṃdassa bâlayâ.[4] niyaṭṭamâṇâ v' ege âyâragoyaram âikkhaṃti.[5] nâṇabbhaṭṭhâ daṃsa-
328 ṇalûsiṇo namamâṇâ ege jîviyaṃ vippariṇâmeṃti.[6] puṭṭhâ v' ege niyaṭṭaṃti jîviyass' eva kâraṇâ. nikkhaṃtaṃ pi tesiṃ dunnikkhaṃtaṃ bhavati. ||1|| bâla vayaṇijjâ[7] hu te narâ puṇo puṇo jâ*t*iṃ pagappĕṃti.[8] ahe saṃbhavaṃtâ[9] viddâyamâṇâ aham aṃsî 'ti viukkase; udâsîṇe pharusaṃ vayaṃti. paliyaṃ pagaṃthe aduvâ pagaṃthe atahehiṃ. taṃ mehâvî jâṇĕjjâ dhammaṃ. ahaṃmaṭṭhî tumaṃ si nâma
330 bâle ârambhaṭṭhî aṇuvayamâṇe: haṇa pâṇe! ghâ*t*amâṇe haṇao yâvi samaṇujâṇamîṇe[10]: ghore dhamme udîri*t*e; uvehai ṇaṃ aṇâṇâe, esa visaṇṇe vitaṃḍe[11] viyâhie. tti bemi. ||2||

kim aṇeṇa bho yaṇeṇa karissâmi tti mannamâṇâ evaṃ ege[12] viditta[13] mâtaraṃ piyaraṃ [14]hĕccâ nâyao pariggahaṃ; vîrâyamâṇâ[15] samuṭṭhâe avihiṃsâ suvva*t*â daṃtâ pâsa[16] dîṇe; uppaie paḍivayamâṇe. vasaṭṭâ kâyarâ jaṇâ lûsagâ bhavaṃti. aham egesiṃ siloe pâvae bhava*t*i: se samaṇavibbhaṃte 2
332 pâsah' ege samannâga*t*ehiṃ[17] asamannâgate namamâṇehiṃ aṇamamâṇe vira*t*ehiṃ avira*t*e daviehiṃ addavie. abhisamĕccâ paṃḍie mehâvî niṭṭhiyaṭṭhe vîre âgameṇaṃ sayâ parakkamĕjjâ si tti bemi. ||3||**4**||

cauttho uddesao.

se gihesu vâ gihaṃtaresu vâ gâmesu vâ gâmaṃtaresu vâ nagaresu vâ nagaraṃtaresu vâ jaṇavaesu vâ jaṇavayaṃtaresu vâ saṃtegaiyâ jaṇâ lûsagâ bhavaṃti, aduvâ phâsâ phusaṃti. te phâse phuṭṭho vîro ahiyâsae.[1] ||1|| oe samiyadaṃsaṇe dayaṃ logassa jâṇittâ pâîṇaṃ paḍîṇaṃ[2] dâhiṇaṃ u*d*îṇaṃ
335 âikkhe vibhae kiṭṭe ve*d*avî.[3] se uṭṭhi*t*esu vâ aṇuṭṭhi*t*esu vâ

[3] A ajo°. [4] B bâliyâ. [5] A âti°. [6] B vipari°, A °aṃti. [7] B vaiṇ°. [8] B pakappiṃti. [9] A °to. [10] B °mâṇe. [11] B viadde. [12] B pege. [13] B caittâ. [14] Nâgârjunîyâs tu paṭhanti: samaṇâ bhavissâmo aṇagârâ akiṃcaṇâ aputtâ apasû ahiṃsagâ suvvayâ daṃtâ paradattabhoiṇo pâvaṃ kammaṃ karessâmo samuṭṭhâe. [15] A °ṇe. [16] B passa. [17] B adds saha.

[1] A hiy°. [2] A paḍiṇaṃ. [3] Nâgârjunîyâs tu paṭhanti: je khalu bhikkhû bahussue vajjhâgame âharaṇaheo kusale dhammakahâladdhisaṃpanno khettaṃ kâlaṃ purisaṃ samâsajja kah' eyaṃ purise kaṃ vâ darisaṇam abhisaṃpanno evaṃ puṇa jâtîe pabhû dhammassâ âghavittae.

sussûsamâṇesu pavedae. ‖2‖ saṃtiṃ viratiṃ uvasamaṃ nivvâṇaṃ soyaṃ[4] ajjaviyaṃ maddaviyaṃ lâghaviyaṃ aṇativattiya[5] savvesiṃ pâṇâṇaṃ savvesiṃ bhû*t*âṇaṃ savvesiṃ jîvâṇaṃ savvesiṃ sattâṇaṃ aṇuvîi bhikkhudhammam âikkhĕjjâ. ‖3‖ aṇuvîi bhikkhuddhammam âikkhamâṇe no attâṇaṃ âsâ*d*ĕjjâ, no paraṃ âsâ*d*ĕjjâ, no annâiṃ pâṇâiṃ bhûtâiṃ jîvâiṃ sattâiṃ âsâ*d*ĕjjâ. se aṇâsâyae aṇâsâyamâṇe vajjhamâ- 337
ṇâṇaṃ pâṇâṇaṃ bhû*t*âṇaṃ jîvâṇaṃ sattâṇaṃ, jahâ se dîve asaṃdîṇe, evaṃ se bhavati saraṇaṃ mahâmuṇî. ‖4‖ evaṃ se uṭṭhie ṭhiyappâ aṇihe acale cale abahilese parivvae:

saṃkhâya[6] pesalaṃ dhammaṃ diṭṭhimaṃ parinivvuḍe |
tamhâ saṃgaṃ ti pâsahâ gaṃthehiṃ gaḍhiyâ narâ. ‖

visannâ kâmakkaṃtâ, tumhâ lûhâo no parivittasĕjjâ. jass' ime âraṃbhâ savvato savvattâe suparinnâyâ bhavaṃti, jass' ime lûsiṇo no parivittasaṃti se vaṃtâ kohaṃ ca mâṇaṃ ca mâyaṃ ca lo*bh*aṃ ca esa tuṭṭe[7] viyâhie tti bemi. ‖5‖ 340
kâyassa viâghâe[8] esa saṃgâmasîse viyâhie. se hu pâraṃgame muṇî avihammamâṇe phalagâva*t*aṭṭhî kâlovaṇîe kaṃkhĕjjâ kâlaṃ jâva sarîrabhe*d*ŏ tti bemi. ‖6‖**5**‖

paṃcamo uddesao.

chattham ajjhayaṇaṃ.

dhûtaṃ samattaṃ.

[4] A soviyaṃ. [5] MSS. °iyaṃ, Comm. = anatipatya. [6] A saṃkhâta. [7] AC tiuṭṭe.
[8] AB viâvâe.

SATTAMAM AJJHAYAṆAṂ.

MAHÂPARINNÂ.

se bemi: samaṇunnassa vâ asamaṇunnassa vâ asaṇaṃ vâ pâṇaṃ vâ khâimaṃ vâ sâimaṃ vâ vatthaṃ vâ paḍiggahaṃ[1] vâ pâyapuṃchaṇaṃ vâ no pâĕjjâ no nimaṃtijjâ no kujjâ veyâvaḍiyaṃ paraṃ âḍhâyamîṇe tti bemi. ‖1‖ dhuvaṃ[2]
346 c' eyaṃ jâṇĕjjâ asaṇaṃ vâ *jâva*[3] pâyapuṃchaṇaṃ vâ labhiya[4] no labhiya,[4] bhuṃjiya[4] no bhuṃjiya[4] paṃthaṃ viyattûṇa viukkamma[11] vibhattaṃ dhammaṃ jhosemâṇe samemâṇe palemâṇe[5] pâĕjjâ nimaṃtĕjjâ kujjâ veyâvaḍiyaṃ paraṃ aṇâḍhâyamîṇe tti bemi. ‖2‖ iham egesiṃ âyâragoyare no suṇisaṃte bhava*t*i. te iha âraṃbhaṭṭhî aṇuvayamâṇâ:[6] haṇa pâṇe; ghâyamâṇâ haṇao âvi samaṇujâṇamîṇâ,[7] aduvâ adinnam âiyaṃti, aduvâ vâyâo vippauṃjaṃti; taṃ jahâ: atthi loe, n'atthi loe; dhuve loe, adhuve loe; sâie loe, aṇâie loe;
349 sapajjavasie loe, apajjavasie loe; sukaḍe tti vâ, dukkaḍe tti vâ; kallâṇe ti[8] vâ, pâvae[9] ti vâ; sâ*dh*û ti[8] vâ, asâ*dh*û ti[8] vâ; siddhî ti[8] vâ, asiddhî ti[8] vâ; nirae ti[8] vâ, anirae ti[8] vâ—jam iṇaṃ vipaḍivannâ mâmagaṃ dhammaṃ pannavemâṇâ[10] ĕttha vi jâṇa[11] akasmât. evaṃ tesiṃ no suyakkhâe no supannatte dhamme bhava*t*i; se jah' eyaṃ bhagava*t*â pave*d*i*t*aṃ âsupanneṇaṃ jâṇayâ pâsayâ; aduvâ guttî vaogoyarassa tti bemi. ‖3‖ savvattha saṃmayaṃ pâvaṃ, tam eva uvâ*t*ikkamma esa
351 mahaṃ vivege viyâhie. gâme vâ aduvâ raṇṇe, n'eva gâme n'eva raṇṇe dhammam âyâṇaha paveiyaṃ. mâhaṇeṇa ma*t*imayâ jâmâ tinni udâhiyâ, jesu ime âriyâ saṃbujjhamâṇâ samuṭṭhi*t*â nivvuyâ pâvehiṃ kammehiṃ aṇi*d*âṇâ te viyâhiyâ. ‖4‖ uḍḍhaṃ ahaṃ tiriyaṃ disâsu savvao savvâvaṃti ca ṇaṃ paḍikkaṃ[1] jîvehiṃ kammasamâraṃbhe ṇaṃ; taṃ parinnâya mehâvî n'eva sayaṃ eehiṃ kâehiṃ daṃḍaṃ samâraṃbhĕjjâ, n' ev' annehiṃ eehiṃ kâehiṃ

[1] A pari°. [2] A dhuyaṃ. [3] A full phrase. [4] AB iyâ. [5] B vale°. [6] B °mâṇe. [7] A adds ahaṇao. [8] B tti preceded by the short vowel. [9] B pâve. [10] A °ṇe. [11] BC jâṇeha.

damḍaṃ samârambhâvĕjjâ, n' ev' anne eehiṃ[11] kâehiṃ
damḍaṃ samârambhaṃte vi samaṇujâṇĕjjâ; je[12] v' anne 353
eehiṃ kâehiṃ damḍaṃ samârambhaṃti, tesiṃ vayaṃ lajjâmo.
taṃ parinnâya mehâvî taṃ vâ damḍaṃ annaṃ vâ damḍaṃ no
damḍaṃ bhîdamḍaṃ samârambhâvĕjjâ si tti bemi. ||5||**1**||

padhamo uddesao.

se bhikkhû parakkamejja vâ ciṭṭhejja vâ nisiejja vâ
tuyaṭṭejja vâ susâṇaṃsi vâ sunnâgâraṃsi vâ giriguhaṃsi vâ
rukkhamûlaṃsi vâ kuṃbhârâyayaṇaṃsi vâ huratthâ vâ kahiṃ
ci viharamâṇaṃ taṃ bhikkhuṃ uvasaṃkamittu gâhâvatî
bûyâ: âusaṃto[1] samaṇâ! ahaṃ khalu tava aṭṭhâe asaṇaṃ vâ 4 354
vatthaṃ vâ paḍiggahaṃ vâ kaṃbalaṃ vâ pâyapuṃchaṇaṃ vâ
pâṇâiṃ bhûtâiṃ jîvâiṃ sattâiṃ samârabbha samuddissa
kîyaṃ pâmiccaṃ acchejjaṃ aṇisaṭṭhaṃ abhihaḍaṃ âhaṭṭu
cetemi, âvasa*h*aṃ vâ samussiṇâmi; se bhuṃjaha, vasaha! ||1||
âusaṃto[1] samaṇâ! bhikkhû[2] taṃ[2] gâhâva*t*iṃ samaṇasaṃ
savayasaṃ paḍiyâikkhe: âusaṃto gâhâva*t*î![3] no khalu te
vayaṇaṃ âḍhâmi,[4] no khalu te vayaṇaṃ parijâṇâmi, jo tumaṃ
mama aṭṭhâe asaṇaṃ vâ 4[5] vatthaṃ vâ 4[5] pâṇâiṃ 4[5] samârabbha 356
samuddissa kîyaṃ pâmiccaṃ acchejjaṃ aṇisaṭṭhaṃ abhihaḍaṃ âhaṭṭu ce*t*esi, âvasahaṃ samussiṇâsi. se virato âuso
gâhâva*t*î eyassâ 'karaṇâe.[6] ||2|| se bhikkhû parakkamejja
vâ *jâva* huratthâ vâ kahiṃci viharamâṇaṃ taṃ bhikkhuṃ
uvasaṃkamittu gâhâva*t*î âyaga*t*âe pehâe asaṇaṃ vâ 4[5] vatthaṃ
vâ 4[5] pâṇâiṃ 4 samârabbha *jâva* âhaṭṭu ceteti, âvasahaṃ vâ
samussiṇâe,[7] taṃ bhikkhuṃ parighâseuṃ.[8] taṃ ca bhikkhû 357
jâṇejjâ sahasammaiyâe[9] paravâgaraṇeṇaṃ annesiṃ vâ soccâ:
ayaṃ khalu gâhâva*t*î[10] mama aṭṭhâe asaṇaṃ vâ 4 vatthaṃ vâ
4[5] pâṇâiṃ vâ 4 samârabbha *jâva* âhaṭṭu ceteti, âvasahaṃ vâ
vâ samussiṇâ*t*i.[10] taṃ ca bhikkhû paḍilehâe âgamettâ âṇa-
vejjâ aṇâsevaṇâe tti bemi. ||3|| bhikkhuṃ ca khalu puṭṭhâ
vâ apuṭṭhâ vâ, je ime âhacca gaṃthâ phusaṃti, se haṃtâ
haṇaha, khaṇaha, chiṃdaha, dahaha, pacaha, âluṃpaha,
viluṃpaha, sahasakkâreha,[11] vipparâmusaha! te phâse 358

[11] A annehiṃ. [12] A ne.

[1] MSS. âusaṃbho. [2] A taṃ bhikkhuṃ. [3] A. °iṃ. [4] B âḍhâemi.
[5] B hva 4. [6] B kâraṇayâe. [7] B °ṇati. [8] B °settum; add ahivâseuṃ or a similar
word. [9] B °mutiyâe. [10] A no *t*. [11] B °sâkâŗeha.

puṭṭho vîro ahiyâsae, aduvâ âyâragoyaram âikkhe takkiyâ ṇam aṇelisaṃ, aduvâ vaiguttîe goyarassa aṇupuvveṇaṃ sammaṃ paḍilehâe âyagutte. buddhehiṃ eyaṃ paveditaṃ: se samaṇunne asamaṇunnassa asaṇaṃ vâ 4 [12]vatthaṃ vâ 4 no pâejjâ, no nimaṃtejjâ, no kujjâ veyâvaḍiyaṃ paraṃ âḍhâyamîṇe tti bemi. ||4|| dhammam âyâṇaha pavedi*t*aṃ mâhaṇeṇaṃ ma*t*imayâ: samaṇunne samaṇunnassa asaṇaṃ vâ 4
360 vatthaṃ vâ 4 pâejjâ, nimaṃtejjâ, kujjâ veyâvaḍiyaṃ paraṃ âḍhâyamîṇe tti bemi. ||5||**2**||

biio uddesao.

majjhimeṇaṃ vayasâ vi ege saṃbujjhamâṇâ samuṭṭhitâ soccâ medhâvî vayaṇaṃ paṃḍiyâṇaṃ nisâmittâ.[1] samiyâe dhamme âriehiṃ pavedite. te aṇavakaṃkhamâṇâ aṇativâtemâṇâ apariggahamîṇâ. no pariggahavaṃtî[2] savvâvaṃtî[2] ca ṇaṃ logaṃsi nihâya daṃḍaṃ[3] pâṇehiṃ pâvaṃ kammaṃ akuvvamâṇe esa mahaṃ agaṃthe viyâhie. ||1|| oe jutimaṃtassa[4] khe*t*anne uvavâyaṃ cavaṇaṃ ca naccâ âhârovacayâ dehâ
362 parîsahapabhaṃgurâ. pâsah' ege savviṃdiehiṃ parigilâyamâṇehiṃ oe dayaṃ dayati; je saṃnihâṇasatthassa kheyanne se bhikkhû kâlanne balanne[5] mâyanne[5] khaṇanne[5] viṇayanne[5] samayanne[5] pariggahaṃ amamâyamîṇe kâle 'ṇuṭṭhâî apaḍinne duhao chettâ niyâti. ||2|| taṃ bhikkhuṃ sîyaphâsapaḍivevamâṇagâtaṃ[6] uvasaṃkamittu gâhâva*t*î bûyâ: âusaṃto samaṇâ! no khalu te gâma*dh*ammâ uvvâhaṃti? âusaṃto gâhâva*t*î! no khalu mama gâmadhammâ uvvâhaṃti.
364 sîyaphâsaṃ ca no khalu ahaṃ saṃcâemi ahiyâsettae; no khalu me kappati agaṇikâyaṃ ujjâlettae pajjâlĕttae vâ kâyaṃ âyâvĕttae vâ payâvĕttae vâ, annesiṃ vâ vayaṇâo. siyâ s' evaṃ va*d*aṃtassa paro agaṇikâyaṃ ujjâlĕttâ pajjâlĕttâ âyâvejja[7] vâ payâvĕjja[7] vâ. taṃ ca bhikkhû paḍilehâe âgamettâ âṇavejjâ aṇâsevaṇâe tti bemi. ||3||**3**||

taio uddesao.

je bhikkhû tihiṃ vatthehiṃ parivusi*t*e[1] pâyacautthehiṃ,

[12] A om.
[1] B nisâmiyâ. [2] B °i. [3] B ḍa°. [4] MSS. jj. [5] MSS. ṇṇ. [6] A °veya° B parîve°. [7] B °â.
[1] B pariosite pâda°.

tassa ṇaṃ no evaṃ bhavati: cautthaṃ vatthaṃ jâissâmi. se ahesaṇijjâiṃ jâejjâ, ahâpariggahiyâiṃ vatthâiṃ dhârejjâ, no 366
dhovĕjjâ,[2] no raejjâ,[3] no dhotarattâiṃ vatthâiṃ dhârejjâ, apaliuṃcamâṇe[4] gâmaṃtaresu omacelie. eyaṃ[5] khu vatthadhârissa sâmaggiyaṃ. a*h*a puṇa evaṃ jâṇejjâ: uvâ*t*ikkaṃte[6] khalu hemaṃte, gimhe paḍivanne; a*h*âparijuṇṇâiṃ vatthâiṃ pariṭṭhavejjâ, ahâparijuṇṇaiṃ vatthâiṃ pariṭṭhavettâ aduvâ saṃtaruttare, aduvâ omacelae,[7] aduvâ egasâḍe, aduvâ acele lâghaviyaṃ âgamamîṇe. tave se abhisamannâgate bhavati.
jam e*t*aṃ bhagava*t*â paveditaṃ, tam eva abhisameccâ savvato 367
savvayâe[8] samattam eva samabhijâṇiyâ. ‖1‖ jassa ṇaṃ bhikkhussa evaṃ bhavati: puṭṭho khalu aham aṃsi, nâ 'lam aham[9] aṃsi[9] sîyaphâsaṃ a*h*iyâsĕttae,[10] se vasumaṃ savvasamannâgatapannâṇeṇaṃ appâṇeṇaṃ kei akaraṇayâe[11] âvaṭṭe. tavassiṇo hu taṃ seyaṃ[12] jam ege vihamâdie. tatthâ 'vi tassa kâlapariyâe se vi tattha viyaṃtikârae. icc etaṃ[12] vimohâyataṇaṃ hiyaṃ suhaṃ khamaṃ nisseyasaṃ âṇugâmiyaṃ ti bemi. ‖2‖4‖

cauttho uddesao.

je bhikkhû dohiṃ vatthehiṃ parivusi*t*e pâ*t*atatiehiṃ, tassa 370
ṇaṃ no evaṃ bhavati: tatiyaṃ vatthaṃ jâissâmi. se ahesaṇijjâiṃ vatthâiṃ jâejjâ *jâva* eyaṃ khu[1] tassa bhikkhussa sâmaggiyaṃ. aha puṇa evaṃ jâṇĕjjâ: uvâ*t*ikkaṃte khalu hemaṃte, gimhe paḍivanne; a*h*âparijuṇṇâiṃ[2] vatthâiṃ pariṭṭhavejjâ, ahâparijuṇṇâiṃ vatthâiṃ pariṭṭhavettâ aduvâ[3] saṃtaruttare,[3] aduva egasâḍe, aduvâ acele lâghaviyaṃ âgamamîṇe. tave se abhisamannâgate bhavati. jam[4] eyaṃ bhagava*t*â paveditaṃ,
tam eva abhisameccâ savvato savvayâe[5] samattam eva sama- 371
bhijâṇiyâ.[6] jassa ṇaṃ bhikkhussa evaṃ bhavati: puṭṭho abalo aham aṃsi, nâ 'lam aham aṃsi gihaṃtarasaṃkamaṇaṃ bhikkhâyariyaṃ gamaṇâe. ‖1‖ se evaṃ vadaṃtassa paro abhihaḍaṃ asaṇaṃ vâ 4 âhaṭṭu dalaejjâ. se puvvâm eva

[2] A dhoejjâ. [3] B om. [4] B °ṇo. [5] A evaṃ. [6] A uvâikaṃte. [7] A avama°, B °le. [8] B savvattâe. [9] A om. [10] B adhi°, A °settae. [11] B keti akaraṇâe, A âuḍḍhe. [12] B se taṃ.

[1] B khalu. [2] B adhâ°. [3] A om. B adds aduvâ omacele. [4] B jadh. [5] B savvattâe. [6] A °ṇayâ, B °ṇitâ.

âloejjâ: âusaṃto gâhâva*tî*! no khalu me kappati abhihaḍe
asaṇe vâ 4 bhottae vâ pâyae vâ anne vâ tahappagâre.[6] ||2||
jassa ṇaṃ bhikkhussa ayaṃ pagappe: ahaṃ ca khalu paḍi-
372 ṇnatto[7] apaḍinnattehiṃ[7] gilâṇo agilâṇehiṃ abhikaṃkha sâ-
hammiehiṃ kîramâṇaṃ veyâvaḍiyaṃ sâijjissâmi[8]; ahaṃ câvi
khalu apaḍinnatto[7] paḍinnattassa,[7] agilâṇo gilâṇassa abhikaṃ-
kha sâ*dh*ammiyassa kujjâ veyâvaḍiyaṃ karaṇâe. ||3|| âhaṭṭu
parinnaṃ[9] âṇakkhessâmi âhaḍaṃ ca sâijjissâmi[8]; âhaṭṭu
parinnaṃ[9] âṇakkhessâmi âhaḍaṃ ca no sâijjissâmi[8]; âhaṭṭu
parinnaṃ[9] no âṇakkhessâmi âhaḍaṃ ca sâijjissâmi[8]; âhaṭṭu
374 parinnaṃ[9] no âṇakkhessâmi âhaḍaṃ ca no sâijjissâmi.[8] evaṃ
se a*h*âkiṭṭitam[2] eva dhammaṃ sama*bh*ijâṇamâṇe saṃte virate
susamâhi*t*alesse. tatthâ 'vi tassa kâlapariyâe se tattha viaṃti-
kârae.[10] icc etaṃ vimohâyataṇaṃ hiyaṃ suhaṃ khamaṃ
nisseyasaṃ[11] âṇugâmiyaṃ ti bemi. ||4||**5**||

pamcamo uddesao.

je bhikkhû egeṇa vattheṇa parivusi*t*e pâyabitieṇa, tassa no
evaṃ bhava*t*i: bitiyaṃ vatthaṃ jâissâmi. se ahesaṇijjaṃ[1]
vatthaṃ jâejjâ, a*h*âpariggahi*t*aṃ vatthaṃ dhârejjâ *jâva*
gimhe paḍivanne; ahâparijuṇṇaṃ vatthaṃ pariṭṭhavejjâ,
375 aduvâ egasâḍe, aduvâ acele lâghaviyaṃ âgamamîṇe *jâva*
samattam eva samabhijâṇiyâ. jassa ṇaṃ bhikkhussa evaṃ
bhava*t*i: ego aham aṃsi, no me atthi koi na yâ'ham avi
kassai—evaṃ 'sa egâṇiyam[2] eva appâṇaṃ samabhijâṇĕjjâ
lâghaviyaṃ âgamamîṇe. tave se abhisamannâgate bhava*t*i.
jah' eyaṃ bhagava*t*â pave*dit*aṃ, tam eva abhisamĕccâ savva-
to savvayâe[3] samattam eva samabhijâṇiyâ. ||1|| se bhikkhû vâ
376 bhikkhuṇî vâ asaṇaṃ vâ 4 âhâremâṇe no vâmâo haṇuyâo dâhiṇaṃ haṇuyaṃ saṃcârejjâ âsâemîṇe[4] dâhiṇâo[5] vâ haṇuyâo[5]
vâmaṃ haṇuyaṃ no saṃcârejjâ âsâemîṇe, aṇâsâemîṇe lâghaviyaṃ âgamamîṇe.[6] tave se abhisamannâgate bhavati. jah'
eyaṃ bhagava*t*â paveditaṃ, tam eva abhisameccâ savvato

[6] B eyapp°.—pâṭhântaraṃ vâ: gâhâvatî uvasaṃkamittu bûyâ: âusaṃto samaṇâ! ahaṃ ṇaṃ tava aṭṭhâe asaṇaṃ vâ 4 abhihaḍaṃ dalâmi. se puvvâm eva jâṇejjâ: âusaṃto gâhâvaî! jannaṃ tumaṃ mamaṃ aṭṭhâe asaṇaṃ vâ 4 bhottae vâ pâyae vâ anne vâ tahappagâre. [7] A padiṇa°. [8] A sâti°. [9] A ṇṇ. [10] B viaṃti. [11] A nisesaṃ.

[1] A adh°. [2] B egâgiṇam. [3] B *t*ttâe. [4] B om. [5] B °âto. [6] A °mâṇe.

savvayâe[3] samattaṃ eva samabhijâṇiyâ. ||2|| jassa ṇaṃ bhikkhussa evaṃ bhavati: se gilâmi ca khalu ahaṃ imaṃmi samae imaṃ sarîragaṃ aṇupuvveṇa parivahittae, se aṇupuvveṇaṃ[7] âhâraṃ saṃvaṭṭejjâ, aṇupuvvenaṃ[7] âhâraṃ 377
saṃvaṭṭittâ kasâe pataṇue[8] kiccâ samâhiyacce phalagâva*t*aṭṭhî utthâya bhikkhû abhinivvuḍacce. ||3|| aṇupavisittâ gâmaṃ vâ nagaraṃ vâ kheḍaṃ vâ kabbaḍaṃ vâ maḍaṃbaṃ vâ paṭṭaṇaṃ vâ doṇamuhaṃ vâ âgaraṃ vâ âsamaṃ vâ saṃnivesaṃ vâ nigamaṃ vâ râyahâṇiṃ vâ taṇâiṃ jâejjâ, taṇâiṃ jâĕttâ se ttam âyâe e*g*aṃtam avakkamejjâ, egaṃtam avakkamittâ appaṃḍe appapâṇe appabîe appaharie appose appudae[9] apputtiṃgapaṇagadagamaṭṭiyamakkaḍâsaṃtâṇae paḍilehiya 2 pamajjiya 2 taṇâiṃ 379
saṃtharejjâ, saṃtharĕttâ ettha vi samae ittiriyaṃ kujjâ. ||4|| taṃ saccaṃ: saccavâdî oe tiṇṇe chinnaka*h*aṃka*h*e âtî*t*aṭṭhe aṇâtî*t*e ceccâṇa bhe*d*uraṃ kâyaṃ saṃvi*dh*uṇiya virûvarûve parîsahovasagge assiṃ vissaṃbhaṇayâe bheravam aṇuciṇṇe· tattha vi tassa kâlapariyâe se tattha viaṃtakârae.[10] icc etaṃ vimohâyataṇaṃ hiyaṃ suhaṃ khamaṃ nisseyasaṃ âṇugâmiyaṃ ti bemi. ||5|| **6**||

chaṭṭho uddesao.

je bhikkhû acele parivusite, tassa ṇaṃ evaṃ bhavati: câemi ahaṃ taṇaphâsaṃ a*h*iyâsĕttae,[1] sîyaphâsaṃ a*h*iyâsĕttae, 382
teuphâsaṃ ahisâyettae,[1] daṃsamasagaphâsaṃ ahiyâsettae, ega*t*are annatare[1] virûvarûve phâse ahiyâsettae, hiripaḍicchâ*d*aṇaṃ ca 'haṃ[2] no[3] saṃcâemi ahiyâsettae.[2] evaṃ se kappati kaḍibaṃdhaṇaṃ dhârittae. aduvâ tattha parakkamaṃtaṃ bhujjo acelaṃ taṇaphâsâ phusaṃti, sîyaphâsâ phusaṃti, teuphâsâ phusaṃti, daṃsamasagaphâsâ phusaṃti, egatare annatare virûvarûve phâse a*h*iyâseti acele lâghaviyaṃ âgamamîṇe. tave 383
se abhisamannâgate bhavati. ja*h*' etaṃ bhagava*t*â paveditaṃ *jîva* tam eva abhisamĕccâ savvaso savvattâe samattam eva samabhijâṇiyâ. ||1|| jassa ṇaṃ bhikkhussa evaṃ bhavati: ahaṃ ca khalu annesiṃ bhikkhûṇaṃ asaṇaṃ 4 âhaṭṭu

[7] BC âṇupuvveṇa. [8] B payaṇu. [9] B appodae. [10] B viaṃti°.
[1] A om. [2] B om. [3] B ṇ.

dalaissâmi, âhaḍaṃ ca sâijjissâmi:[4] jassa ṇaṃ bhikkhussa evaṃ bhavati: ahaṃ ca khalu annesiṃ bhikkhûṇaṃ asaṇaṃ 4 âhaṭṭu dalaissâmi, âhaḍaṃ ca no[3] sâijjissâmi; jassa ṇaṃ etc . . . asaṇaṃ 4 âhaṭṭu no[3] dâsâmi,[5] âhaḍaṃ ca sâijjissâmi; jassa ṇaṃ etc . . . asaṇaṃ 4 âhaṭṭu no[4] dâsâmi, âhadaṃ ca no sâijjissâmi; ||2|| ahaṃ ca khalu teṇaṃ ahâtiritteṇaṃ ahesaṇijjeṇaṃ ahâpariggahieṇaṃ asaṇeṇaṃ vâ 4 abhikaṃkha sâhammiyassa kujjâ veyâvaḍiyaṃ karaṇâe; ahaṃ câvi teṇaṃ ahâtiritteṇaṃ ahesaṇijjeṇaṃ ahăpariggahieṇaṃ asaṇeṇaṃ 4. abhikaṃkha sâhammiehiṃ kîramâṇaṃ veyâvaḍiyaṃ sâijjissâ-
384 mi. ||3|| lâghaviyaṃ âgamamîṇe *jâva* samattam eva samabhijâṇiyâ. ||4|| jassa ṇaṃ bhikkhussa evaṃ bhavati: se gilâmi, na khalu ahaṃ imammi samae imaṃ sarîragaṃ aṇupuvveṇa parivahittae etc. (6 § 3–5). ti bemi ||5||**7**||

sattamo uddesao.

aṇupuvveṇaṃ vimohâiṃ jâiṃ dhîrâ samâsajja |
vasumaṃto matimaṃto savvaṃ naccâ aṇelisaṃ ||i||
duvihaṃ pi viditttâ ṇaṃ buddhâ dhammassa pâragâ |
aṇupuvviya[1] saṃkhâe kammuṇâu tiuṭṭati[2] ||ii||
kasâe payaṇue kiccâ appâhâro titikkhae |
387 aha bhikkhû gilâejjâ âhârass' eva aṃtiyaṃ ||iii||
jîviyaṃ nâ 'bhikaṃkhejjâ maraṇaṃ no vi patthae |
duhato vi na sajjejjâ jîviṭe maraṇe tahâ ||iv||
majjhattho nijjarâpehî samâhim aṇupâlae |
aṃto bahiṃ viosajja ajjhatthaṃ suddham esae ||v||
jaṃ kiṃc' uvakkamaṃ jâṇe âukkhemassa-m-appaṇo |
tass' eva aṃtaraddhâe khippaṃ sikkhejja paṃḍie ||vi||
gâme vâ aduvâ raṇṇe thaṃḍilaṃ paḍilehiyâ |
appapâṇaṃ tu vinnâya taṇâiṃ saṃthare muṇî ||vii||
aṇâhâro tuyaṭṭejjâ puṭṭho tatth' ahiyâsae |
389 nâ' tivelaṃ uvacare mâṇussehi[3] vi puṭṭhavaṃ ||viii||
saṃsappagâ ya je pâṇâ je ya uḍḍham ahecarâ |
bhuṃjaṃti[4] maṃsaṃ[5] soṇîtaṃ na chaṇe na pamajjae ||ix||
pâṇâ dehaṃ vihiṃsaṃti ṭhâṇâo na viubbhame |
âsavehiṃ vivittehiṃ tippamâṇo 'hiyâsae ||x||

[4] B sâti° always. [5] B dalaissâmi.
[1] B °vîi. [2] B °tî, pâṭhântaraṃ tiuṭṭaha. [3] A ma°, AB °hiṃ. [4] B °te. [5] A saṃ.

gaṃthehiṃ vivittehiṃ âukâlassa pârae |
paggahitataraṃ [6] c' e*t*aṃ daviyassa viyâṇa*t*o ||xi||
ayaṃ se avare dhamme Nâyaputteṇa sâhie |
âyavajjaṃ paḍîyâraṃ vijahejjâ ti*dh*â ti*dh*â ||xii||
hariesu na nivajjejjâ thaṃḍilaṃ muṇiyâ sae |
viosejja aṇâhâro puṭṭho tatth' a*h*iyâsae ||xiii|| 391
iṃdiehiṃ gilâyaṃto samiyaṃ âhare muṇî |
tahâ 'vi se agarahe acale je samâhi*t*e ||xiv||
abhikkame paḍikkame saṃkucae [7] pasârae |
kâyasâhâraṇaṭṭhâe [8] ettha [9] vâ vi aceyaṇe ||xv||
parikkame parikilaṃte aduvâ ciṭṭhe a*h*âyate |
ṭhâṇeṇa parikilaṃte nisiejjâ ya aṃtaso ||xvi||
âsîṇe 'ṇelisaṃ [10] maraṇaṃ iṃdiyâṇi samîrae |
kolâvâsaṃ samâsajjâ [11] 'vitahaṃ pâduresae [12] ||xvii||
jao vajjaṃ samuppajje na tattha avalaṃbae | 392
ta*t*o ukkase appâṇaṃ savve phâse '*h*iyâsae ||xviii||
ayaṃ câ ''yatatare siyâ jo [13] evaṃ aṇupâlae |
savvagâ*t*anirodhe vi ṭhâṇâo na viubbhame ||xix||
ayaṃ se uttame dhamme puvvaṭṭhâṇassa paggahe |
aciraṃ paḍilehittâ vihare ciṭṭha mâhaṇe ||xx||
acittaṃ tu samâsajja ṭhâvae tattha appagaṃ |
vosire savvaso kâyaṃ na me dehe parîsahâ ||xxi||
jâvajjîvaṃ parîsahâ uvasaggâ ya [15] saṃkhayâ [16] |
saṃvuḍe dehabhe*d*âe iti panne '*h*iyâsae ||xxii||
bhiduresu [17] na rajjejjâ kâmesu bahutaresu vâ | 395
icchâlobhaṃ na sevejjâ dhuvaṃ vaṇṇaṃ sapehiyâ ||xxiii||
sâsaehiṃ nimaṃtejjâ divvaṃ mâyaṃ na saddahe |
taṃ paḍibujjha mâhaṇe savvaṃ nûmaṃ vi*h*ûṇiyâ ||xxiv||
savvaṭṭhehiṃ amucchie âukâlassa pârae |
titikkhaṃ paramaṃ naccâ vimohanna*t*araṃ hitaṃ ||xxv||

ti bemi. ||**8**||

atthamo uddesao.

[6] B pagahitatarâgaṃ. [7] A °kuṃ°. AC °ie. [8] A °har°. [9] AC °ṃ. [10] AC aṇelisaṃ. [11] BC °jja. [12] B pâuḍuesae. [13] B je. [15] B iti. [16] B saṃkhatâ. [17] B bheuresu.

OHÂṆASUYAṂ.

a*h*âsuyaṃ vadissâmi jahâ se samaṇe bhagavaṃ uṭṭhâya saṃkhâe taṃsi hemaṃte ahuṇo pavvaie rîitthâ.[1]

no c' ev' imeṇa vattheṇaṃ
pehissâmi taṃsi hemaṃte |
se pârae âvakahâe
401 e*t*aṃ khu aṇudhammiyaṃ [2] tassa || i ||
cattâri sâhie mâse
bahave pâṇajâ*t*i âgamma |
abhirujjha kâyăṃ vihariṃsu
ârusiyâ ṇăṃ tattha hiṃsiṃsu || ii ||
saṃvaccharăṃ [3] sâ*h*iyaṃ mâsaṃ
jaṇ na rikkâsi vatthagaṃ bhagavaṃ |
acele tatto [4] câî
taṃ vosajja vattham aṇagâre || iii ||
adu porisiṃ tiriyabhittiṃ [5]
cakkhum âsajja aṃtaso jjhâti |
a*h*a cakkhubhîtasahi*t*â [6]
te haṃtâ kaṃtâ bahave kaṃdiṃsu || iv ||
sayaṇehiṃ vitimissehiṃ [7]
itthîo se tattha parinnâyâ |
sâgâriyaṃ na seve
iti se sayaṃ [8] pavesiyâ jhâti || v ||
je kei ime agâratthâ
403 mîsîbhâvaṃ pahâya se jhâti |
[9] puṭṭho vi nâ 'bhibhâsiṃsu
gacchati nâ 'tivattatî aṃjû || vi ||
no sugaram [10] etaṃ [11] egesiṃ

[1] B rîyatthâ. [2] BC âṇu°. [3] read vâsaṃ ca. [4] B acelae tato. [5] B tiriyaṃ. [6] A saṃhitâ. [7] AC vimissehiṃ. [8] B sesaṃ. [9] Nâgârjunîyâs tu paṭhanti: puṭṭho va se apuṭṭho va no aṇunnâi pâvagavaṃ. [10] A sukaram. [11] B om.

nâ 'bhibhâse abhivâyamîṇe[12] |
hatapuvvo tattha daṃḍehiṃ[13]
lûsiyapuvvo appapuṇṇehiṃ || vii ||
pharusâiṃ duttittikkhâiṃ[14]
atiyacca muṇî parakkamamâṇe |
âghâtaṇaṭṭagîtâiṃ
daṃḍajujjhâiṃ[15] muṭṭhijujjhâiṃ[15] || viii ||
gaḍhie miho kahâsu[16] samayaṃmi
Nâtisute visoe addakkhu[17] |
etâi[18] sourâlâiṃ
gacchati Nâyaputte saraṇâe || ix ||
avi sâhie duve vâse
sîtodagam[19] abhŏcca[20] nikkhaṃte | 405
egattagate pihitacce
se 'bhinnâyadaṃsaṇe[21] saṃte || x ||
puḍhaviṃ ca âukâyaṃ[22] ca
teukâyaṃ[22] ca vâukâyaṃ ca |
paṇagâi[18] bîyahariyâiṃ
tasakâyaṃ ca savvaso naccâ || xi ||
eyâi[18] saṃti paḍilehe
cittamaṃtâi[18] se abhinnâya |
parivajjiyâṇa viharitthâ
iti saṃkhâya se Mahâvîre || xii ||
adu thâvarâ ya tasatâe[23]
tasajîvâ ya thâvarattâe |
adu[24] savvajoṇiyâ sattâ
kammuṇâ kappiyâ puḍho bâlâ || xiii ||
bhagavaṃ ca evam annesî[25]
sovahie hu luppatî bâle |
kammaṃ ca savvaso naccâ
taṃ paḍiyâikkhe[26] pâvagaṃ bhagavaṃ || xiv || 407
duvihaṃ samecca medhâvî
kiriyam akkhâya 'ṇelisaṃ nâṇî |
âyâṇasotam ativâtasoyăṃ
jogaṃ ca savvaso naccâ || xv ||

[12] A °vîṇe. [13] B °ḍaṃ°. [14] A dutitti°, BC duttiti. [15] B juddhâiṃ cf.[13]. [16] B mihukahâ. [17] B Nâyasute visoge ada°. [18] MSS. °iṃ. [19] B sîtodaṃ. [20] B abhoccâ. [21] B ahi°. [22] B kk. [23] B °ttâe. [24] MSS. °duvâ. [25] A annesi. [26] B pari°.

* ativâtiyaṃ aṇâuttiṃ
saṭam annesiṃ akaraṇayâe ²⁷ |
jass' itthîŏ ²⁸ parinnâyâ
savvakammâvahâŏ addakkhû ²⁹ ‖xvi‖
âhâkaḍaṃ ³⁰ na se seve
savvaso kammuṇâ ya addakkhû ³¹ |
jaṃ kiṃci pâvagaṃ bhagavaṃ
taṃ akuvvaṃ viꞡaḍaṃ bhuṃjitthâ ‖xvii‖
no sevatî ³² ya paravatthaṃ
parapâe ³³ vi ³⁴ se ṇa bhuṃjitthâ |
parivajjiyâṇa omâṇaṃ

408   gacchati saṃkhaḍiṃ asaraṇâe ‖xviii‖
mâyanne asaṇapâṇassa
nâ 'ṇugiddhe rasesu apaḍinne |
acchiṃ pi no pamajjiyâ
no vi ya kaṃḍuyae muṇî gâyaṃ ‖xix‖
appaṃ tiriyaṃ pehâe
appaṃ piṭṭhao ³⁵ va pehâe ³⁶ |
appaṃ buie paḍibhâṇî
paṃthapehî care jaṭamâṇe ‖xx‖
sisiraṃsi addhapaḍivanne
taṃ vosajja vattham aṇagâre |
pasârettu bâhu parakkame
no avalaṃbiyâṇa kaṃdhaṃsi ³⁷ ‖xxi‖
esa vihî aṇokkaṃto
mâhaṇeṇa maîmayâ bahuso |
apaḍinneṇa bhagavaṭâ
evaṃ rîyaṃtĕ tti bemi ‖xxii‖1‖
paḍhamo uddesao.

410   cariyâsaṇâi ¹ sejjâo
egaiyâu jâu buiṭâo
âikkhaṭâi ¹ sayaṇâ
saṇâi¹ jâiṃ sevittha ² se Mahâvîre ‖i‖
âvesaṇasabhapavâsu ³

---

²⁷ B akaraṇâe.   ²⁸ B itthio.   ³⁹ BC se ada°.   ³⁰ B ahâ.   ³¹ A ada°.   ³² B sevai.
³³ B pâde.   ³⁴ B vî.   ³⁵ MSS. °au.   ³⁶ A uppehâe.   ³⁷ A kkhaṃdhaṃsi.
¹ MSS. °iṃ.   ² B °â.   The metre requires: sayaṇâi jâi.   ³ A °bhapp°,
B °bhâp°.   c

paṇiyasâlâsu egadâ vâso |
aduvâ paliyaṭṭhâṇesu
palâlapuṃjesu egad*â* vâso ||ii||
âgaṃtâre ârâmâ
gâre na*g*are vi egad*â* vâso |
susâṇe sunnagâresu vâ
rukkhamûle vi egad*â* vâso ||iii||
etehi[1] muṇî sayaṇehiṃ
samaṇe âsi[4] paterasa[5] vâse |
raiṃdiyaṃ pi jayamâṇe
appamatte samâhie jhâtî[6] ||iv||
niddaṃ pi no pagâmâe
sevai ya bhagavaṃ uṭṭhâe | 411
jaggâvatî ya appâṇaṃ
îsiṃ sâ*t*iya apaḍinne ||v||
saṃbujjhamâṇe puṇar avi
âsaṃsu bhagavaṃ uṭṭhâe[7] |
nikkhamma egad*â* râo
bahiṃ caṃkammiyâ muhuttâgaṃ ||vi||
sayaṇehiṃ tass[8] uvasaggâ[9]
bhîm' âsî aṇegarûvâ ya |
saṃsappagâ ya je pâṇâ
aduvâ je pakkhiṇo uvacaraṃti ||vii||
adu kucarâ[10] uvacaraṃti
gâmarakkhâ ya sattihatthâ ya |
adu gâmiyâ uvasaggâ
itthî egatiyâ puriso vâ ||viii||
ihaloiyâi[1] paraloiyâi[1]
bhîmâ[1] aṇegarûvâiṃ |
avi subbhidubbhigaṃdhâiṃ 413
saddâiṃ aṇegarûvâiṃ ||ix||
a*h*iyâsae sayâ sami*t*e
phâsâi[1] virûvarûvâiṃ |
aratiṃ[11] ratiṃ abhibhûya
rîyatî mâhaṇe abahuvâî ||x||
sa jaṇehi[12] tattha pucchiṃsu

[4] B vâse. [5] MSS. patelasa. [6] A jjhâdî. [7] A °âî. [8] B tattha. [9] A ss. [10] read kuccarâ. [11] B arati. [12] A ya° cf.[1] "

egacarâ vi egadâ râto |
avvâhite kasâitthâ
pehamâṇe samâhiṃ apaḍinne || xi ||
ayam aṃtaraṃsi ko etthaṃ
aham aṃsî ti[14] bhikkhu âhaṭṭu |
ayam uttame se dhamme
tusiṇîe saṃkasâie[15] jhâtî || xii ||
jaṃsi pp ege pavevaṃti[16]
sisire mâru*t*e pavâyaṃte |
taṃsi pp ege aṇagârâ
himavâ*t*e nivâyam esaṃti || xiii ||
415 saṃghâḍîo pavisissâmo
pa*h*â ya samâdahamâṇâ |
pihi*t*â vâ sakkhâmo
atidukkhahimagasaṃphâsâ || xiv ||
taṃsi bhagavaṃ apaḍinne
adhoviyaḍe[17] ahiyâsae davie |
nikkhamma egadâ râo
câeti bhagavaṃ samiyâe || xv ||
esa vihî aṇŏkkaṃto[18]
mâhaṇeṇa ma*t*îma*t*â bahuso |
apaḍinneṇaṃ bhagava*t*â
evaṃ rîyaṃte tti bemi || xvi || **2** ||
biio uddesao.

taṇaphâsasîyaphâse ya
teuphâse ya daṃsamasa*g*e ya |
ahiyâsae sayâ samie
phâsâiṃ virûvarûvâiṃ || i ||
aha duccaraLâḍham[1] acârî
Vajjabhûmiṃ ca Subbhabhûmiṃ ca |
416 paṃtaṃ sĕjjaṃ seviṃsu
âsaṇa*g*âi[2] ceva paṃtâiṃ || ii ||
Lâḍhehiṃ[3] tass' uvasaggâ
bahave jâṇavayâ lûsiṃsu |

[13] sic! for ettha. [14] B aṃsi tti. [15] B sak°. [16] AC pavedamti, B pavedeṃti.
[17] B adhevigaḍe. [18] B anno°.

[1] read ducara°. [2] A °âiṃ, B °âṇi. [3] B lâḍhesu.

aha lukkhadesie[4] bhatte
kukkurâ tattha hiṃsiṃsu nivatiṃsu ||iii||
appe jaṇe nivârei
lûsaṇae suṇae dasamâṇe[5] |
chucchû kareṃti âhaṃtuṃ
samaṇaṃ kukkurâ dasaṃtu tti. ||iv||
elikkhae jaṇo bhujjo
bahave Vajjabhûmĭṃ pharusâsî |
laṭṭhiṃ gahâya ṇâlîyaṃ
samaṇâ tattha eva vihariṃsu ||v||
evaṃ pi tattha viharaṃtâ
puṭṭhapuvvâ ahesi suṇaehiṃ |
saṃlucamâṇâ[6] suṇaehiṃ
duccaragâṇi[7] *tattha* Lâḍhehiṃ ||vi||
ni*h*âya daṃḍaṃ pâṇehiṃ 418
taṃ vosajja kâyam aṇagâre |
aha[8] gâmakaṃṭae bhagavaṃ
te a*h*iyâsae abhisameccâ ||vii||
nâo saṃgâmasîse va[9]
pârae tattha se Mahâvîre |
evaṃ pi tattha Lâḍhehiṃ
aladdhapuvvo vi ega*d*â gâmo ||viii||
uvasaṃkamaṃtam apaḍinnaṃ
gâmaṃtiyaṃ pi appattaṃ[10] |
paḍiṇikkhamittu lûsiṃsu
etâo paraṃ palehi tti ||ix||
hayapuvvo tattha daṃḍeṇaṃ
aha[8] vâ muṭṭhiṇâ aha[11] phaleṇaṃ |
aha[8] leluṇâ kavâleṇaṃ
haṃtâ haṃtâ bahave kaṃdiṃsu ||x||
maṃsûṇi chinnapuvvâiṃ
oṭṭhabhiyâe ega*d*â kâyaṃ | 419
parissahâiṃ luṃciṃsu[12]
aha[8] vâ paṃsuṇâ uvakariṃsu ||xi||
uccâlaiya nihaṇiṃsu

[4] B lûha. [5] B ḍas°. [6] B °luṃc°. [7] A °râiṃ. [8] B adu. [9] A vâ. [10] BC apattaṃ. read pattam appattaṃ. [11] cf.[8] MSS. add kuṃtâdi, apparently a gloss. [12] B lûsiṃsu.

aha[8] vâ âsaṇâo khalaiṃsu |
vosaṭṭhakâe paṇa*t*âsî
dukkhasahe[13] bhagavaṃ apaḍinne ||xii||
sûro saṃgâmasîse va[14]
saṃvuḍe tattha se Mahâvîre |
paḍisevamâṇo pharusâiṃ
acale bhagavaṃ rîitthâ[15] ||xiii||
esa vihî aṇokkaṃto[16]
mâhaṇeṇaṃ maîmayâ[17] bahuso |
apaḍinneṇaṃ bhagava*t*â
rîyaṃti tti bemi. ||xiv|| **3** ||

taio uddesao.

omodariyaṃ câeti
apuṭṭhe vi bhagavaṃ rogehiṃ |
puṭṭho va[1] se apuṭṭho vâ
no se sâijjatî teicchaṃ ||i||
saṃsohaṇaṃ ca vamaṇaṃ ca
gâyabbhaṃgaṇaṃ siṇâṇaṃ ca |
saṃbâhaṇaṃ na se kappe
daṃtakkhâlaṇaṃ parinnâe ||ii||
virae ya[2] gâma*dh*ammehiṃ
rîyai[3] mâhaṇe abahuvâî |
sisirammi[4] egadâ bhagavaṃ
châyâe jhâ*t*i âsî ya ||iii||
âyâvaî ya gimhâṇaṃ
acchati ukkuḍue abhitâve |
aha[6] jâvaittha lûheṇaṃ
oyaṇamaṃthukummâseṇaṃ ||iv||
e*t*âṇi tinni paḍiseve
aṭṭha mâse ajâvae[5] bhagavaṃ |
apiittha egayâ bhagavaṃ
addhamâsaṃ aduvâ[6] mâsaṃ pi ||v||
avi sâ*h*ie duve mâse

[13] A dukkhaṃ. [14] MSS. vâ. [15] B rîyattha. [16] B aṇṇo°. [17] B mâhaṇeṇa matîmatâ.

[1] B vâ. [2] B hi. [3] B rîyaṃti. [4] A ṃsi. [5] B ya jâvagaṃ. [6] B adu.

chap pi mâse aduvâ apivvitthâ [7] |
râovarâyam [8] apaḍinne 422
annagilâyam [9] egayâ bhuṃje ||vi||
chaṭṭheṇam [8] egayâ bhuṃje
aha [6] vâ aṭṭhameṇa [8] dasameṇaṃ |
duvâlasameṇa egayâ bhuṃje
pehamâṇe samâhim [8] apaḍinne ||vii||
naccâṇa se Mahâvîre
ṇo vi ya pâvagaṃ sayam akâsî |
annehiṃ pi [10] na kârĕtthâ
kîraṃtaṃ pi nâ 'ṇujâṇitthâ ||viii||
gâmaṃ pavissa nagaraṃ vâ
ghâsam ese kaḍaṃ paraṭṭhâe |
suvisuddham esiyâ bhagavaṃ
ajâtajoga*t*âe sevitthâ ||ix||
adu vâyasa digicchaṃtâ [11]
je anne rasesiṇo sattâ |
ghâsesaṇâe ciṭṭhaṃte 423
sayayaṃ nivatite ya pehâe ||x||
adu mâhaṇaṃ va samaṇaṃ vâ
gâmapiṃḍolagaṃ va atihiṃ vâ |
sovâgamûsiyâriṃ vâ
kukkuraṃ vâ viṭṭhiyaṃ [12] pura*t*o ||xi||
vitticchedaṃ vajjaṃto
tes' appattiyaṃ [13] parihaṛaṃto |
maṃdaṃ parakkame [14] bhagavaṃ
ahiṃsamâṇe ghâsam esitthâ ||xii||
avi sûiyaṃ va [15] sukkaṃ vâ
sîyapiṃḍaṃ purâṇakummâsaṃ |
adu vakkasaṃ pulâgaṃ vâ
laddhe piṃḍe aladdhae davie ||xiii||
avi jhâti se Mahâvîre
âsaṇatthe akukkue jhâṇaṃ | 425
uḍḍhaṃ ahe ya tiriyaṃ ca
loe [16] jhâya*t*i samâhim apaḍinne ||xiv||

[7] C viharitthâ, A had so originally, but changed it in apivitthâ. [8] MSS. ṃ. [9] A annâi°, B °lâgam. [10] A vi, B vî. [11] B digiṃchantâ. [12] B vivihaṃ ṭhitaṃ purato. [13] A tassapattiyaṃ. [14] A pari°. [15] B vâ. [16] B savvaloea jhâyaî samiyaṃ pehâmâṇo samâhimapaḍinne.

akasâi vigatagehî ya
saddarûvesu amucchite jhâî [17] |
chaumatthe [18] parakkamamâṇe
na pamâyaṃ sayaṃ pi kuvvitthâ [19] || xv ||
sayaṃ eva abhisamâgamma
âyatajogam âyasohîe |
abhinivvuḍe amâille
âvakahaṃ bhagavaṃ samîtâsî [20] || xvi ||
esa vihî aṇŏkkaṃte [21]
mâhaṇeṇaṃ maîmayâ [22] bahuso |
apaḍinneṇaṃ bhagavatâ
evaṃ rîyaṃti tti bemi || xvii || **4** ||

cauttho uddesao.

aṭṭhamam ajjhayaṇaṃ.

ohâṇasuyam samattam.

paḍhame suyakkhaṃdhe samatte.

[17] B jhâtî. [18] A °o. MSS. add vi. [19] A saṃpakuvitthâ. [20] AC samit°. [21] B anno°. [22] B matîmatâ.

BIIE SUYAKKHAṂDHE.

PAḌHAMAM AJJHAYAṆAṂ

PIṂḌESEṆÂ.

se bhikkhû vâ bhikkhuṇî vâ gâhâvaikulaṃ piṃḍavâya- 1
*p*aḍiyâe aṇupaviṭṭhe samâṇe, se jjaṃ[1] puṇa jâṇejjâ : asaṇaṃ
vâ pâṇaṃ vâ khâimaṃ vâ sâimaṃ vâ pâṇehiṃ vâ paṇaehiṃ
vâ bîehiṃ[2] vâ[2] hariehiṃ vâ saṃsattaṃ ummissaṃ sî*t*odaeṇa
vâ osittaṃ rayasâ vâ parighâsiyaṃ, tahappagâraṃ asaṇaṃ vâ
4 parahatthaṃsi vâ parapâyaṃsi vâ aphâsuyaṃ aṇesaṇijjaṃ
ti mannamâṇe lâbhe vi saṃte no paḍigâhejjâ.[3] ‖ 1 ‖
se âhacca paḍigâhe[4] siyâ, se ttaṃ[5] â*d*âe egaṃtam avakka- 5
mejjâ, egaṃtam avakkamittâ a*h*e ârâmaṃsi vâ a*h*e uvassayaṃsi
vâ appaṃḍe appapâṇe appabîe appaharie appose appudae
apputtiṃgadagamaṭṭiyamakkaḍâsaṃtâṇae vigiṃciya 2 ummissaṃ visohiya tato saṃjatâm eva bhuṃjejja vâ piejja[6]
vâ ; jaṃ ca no saṃcâejjâ bhottae vâ pâyae[7] vâ, se ttam âyâe
egaṃtam avakkamĕjjâ a*h*e jhâmathaṃḍilaṃsi vâ aṭṭhirâsiṃsi
vâ kiṭṭharâsiṃsi vâ tusarâsiṃsi vâ gomayarâsiṃsi vâ annayaraṃsi vâ tahappagâraṃsi thaṃḍilaṃsi[8] paḍilehiya 2 pa- 6
majjiya 2 tato saṃjayâm eva pariṭṭhavejjâ. ‖ 2 ‖
se bhikkhû vâ bhikkhuṇî vâ *jâva* paviṭṭhe samâṇe, se jjâo
puṇa osahîo jâṇejjâ : ḵasiṇâo sâsiyâo avidalakaḍâo atiriccha-
chinnâo avocchinnâo taruṇiyaṃ vâ chivâḍiṃ aṇabhikkaṃta-
bhajjiyaṃ pehâe aphâsuyaṃ aṇesaṇijjaṃ ti mannamâṇe
lâbhe saṃte no paḍigâhejjâ. ‖ 3 ‖
se bhikkhû vâ *jâva* samâṇe, se jjaṃ puṇa jâṇejja : akasiṇâo 7
viyalakaḍâo tiricchachinnâo[9] vocchinnâo, taruṇiyaṃ vâ
chivâḍiṃ abhikkaṃtabhajjiyaṃ pehâe phâsuyaṃ esaṇijjaṃ
ti[10] mannamâṇe lâbhe saṃte paḍigâhejjâ. ‖ 4 ‖

[1] B jaṃ. [2] B om. [3] A gg. [4] B gg. [5] A taṃ. [6] B pîejja. [7] B. pâittae.
[8] A ll. [9] A cchinnâo. [10] A om.

se bhikkhû vâ *jâva* jâṇejjâ: pi*h*uyaṃ vâ bahurayaṃ vâ
bhujjiyaṃ vâ maṃthuṃ vâ câulaṃ vâ câulapalaṃbaṃ vâ
saiṃ bhajjiyaṃ aphâsuyaṃ *jâva* no paḍigâhejjâ. ||5|| se
8 bhikkhû vâ . . . (§ 5) . . . câulapalaṃbaṃ vâ asaiṃ bhajji-
yam, dukkhutto vâ tikkhutto vâ bhajjiyaṃ phâsuyaṃ *jâva*
lâbhe saṃte paḍigâhejjâ. ||6||
se bhikkhû vâ 2 gâhâvaikulaṃ piṃḍavâyavaḍiyâe pavisi-
ttukâme no annautthieṇa vâ gâratthieṇa vâ parihârio
aparihârieṇa saddhiṃ gâhâvaikulaṃ piṃḍavâyapaḍiyâe pa-
visejja vâ nikkhamejja vâ. ||7|| se bhikkhû vâ 2 bahiyâ
9 viyârabhûmiṃ vâ vihârabhûmiṃ vâ nikkhamamâṇe[11] vâ
pavisâmâṇe vâ no annautthieṇa vâ . . . (§ 7) . . . saddhiṃ
bahiyâ viyârabhûmiṃ vâ vihârabhûmiṃ vâ nikkhamejja vâ
pavisejja vâ. ||8|| se bhikkhû vâ 2 gâmâṇugâmaṃ dûijjamâṇe[12]
no annautthieṇa vâ . . . (§ 7) . . . saddhiṃ gâmâṇugâmaṃ
dûijjejjâ.[12] ||9||
11 se bhikkhû vâ 2 *jâva* paviṭṭhe samâṇe no annautthiyassa
vâ[16] gâratthiyassa[13] vâ pahârio apahâriyassa vâ asaṇaṃ vâ
4 dejja vâ aṇupadejja vâ. ||10||
se bhikkhû vâ 2 *jâva* paviṭṭhe samâṇe, se jjaṃ jâṇejjâ:
asaṇaṃ vâ 4 assiṃ[14] paḍiyâe egaṃ sâhammiyaṃ samuddissa
pâṇâiṃ bhû*t*âiṃ jîvâiṃ sattâiṃ samârabbha[15] samuddissa
kî*t*aṃ pâmiccaṃ acchejjaṃ aṇisaṭṭhaṃ abhihaḍaṃ âhaṭṭu
ceteti, taṃ tahappagâraṃ asaṇaṃ vâ 4 purisaṃtarakaḍaṃ vâ
apurisaṃtarakaḍaṃ vâ bahiyâ nîhaḍaṃ vâ aṇîhaḍaṃ vâ
12 attaṭṭhiyaṃ vâ aṇattaṭṭhiyaṃ vâ paribhuttaṃ vâ aparibhuttaṃ
vâ âsevitaṃ vâ aṇâsevitaṃ vâ aphâsuyaṃ *jâva* no paḍigâhejjâ. evaṃ bahave sâhammiyâ, egâ sâhammiṇî, bahave
sahammiṇîo samuddissa cattâri âlâvagâ bhaṇiyavvâ. ||11||
se bhikkhû vâ 2 *jâva* paviṭṭhe samâṇe, se jjaṃ puṇa
jâṇejjâ: asaṇaṃ vâ 4 bahave samaṇamâhaṇe ati*h*ikivaṇava-
ṇîmae pagaṇiya 2 samuddissa pâṇâiṃ *jâva* samârabbha
13 âseviyaṃ vâ aṇâseviyaṃ vâ aphâsuyaṃ aṇesaṇijjaṃ ti
mannamâṇe lâbhe saṃte no paḍigâhejjâ. ||12||
se bhikkhû vâ 2 . . . (§ 12) . . . vaṇîmae samuddissa
pâṇâiṃ *jâva* âhaṭṭu cetitaṃ, tahappagâraṃ asaṇaṃ vâ 4

[11] A °khamâṇe, B °khammamâṇe. [12] B dûti°. [13] A gihatthassa. [14] AB assaṃ.
[15] A °ṃbhaṃ.

apurisaṃtarakaḍaṃ [16] bahiyâ aṇîhaḍaṃ [17] aṇattaṭṭhiyaṃ aparibhuttaṃ aṇâseviyaṃ aphâsuyaṃ aṇesaṇijjaṃ *jâva* no paḍigâhejjâ. aha puṇa evaṃ jâṇejjâ : purisaṃtarakaḍaṃ [16] 14 bahiyâ nîhaḍaṃ attaṭṭhiyaṃ paribhuttaṃ âsevi*t*aṃ phâsuyaṃ esaṇijjaṃ *jâva* paḍigâhejjâ. || 13 ||

se. bhikkhû vâ 2 . . . (§ 7) . . . kâme, se jjâiṃ puṇa kulâiṃ jâṇejjâ : imesu khalu kulesu nitie piṃḍe dijjati, nitie aggapiṃḍe dijjati, nitie bhâe dijja*t*i, nitie avaḍḍhabhâe dijja*t*i, tahappagârâiṃ ni*t*iyâiṃ nitiomâṇâiṃ [18] no bhattâe vâ pâṇae vâ pavisejja vâ nikkhamejja vâ.

eyaṃ khalu tassa bhikkhussa vâ [10] bhikkhuṇîe vâ [2] sâmaggi- 15 yaṃ, jaṃ savvaṭṭhehiṃ samite sahite sayâ jaejjâ si tti bemi. || 14 || 1 ||

paḍhamo uddesao.

se bhikkhû vâ 2 . . . (1 § 1) . . . asaṇaṃ vâ 4 aṭṭha-miposahiesu vâ addhamâsiesu vâ mâsiesu va domâsiesu vâ temâsiesu vâ câummâsiesu [1] vâ paṃcamâsiesu vâ chammâsiesu 16 vâ uûsu vâ uusaṃdhîsu vâ uupariyaṭṭesu vâ bahave samaṇa-mâhaṇe atihikivaṇavaṇîmage [2] egâo ukkhâo pariesejjamâṇe pehâe dohiṃ ukkhâhiṃ pariesejjamâṇe pehâe tihiṃ ukkhâhiṃ p. p. cauhiṃ u. p. p. kâlovatîo vâ kuṃbhimuhâo vâ sannihi-sannicayâo vâ pariesejjamâṇe pehâe, tahappagâraṃ asaṇaṃ vâ [4] apurisaṃtarakaḍaṃ *jâva* aṇâsevitaṃ aphâsuyâṃ aṇesa- 17 ṇijjaṃ *jâva* no paḍigâhejjâ. aha puṇa evaṃ jâṇejjâ : puri-saṃtarakaḍaṃ *jâva* âsevi*t*aṃ phâsuyaṃ *jâva* paḍigâhejjâ. || 1 ||

se bhikkhû vâ 2 *jâva* paviṭṭhe samâṇe, se jjâiṃ puṇa kulâiṃ jâṇejjâ, taṃ jahâ : uggakulâṇi vâ bhogakulâṇi vâ râinnakulâṇi vâ khattiyakulâṇi vâ Ikkhâgakulâṇi vâ Hari-vaṃsakulâṇi vâ esiya*k*ulâṇi vâ vesiyakulâṇi vâ gaṃdâga-kulâṇi vâ kŏṭṭâgakulâṇi vâ gâmarakkhakulâṇi vâ pokkasâ-liyakulâṇi [3] vâ, anna*t*aresu [4] vâ tahappagâresu kulesu 18 adugucchiesu [5] vâ agarahiesu vâ asaṇaṃ vâ 4 phâsuyaṃ *jâva* paḍigâhejjâ. || 2 ||

se bhikkhû vâ 2 *jâva* paviṭṭhe samâṇe, se jjaṃ puṇa

---

[16] B °gaḍaṃ.   [17] B abahiyâ nîhaḍaṃ.   [18] A nitiaummâṇâiṃ.
[1] A caumâsiesu.   [2] B vaṇimage ; in § 3 atithikiviṇa.   [3] A vokk".   [4] B has generally annatar°.   [5] B °gumch".

jâṇejjâ : asaṇaṃ vâ 4 samavâesu vâ piṃḍaṇîyaresu vâ
Iṃdamahesu vâ Khaṃdamahesu vâ evaṃ Ruddamahesu vâ
Muguṃdamahesu vâ bhû*t*amahesu vâ jakkhamahesu vâ
nâgamahesu vâ thûbhamahesu [6] vâ [6] ceiyamahesu vâ rukkha-
19 mahesu vâ girimahesu vâ darimahesu [6] vâ [6] agaḍamahesu vâ
taḍâgamahesu vâ dahamahesu vâ nadimahesu [6] vâ [6] sarama-
hesu [6] vâ [6] sâgaramahesu [6] vâ [6] âgaramahesu vâ annataresu
vâ tahappagâresu vâ virûvarûvesu mahâmahesu vaṭṭa-
mâṇesu bahave samaṇamâhaṇe . . . (§ 1) . . . *jâva* no
paḍigâhejjâ. ||3|| aha puṇa evaṃ jâṇejjâ : dinnaṃ jaṃ tesiṃ
dâyavvaṃ, aha tattha bhuṃjamâṇe pehâe—gâhâva*t*ibhâriyaṃ
vâ gâhâva*t*ibhagiṇiṃ vâ gâhâva*t*iputtaṃ vâ dhûyaṃ vâ
suṇhaṃ vâ dhâiṃ vâ dâsaṃ vâ dâsiṃ vâ kammakaraṃ vâ
kammakariṃ vâ—se puvvâm eva âloejjâ : âuso tti vâ bhagiṇî
ti [7] vâ, dâhisi me etto anna*t*araṃ bhoyaṇajâyaṃ ; [8] se s'evaṃ
vadaṃtassa paro asaṇaṃ vâ 4 âhaṭṭu dalaejjâ, tahappagâraṃ
asaṇaṃ vâ 4 sayaṃ vâ ṇaṃ jâejjâ, paro vâ se dejjâ, phâsuyaṃ
jâva paḍigâhejjâ. ||4||
20 se bhikkhû vâ 2 paraṃ addhajoyaṇamerâe saṃkhaḍiṃ
naccâ saṃkhaḍipaḍiyâe no abhisaṃdhârejjâ gamaṇâe. ||5||
se bhikkhû vâ 2 pâîṇaṃ saṃkhaḍiṃ naccâ paḍîṇaṃ gacche
aṇâḍhâyamîṇe, paḍîṇaṃ saṃkhaḍiṃ naccâ pâîṇaṃ gacche
aṇâḍhâyamîṇe, dâhiṇaṃ saṃkhaḍiṃ naccâ udîṇaṃ gacche
aṇâḍhâyamîṇe, udîṇaṃ saṃkhaḍiṃ naccâ dâhiṇaṃ gacche
aṇâḍhâyamîṇe; jatth' eva saṃkhaḍî siyâ, taṃ jahâ : gâmaṃsi
vâ nagaraṃsi vâ kheḍaṃsi vâ kabbaḍaṃsi vâ maṃḍavaṃsi
vâ paṭṭaṇaṃsi vâ doṇamuhaṃsi vâ âgaraṃsi vâ âsamaṃsi vâ
21 saṃnivesaṃsi vâ nigamaṃsi vâ râyahâṇiṃsi vâ—, saṃkhaḍiṃ saṃkhaḍipaḍiyâe no abhisaṃdhârejjâ gamaṇâe. kevalî
bûyâ : âyâṇam [9] e*t*aṃ ; saṃkhaḍiṃ saṃkhaḍipaḍiyâe abhi-
saṃdhâremâṇe âhâkammiyaṃ [10] vâ uddesiyaṃ vâ mîsajjâyaṃ
vâ kîyagaḍaṃ vâ pâmiccaṃ vâ acchejjaṃ vâ aṇisaṭṭhaṃ vâ
abhihaḍaṃ vâ âhaṭṭu dijjamâṇaṃ bhuṃjejjâ. ||6||
asaṃja*t*e bhikkhupaḍiyâe khuḍḍiyaduvâriyâo mahalliyâo
22 kujjâ, mahalliyaduvâriyâo khuḍḍiyâo kujjâ, samâo sejjâo
visamâo kujjâ, visamâo sĕjjâo samâo kujjâ, pavâtâo sĕjjâo
nivâ*t*âo kujjâ, nivâ*t*âo sejjâo pavâ*t*âo kujjâ, aṃto vâ bahiṃ

[6] A om. [7] B bhagiṇi tti vâ. [8] A °jâiṃ. [9] pâṭhantaram : âyayaṇaṃ.
[10] A ahâ°, B °ie. [11] B ass°.

vâ uvassayassa hariyâṇi chiṃdiya 2 dâliya 2 saṃthâragaṃ
saṃtharejjâ. esa vi luṃgayâmo sejjâe akkhâto.[12] tamhâ se
saṃja*t*e niyaṃṭhe [13] annayare [6] vâ [6] tahappagâre puresaṃkhaḍiṃ vâ pacchâsaṃkhaḍiṃ vâ saṃkhaḍiṃ[14] saṃkhaḍipaḍiyâe no
abhisaṃdhârejjâ gamaṇâe.

eyaṃ khalu tassa bhikkhussa vâ bhikkhuṇîe vâ sâmaggiyam, 23
jaṃ savvatthehiṃ samite sahite sayâ jaejjâ si 'tti bemi. ‖ 7 ‖ **2** ‖

biio uddesao.

se egao annataraṃ saṃkhaḍiṃ asitta pivittâ chaḍḍejjâ,
bhutte vâ se no sammaṃ pariṇamejjâ, anna*t*are vâ se dukkhe
ro*g*âtaṃke samuppajjejjâ. kevalî bûyâ: âyâṇam e*t*aṃ; ‖ 1 ‖
iha khalu bhikkhû gâhâvatîhiṃ gâhâvatiṇîhi vâ parivâyaehi
vâ parivâiyâhi vâ egajjhaṃ saddhiṃ soḍaṃ pâuṃ bho vati- 24
missaṃ; huratthâ vâ uvassayaṃ paḍilehamâṇe no labhejjâ,
tam eva uvassayaṃ sammissîbhâvaṃ âvajjejjâ, annamâṇe vâ
se matte vippariyâsiyabhû*t*e itthiviggahe vâ kilîve [1] vâ taṃ
bhikkhuṃ uvasaṃkamittu: âusaṃto samaṇâ! ahe [2] ârâmaṃsi
vâ ahe [2] uvassayaṃsi vâ râo vâ viyâle vâ gâmadhammani-
yaṃti*t*aṃ kaṭṭu rahassiyaṃ mehuṇadhammaṃ pariyâraṇâe
âuṭṭâmo. taṃ c' egatio sâtijjejjâ akaraṇijjaṃ c' eyaṃ saṃkhâe 25
ete âyâṇâ [3] saṃti saṃcijjamâṇâ paccâvâyâ bhavaṃti, tamhâ
se saṃjae niyaṃṭhe tahappagâraṃ puresaṃkhaḍiṃ vâ . . .
(**2**. § 7) . . . gamaṇâe. ‖ 2 ‖

se bhikkhû vâ 2 annayariṃ [4] saṃkhaḍiṃ soccâ nisamma
saṃparihâvati [5] ussuyabhû*t*eṇa appâṇeṇaṃ dhuvâ saṃkhaḍî;
no saṃcâeti tattha itarehiṃ kulehiṃ samudâṇiyaṃ [6] esiyaṃ
vesiyaṃ piṃḍavâyaṃ paḍigâhettâ âhâraṃ âhârettae; mâiṭṭhâṇaṃ saṃphâse, no evaṃ karejjâ; se tattha kâleṇa 27
aṇupavisittâ tatth' itarehiṃ kulehiṃ samudâṇiyaṃ [6] esiyaṃ
vesiyaṃ piṃḍavâyaṃ paḍigâhettâ âhâraṃ âhârejjâ.[7] ‖ 3 ‖

se bhikkhû vâ 2, se jjaṃ puṇa jâṇejjâ: gâmaṃ vâ *jâva*
râyahâṇiṃ vâ, imaṃsi khalu gâmaṃsi vâ *jâva* râyahâṇiṃsi
vâ saṃkhaḍî siyâ,[8] taṃ pi yâiṃ gâmaṃ vâ *jâva* râyahâṇiṃ

[12] B esa khalu bhagavayâ momî sajjâe akkhâe. A adds bhagavatâ before sejjâe. [13] B ṇiggaṃthe. [14] B om.

[1] A kiliddha. [2] A adhe. [3] avaṇâṇi. [4] B annataraṃ. [5] A °haveti, B saṃpahâveti. [6] B sâm°. [7] B om. the end of the sentence from itarehiṃ. [8] A saṃkhaḍiṃ sivâ. [9] B pi ya.

vâ saṃkhaḍipaḍiyâe no abhisaṃdhârejjâ gamaṇâe. kevalî
bûyâ : âyâṇam eyaṃ ; âiṇṇomâṇaṃ[10] saṃkhaḍiṃ aṇupavissa-
28 mâṇassa pâeṇa vâ pâe akkaṃtapuvve bhavati, hattheṇa vâ
hatthe saṃcâliyapuvve bhavati, pâeṇa vâ pâe âvaḍiyapuvve
bhavati, sîseṇa vâ sîse saṃghaṭṭiyapuvve bhavati, kâeṇa vâ
kâe saṃkhobhitapuvve bhavati, daṃḍeṇa vâ aṭṭhîṇa[11] vâ[11]
muṭṭhîṇa vâ lelûṇa[12] vâ kavâleṇa vâ abhihayapuvve bhavati,
sîtodaeṇa vâ ussittapuvve bhavati, rayasâ vâ parighâsi*t*apuvve
bhavati, aṇesaṇijje vâ paribhuttapuvve[13] bhavati, annesi
vâ dijjamâṇe paḍigâhitapuvve bhavati. tamhâ se saṃjae
29 niyaṃthe tahappagâraṃ âiṇṇomâṇaṃ saṃkhaḍiṃ saṃkhaḍipaḍiyâe no abhisaṃdhârejjâ gamaṇâe. ‖4‖

se bhikkhû vâ 2 *jâva* paviṭṭhe samâṇe, se jjaṃ puṇa
jâṇejjâ : asaṇaṃ vâ 4 esaṇijje siyâ aṇesaṇijje siyâ vitigiccha-
samâvanneṇaṃ appâṇeṇaṃ asamâhaḍâe lessâe tahappagâraṃ
asaṇâṃ vâ 4 lâbhe saṃte no paḍigâhejjâ. ‖5‖

se bhikkhû vâ 2 gâhâva*t*ikulaṃ pavisiukâme savva-
30 bhaṃḍagam âyâe gâhâvatikulaṃ piṃḍavâ*t*apaḍiyâe pavisejja
vâ nikkhamejja vâ. ‖6‖ se bhikkhû vâ 2 bahiyâ vihârabhûmiṃ vâ viyârabhûmiṃ vâ nikkhamamâṇe vâ pavisamâṇe
vâ savvabhaṃḍagam âyâe bahiyâ vihârabhûmiṃ vâ
viyârabhûmiṃ vâ nikkhamejja vâ pavisejja vâ. ‖7‖ se
bhikkhû vâ 2 gâmâṇugâmaṃ dûijjamâṇe[14] savvabhaṃḍagam âyâe gâmâṇugâmaṃ dûijjejjâ.[14] ‖8‖

se bhikkhû vâ 2 aha puṇa evaṃ jâṇejjâ : tivvadesiyaṃ vâ
31 vâsaṃ vâsamâṇaṃ pehâe, tivvadesiyaṃ vâ mahiyaṃ saṃniva-
yamâṇiṃ[15] pehâe, mahâvâeṇa vâ rayaṃ samubbhû*t*aṃ pehâe,
tiricchapâtimâ vâ pâṇâ saṃthaḍâ saṃnivayamâṇâ pehâe,
s' evaṃ naccâ no savvabhaṃḍagam âyâe gâhâvaikulaṃ
piṃḍavâyapaḍiyâe pavisejja vâ nikkhamejja vâ, bahiyâ
vihârabhûmiṃ vâ viyârabhûmiṃ vâ pavisejja vâ nikkhamejja vâ, gâmâṇugâmaṃ dûijjejjâ.[14] ‖9‖

se bhikkhû vâ 2, se jjâiṃ puṇa kulâiṃ jâṇejjâ, taṃ jahâ ;
32 khattiyâṇa vâ râîṇa vâ râyapesiyâṇa vâ râyavaṃsaṭṭhiyâṇa
vâ aṃto vâ bahiṃ[16] vâ saṃṇiviṭṭhâṇa vâ nimaṃtemâṇâṇa vâ
asaṇaṃ vâ 4 lâbhe saṃte no paḍigâhejjâ si tti bemi. ‖10‖**3**‖

taio uddesao.

[10] A âyannâvamâṇaṃ ṇaṃ. [11] A om. [12] B loluṇâ. [13] B paribhûta°.
[14] B dûti°. [15] BC saṃṇivada°. [16] A bahiyaṃ. C adds gacchaṃtâṇa vâ.

se bhikkhû vâ 2 *jâva* paviṭṭhe samâṇe, se jjaṃ puṇa
jâṇejjâ: maṃsâ*d*iyaṃ vâ macchâ*d*iyaṃ vâ maṃsakhalaṃ vâ
macchakhalaṃ[1] vâ[1] âheṇaṃ vâ paheṇaṃ vâ hiṃgoliṃ vâ
sammelaṃ vâ hîramâṇaṃ pehâe, aṃtarâ se maggâ bahupâṇâ 33
bahubîyâ bahuhariyâ bahuosâ[2] bahuudayâ bahuuttiṃgapa-
ṇagadagamaṭṭiyamakkaḍâsaṃtâṇagâ, bahave tattha samaṇamâhaṇa atihikivaṇavaṇîmagâ uvâga*t*â[3] uvâgamissaṃti,[3] tatth'
âiṇṇâ vittî: no pannassa nikkhamaṇapavesâe, no pannassa
vâyaṇâpucchaṇâpariyaṭṭaṇâṇupehâe[4] dhammâṇuogaciṃtâe;
se evaṃ naccâ tahappagâraṃ puresaṃkhaḍiṃ vâ pacchâsaṃkhaḍiṃ vâ saṃkhaḍiṃ saṃkhaḍipaḍiyâe no abhisaṃdhârejjâ gamaṇâe. ‖1‖

se bhikkhû vâ . . (§ 1) . . . jâṇejjâ: maṃsâ*d*iyaṃ vâ 34
jâva sammelaṃ vâ hîramâṇaṃ pehâe aṃtarâ se maggâ *jâva*
saṃtâṇagâ, no jattha bahave samaṇamâhaṇâ *jâva* uvâgamissaṃti, appâiṇṇâ vittî; pannassa nikkhamaṇapavesâe,
pannassa vâyaṇâpucchaṇapariyaṭṭaṇâṇupehâe[4] dhammâṇuo-
gaciṃtae, s'evaṃ naccâ tahappagâraṃ puresaṃkhaḍiṃ vâ
pacchâsaṃkhaḍiṃ vâ saṃkhaḍiṃ saṃkhaḍipaḍiyâe abhisaṃdhârejjâ gamaṇae. ‖2‖

se bhikkhû va 2 *jâva* pavisi*t*ukâme, se jjaṃ puṇa jâṇejjâ: 35
khîriṇîo[5] gâvîo khîrijjamâṇîo pehâe, asaṇaṃ vâ 4 uvakkhaḍijjamâṇaṃ[6] pehâe, purâ appajûhie, s'evaṃ naccâ no gâhâvaikulaṃ piṃḍavâyapaḍiyâe nikkhamejja vâ pavisejja vâ.
se ttam âyâe egaṃtam avakkamejjâ aṇâvâyam asaṃloe
ciṭṭhejjâ. ‖3‖ aha puṇa evaṃ jâṇejjâ: khîriṇîo gâvîo
khîriyâo pehâe, asaṇaṃ vâ 4 uvakkhaḍiyaṃ[6] pehâe, purâ
pajûhie, s'evaṃ naccâ tato saṃjatâm eva gâhâvaikulaṃ 36
piṃḍavâyapaḍiyâe nikkhamejja vâ pavisejja vâ. ‖4‖

bhikkhâgâṇâm ege evam âhaṃsu, samâṇe vâ vasamâṇe vâ
gâmâṇugâmaṃ dûijjamâṇe[7]: khuḍḍâe khalu ayaṃ gâme
saṃṇiruddhâe no mahâlae, se haṃtâ bhayaṃtâro bâhiragâṇi
gâmâṇi bhikkhâyariyâe[8] vayaha, saṃti tatth' egatiyassa
bhikkhussa pure saṃthuyâ vâ pacchâ saṃthuyâ vâ parivasaṃti, taṃ jahâ: gâhâvatî[9] vâ gâhâva*t*iṇî vâ gâhâva*t*iputtâ vâ 37
gâhâva*t*idhûyâo vâ gâhâva*t*isuṇhâo vâ dhâ*t*îo vâ dâsâ vâ

[1] A one. [2] B °ossâ. [3] A uva°. [4] A peha. [5] B khîriṇiyâo. [6] A uvakha°.
[7] B dûti°. [8] B piṃḍavâyapaḍiyâe. [9] A °ti.

dâsîo vâ kammakarâ vâ kammakarîo[10] vâ, tahappagârâiṃ kulâiṃ pure saṃthuyâṇi vâ pacchâ saṃthuyâṇi vâ, puvvâm eva bhikkhâyariyâe aṇupavisissâmi; avi ya ittha labhissâmi piṃḍaṃ vâ loyaṃ vâ khîraṃ vâ da*dh*iṃ vâ navaṇîyaṃ vâ ghayaṃ vâ gulaṃ vâ tellaṃ[11] vâ mahuṃ vâ maṃsaṃ vâ majjaṃ vâ saṃkuliṃ vâ phâṇiyaṃ vâ pûyaṃ vâ sihariṇiṃ[12]
38 vâ; taṃ puvvâm eva bhŏccâ peccâ paḍiggahaṃ vâ saṃlihiya sammajjiya tato[13] pacchâ bhikkhûhiṃ saddhiṃ gâhâva*t*ikulaṃ piṃḍavâyapaḍiyâe pavisissâmi[14] vâ nikkhamissâmi vâ. mâiṭṭhâṇaṃ saṃphâse, no[15] evaṃ karejjâ. ||5|| se tattha bhikkhûhiṃ saddhiṃ kâleṇa aṇupavisittâ tatth' itaretarehiṃ[16] kulehiṃ samudâṇiyaṃ[17] esiyaṃ vesiyaṃ piṃḍavâyaṃ paḍigâhettâ âhâraṃ âhâraṃ âhârejjâ.

eyaṃ khalu tassa bhikkhussa vâ 2 sâmaggiyaṃ etc. ||6||**4**||

cauttho uddesao.

se bhikkhû vâ 2 *jâva* paviṭṭhe samâṇe, se jjaṃ puṇa jâṇejjâ:
39 aggapiṃḍaṃ ukkhippamâṇaṃ pehâe, nikkhippamâṇaṃ pehâe, aggapiṃḍaṃ hîramâṇaṃ pehâe, aggapiṇḍaṃ paribhâijjamâṇaṃ pehâe, aggapiṃḍaṃ paribhujjamâṇaṃ[1] pehâe, aggapiṃḍaṃ pariṭṭhavejjamâṇaṃ pehâe, purâ asiṇâd-i-vâ avahârâd-i-vâ, purâ jatth' anne samaṇamâhaṇâ atihikivaṇavaṇîmagâ[2] khaddhaṃ khaddhaṃ uvasaṃkamaṃti se: 'haṃtâ aham avi khaddhaṃ uvasaṃkamâmi'; mâiṭṭhâṇaṃ saṃphâse, no evaṃ karejjâ. ||1||

se bhikkhû vâ 2 *jâva* samâṇe, aṃtarâ se vappâṇi vâ phalihâṇi
40 vâ pâgârâṇi vâ toraṇâṇi vâ aggalâṇi vâ aggalapâsagâṇi vâ sati parakkame saṃjayâm eva parakkamejjâ, no ujjuyaṃ[3] gacchejjâ. kevalî bûyâ: âyâṇam e*t*aṃ; se tattha parakkamamâṇe payalejja vâ[4] pavaḍejja vâ, se tattha payalamâṇe vâ pavaḍamâṇe vâ tattha se kâe uccâreṇa vâ pâsavaṇeṇa vâ kheleṇa vâ siṃghâṇaeṇa vâ vaṃteṇa vâ pitteṇa vâ pûeṇa vâ sukkeṇa vâ soṇieṇa vâ uvalitte siyâ; tahappagâraṃ kâyaṃ no aṇaṃtarahiyâe
41 puḍhavîe, no[5] sasaṇiddhâe[5] puḍhavîe,[5] no sasarakkhâe puḍhavîe, no cittamaṃtâe silâe, no cittamaṃtâe lelûe kolâ-

[10] A °kârîo, B °karî. [11] A telaṃ. [12] A sihiriṇiṃ. [13] A to. [14] A pavississâmi. [15] A se no, B ṇa. [16] B itarâtiyarehiṃ. [17] B sâṃ°.

[1] A °bhuṃj°. [2] B atithikiviṇa, B vaṇi°. [3] AB originally ujjayaṃ. [4] B adds pakkhalejja vâ. [5] A om.

vâsaṃsi vâ dârue jîvapatiṭṭhiyâe sayaṃḍe sapâṇe *jâva*
saṃtâṇae no âmajjejja vâ no pamajjejja vâ saṃlihejja vâ
vâ uvvalejja vâ uvvaṭṭejja vâ âyâvejja vâ payâvejja vâ; se
puvvâm eva appa[6] sasarakkhaṃ taṇaṃ vâ pattaṃ vâ kaṭṭhaṃ[7]
vâ sakkaraṃ vâ jâejjâ, jâittâ se ttam âyâe egaṃtam avakkamejjâ 2, ahe jhâmathaṃḍilaṃsi vâ *jâva* annataraṃsi vâ
tahappagâraṃsi paḍilehiya 2 pamajjiya 2 ta*t*o saṃjayâm eva 42
âmajjejja vâ *jâva* payâvejja vâ. ‖2‖

se bhikkhû vâ 2 *jâva* paviṭṭhe samâṇe, se jjaṃ puṇa
jâṇejjâ: goṇaṃ viyâlaṃ paḍipahe pehâe, mahisaṃ viyâlaṃ
paḍipahe pehâe, evaṃ maṇussaṃ âsaṃ hatthiṃ[8] sîhaṃ
vagghaṃ vagaṃ dîviyaṃ acchaṃ taracchaṃ parisaraṃ siyâ-
laṃ virâlaṃ suṇayaṃ kolasuṇayaṃ kokaṃtiyaṃ cĕttavilla-
ḍagaṃ[9] viyâlaṃ paḍipahe pehâe, sati parakkame saṃjayâm
eva parakkamejjâ, no ujjuyaṃ gacchejjâ. ‖3‖

se bhikkhû vâ 2 *jâva* samâṇe, aṃtarâ se ovâo vâ khâṇuṃ 43
vâ kaṃṭae vâ ghasî[10] vâ bhilugâ, vâ visame vâ vijjale vâ
pariyâvajjejjâ, sati parakkame saṃjayâm eva parakkamejjâ,
no ujjuyaṃ gacchejjâ. se bhikkhû vâ 2 gâhâvaikulassa
duvâravâhaṃ kaṃṭagavoṃdiyâe paḍipihi*t*aṃ pehâe, tesiṃ
puvvâṃ eva ŏggahaṃ aṇaṇunnaviya apaḍilehiya apamajjiya
no avaguṇejjâ vâ pavisejja vâ nikkhamejja vâ; tesiṃ puvvâm
eva ŏggahaṃ aṇunnaviya paḍilehiya pamajjiya tao saṃjayâm 44
eva avaguṇejja vâ pavisejja vâ nikkhamejja vâ. ‖4‖

se bhikkhû vâ 2 *jâva* samâṇe, se jjaṃ puṇa jâṇejjâ: samaṇaṃ vâ mâhaṇaṃ vâ gâmapiṃḍolagaṃ vâ ati*h*iṃ vâ puvva-
paviṭṭhaṃ pehâe, no tesiṃ saṃloe sapaḍiduvâre ciṭṭhejjâ.
kevalî buyâ: âyâṇam eyaṃ; purâ pehâe tass' aṭṭhâe paro
asaṇaṃ vâ 4 âhaṭṭu dalaejjâ; aha bhikkhûṇaṃ puvvova-
iṭṭhaṃ: esâ painnâ, esa hetû, esa uvaese,[11] jaṃ no tesiṃ
saṃloe sapaḍiduvâre ciṭṭhejjâ. se ttam âyâe egaṃtam 45
avakkamejjâ aṇâvâyam asaṃloe ciṭṭhejjâ. se se paro aṇâ-
vâtam asaṃloe ciṭṭhamâṇassa asaṇaṃ vâ 4 âhaṭṭu dalaejjâ,
se ya evaṃ vadejjâ: âusaṃto samaṇâ! ime bhe asaṇe vâ 4
savvajaṇâe[12] nisaṭṭhe,[13] taṃ bhuṃjaha va [14] ṇaṃ, paribhâe*h*a
va ṇaṃ. taṃ c' egatio paḍigâhettâ tusiṇîo uvehejjâ:[15] avi

[6] A appaṃ. [7] A kaḍaṃ. [8] AB hatthî. [9] B °vell°, Com. °cell°. [10] A ghasiṃ.
[11] B uvaeso. [12] B °jâṇâe. [13] B nisiṭṭhe. [14] B vâ. [15] B ohejjâ.

yâiṃ evaṃ mamam eva siyâ. evaṃ mâiṭṭhâṇaṃ saṃphâse,
no evaṃ karejjâ. se ttam âyâe tattha gacchejjâ 2 se puvvâm
46 eva âloejjâ: âusaṃto samaṇâ! ime bhe asaṇe vâ 4 savvajaṇâe[12] nisaṭṭhe; taṃ bhuṃja*h*a va ṇaṃ, paribhâe*h*a va ṇaṃ.
se ṇ' evaṃ vadaṃtaṃ paro vadejjâ: âusaṃto samaṇâ! tumaṃ
c' eva ṇaṃ paribhâehiṃ. se tattha paribhâemâṇe no appaṇo
khaddhaṃ khaddhaṃ ḍâyaṃ 2 ûsaḍhaṃ 2 rasiyaṃ 2 maṇunnaṃ 2 niddhaṃ 2 lukkhaṃ 2; se tattha amucchi*t*e agiddhe
agaḍhie aṇajjhovavanne bahusamam eva paribhâejjâ. se
ṇaṃ paribhâemâṇaṃ paro vadejjâ: âusaṃto samaṇâ! mâ
ṇaṃ tumaṃ paribhâehiṃ, savve v' egatio[16] bhokkhâmo[17] vâ
47 pâhâmo[18] vâ. se tattha bhuṃjamâṇe no appaṇo khaddhaṃ
jâva lukkhaṃ, se tattha amucchie 4 bahusamam eva bhuṃjejja
vâ piejja[19] vâ. ||5||

se bhikkhû vâ 2 *jâva* samâṇe, se jjaṃ puṇa jâṇejjâ . . .
(§ 5) . . . pehâe, no te uvâtikkamma[20] pavisejja vâ obhâsejja
vâ. se ttam[21] âyâe egaṃtam avakkamejjâ, aṇâvâyam
asaṃloe ciṭṭhejjâ. aha puṇa evaṃ jâṇejjâ: paḍisehie vâ
dinne vâ, tao tammi niyaṭṭite,[22] tao saṃjayâm eva pavisejja
vâ obhâsejja vâ.
48 eyaṃ khalu tassa bhikkhussa vâ 2 sâmaggiyaṃ etc. ||6||**5**||

pamcamo uddesao.

se bhikkhû vâ 2 *jâva* samâṇe, se jjaṃ puṇa jâṇejjâ: rase-
siṇo bahave pâṇâ ghâsesaṇâe saṃthaḍe saṃnivaṭie pehâe,
taṃ jahâ: kukkuḍajâtiyaṃ vâ sûyarajâiyaṃ vâ agga-
piṃḍaṃsi vâ vâyasâ saṃthaḍâ saṃnivatiyâ[1] pehâe, sati
parakkame parakkamejjâ, no ujjuyaṃ gacchejjâ. ||1||

se bhikkhû vâ 2 *jâva* samâṇe no gâhâva*t*ikulassa duvâra-
49 sâhaṃ avalaṃbiya 2 ciṭṭhejjâ; no gâhâva*t*ikulassa dagaccha-
ḍḍaṇamattae[2] ciṭṭhejjâ, no gâhâva*t*ikulassa caṃdaṇioyae
ciṭṭhejjâ, no gâhâva*t*ikulassa siṇâṇassa vâ vaccassa vâ saṃloe
sapaḍiduvâre ciṭṭhejjâ, no gâhâvatikulassa âloyaṃ vâ thigga-
laṃ vâ saṃdhiṃ vâ dagabhavaṇaṃ vâ bâhâo pagijjhiya 2
aṃguliyâe vâ uddisiya 2 oṇamiya 2 unnamiya 2 nijjhâejjâ. ||2||

16 A ega. 17 A bhokhâmo. 18 B pahâmo. 19 B om. 20 A uvatikamma.
21 B yam. 22 A niyattie.

1 A °vaḍiyâ. 2 A °cchaḍḍaṇâ°.

no gâhâva*t*iṃ aṃguliyâe uddisiyâ 2 jâejjâ, no gâhâva*t*iṃ
aṃguliyâe câliya 2 jâejjâ, no gâhâva*t*iṃ tajjiya 2 jâejjâ, no 50
gâhâva*t*iṃ aṃguliyâe uggulaṃpiya[3] 2 jâejjâ, no gâhâva*t*iṃ
vaṃdiya 2 jâejjâ, no vayaṇaṃ pharusaṃ vadejjâ. ‖ 3 ‖
aha tattha kaṃci bhuṃjamâṇaṃ pehâe, taṃ jahâ: gâhâ-
vaiṃ vâ *jâva* kammakariṃ vâ, se puvvâm eva âloejjâ: âuso
ti[4] vâ, bhaiṇî[5] ti[4] vâ, dâhisi me etto annayaraṃ bhoyaṇajâ*t*aṃ? se s'evaṃ vadaṃtassa paro hatthaṃ vâ mattaṃ vâ
davviṃ vâ bhâyaṇaṃ[6] va sî*t*odagaviyaḍeṇa vâ usiṇodagaviyaḍeṇa vâ uccholejja vâ padhoejja[7] vâ. se puvvâm eva 51
âloejjâ: âuso ti[4] vâ, bhagiṇî ti[4] vâ, mâ etaṃ tumaṃ hatthaṃ
vâ mattaṃ vâ davviṃ vâ bhâyaṇaṃ vâ sî*t*odagaviyaḍeṇa vâ
usiṇodagaviyaḍeṇa vâ uccholehi vâ pahovehi[8] vâ; abhikaṃkhasi me dâ*t*uṃ, em eva dalayâhi. se s'evaṃ vadaṃtassa
paro hatthaṃ vâ 4 sîodagaviyaḍeṇa vâ usiṇodagaviyaḍeṇa vâ
uccholettâ padhoittâ âhaṭṭu dalaejjâ; tahappagâreṇaṃ pure-
kammakaeṇaṃ hattheṇa vâ 4 aphâsuyaṃ aṇesaṇijjaṃ[9] *jâva*
no paḍigâhejjâ. ‖ 4 ‖ aha puṇa evaṃ jâṇejjâ: no purekamma-
kaeṇa udaulleṇaṃ tahappagâreṇa udaulleṇa hattheṇa vâ
4 asaṇaṃ vâ 4 aphâsuyaṃ aṇesaṇijjaṃ *jâva* no paḍigâhejjâ. ‖ 5 ‖
aha puṇa evaṃ jâṇejjâ; no udaulleṇa, sasiṇiddheṇa,[10] *sesaṃ
taṃ c'eva.* evaṃ sasarakkhe udaulle sasiṇiddhe maṭṭiyâ
ose hariyâle hiṃgulae maṇosilâ aṃjaṇe loṇe geruya-vaṇṇiya-
seḍiya-soraṭṭhiya[9]-piṭṭhakukkusa-kaeya[11]-ukkuṭṭha[12]-saṃsa-
ṭṭheṇa. ‖ 6 ‖
a*h*a puṇa evaṃ jâṇejjâ: no asaṃsaṭṭhe tahappagâreṇa 53
saṃsaṭṭheṇa hattheṇa vâ 4 asaṇaṃ vâ 4 phâsuyaṃ vâ *jâva*
paḍigâhejjâ. aha puṇa evaṃ jâṇejjâ: asaṃsaṭṭhe tahappagâreṇa saṃsaṭṭheṇa hattheṇa vâ 4 asaṇaṃ vâ 4 phâsuyaṃ
jâva paḍigâhejjâ. ‖ 7 ‖
se bhikkhû vâ 2, se jjaṃ puṇa jâṇejjâ: pihuyaṃ vâ
bahurayaṃ vâ *jâva* câulapalaṃbaṃ vâ asaṃjae bhikkhupaḍiyâe
cittamaṃtâe silâe *jâva* makkaḍâsaṃtâṇae koṭṭiṃsu vâ koṭṭeṃti
vâ koṭṭissaṃti vâ, uppaṇiṃsu vâ 3 tahappagâraṃ pihuyaṃ[13]
vâ *jâva* câulapalaṃbaṃ vâ aphâsuyaṃ *jâva* no paḍigâhejjâ. ‖ 8 ‖
se bhikkhû vâ 2 *jâva* samâṇe, se jaṃ puṇa jâṇejjâ: bilaṃ

[3] B ukkhu°. [4] B tti. [5] B °ṇi. [6] B °ṇiṃ. [7] B paho° [8] B °vâhi. [9] A om.
[10] A sasa°. [11] BC om. [12] B uku°. [13] A pihuṃ, B pidhuvaṃ.

54 vâ loṇaṃ, ubbhiyaṃ vâ loṇaṃ, assaṃjae bhikkhupaḍiyâe
cittamaṃtâe silâe *jâva* saṃtâṇae bhidiṃsu[14] vâ bhidaṃti[9]
vâ bhidissaṃti[9] vâ ruciṃsu[9] vâ 3 bilaṃ vâ loṇaṃ,
ubbhiyaṃ vâ loṇaṃ aphâsuyaṃ *jâva* no paḍigâhejjâ. ‖9‖

se bhikkhû vâ 2 *jâva* samâṇe, se jjaṃ puṇa jâṇejjâ: asaṇaṃ
vâ 4 agaṇinikkhittaṃ, tahappagâraṃ asaṇaṃ vâ 4 aphâsuyaṃ
jâva no paḍigâhejjâ. kevalî bûyâ: âyâṇam e*t*aṃ; assaṃjae
55 bhikkhupaḍiyâe osiṃcamâṇe vâ nisiṃcamâṇe[15] vâ âmajjamâṇe
vâ pamajjamâṇe vâ oyâremâṇe[16] vâ uyattemâṇe vâ agganijîve
hiṃsejjâ. aha bhikkhûṇaṃ puvvovadiṭṭhâ, esa painnâ, esa
heue, esa kâraṇe, es' uva*d*ese, jaṃ tahappagâraṃ asaṇaṃ vâ
4 agaṇinikkhittaṃ aphâsuyaṃ aṇesaṇijjaṃ lâbhe saṃte no
paḍigâhejjâ.

eyaṃ khalu tassa bhikkhussa vâ 2 sâmaggiyaṃ etc. ‖10‖**6**‖

chaṭṭho uddesao

se bhikkhû vâ 2 *jâva* samâṇe, se jjaṃ puṇa jâṇejjâ:
56 asaṇaṃ vâ 4 khaṃdhaṃsi vâ thaṃbhaṃsi vâ maṃcaṃsi
vâ mâlaṃsi vâ pâsâyaṃsi vâ hammiyatalaṃsi vâ annayaraṃsi vâ tahappagâraṃsi aṃtalikkhajâyaṃsi uvaṇi-
kkhitte siyâ; tahappagâraṃ mâlohaḍaṃ asaṇaṃ vâ 4
aphâsuyaṃ *jâva* no paḍigâhejjâ. kevalî bûyâ: âyâṇam e*t*aṃ;
assaṃjae bhikkhupaḍiyâe pîḍhaṃ vâ phalahagaṃ[2] vâ nisseṇiṃ
vâ udûhalaṃ vâ âhaṭṭu[3] ussaviya duruhejjâ; se tattha duruhamâṇe payalejja vâ pavaḍejja vâ, se tattha payalamâṇe
57 pavaḍamâṇe hatthaṃ vâ pâyaṃ vâ bâhaṃ vâ ûraṃ[4] vâ
udaraṃ vâ sîsaṃ vâ anna*t*araṃ vâ kâyaṃsi iṃdiyajâyaṃ
lûsĕjjâ, pâṇâṇi vâ 4 abhihaṇejja vâ vattejja vâ lesejja vâ
saṃghâsejja[5] vâ saṃghaṭṭejja vâ pariyâvejja vâ kilâmejja
vâ ṭhâṇâo ṭhâṇaṃ saṃkâmejjâ; taṃ tahappagâraṃ mâlohaḍaṃ
asaṇaṃ vâ 4 *jâva* no paḍigâhejjâ. ‖1‖

se bhikkhû vâ 2 *jâva* samâne, se jjaṃ puṇa jâṇejjâ: asaṇaṃ
vâ 4 koṭṭhitâo vâ kolejjâo vâ assaṃjae bhikkhupaḍiyâe
58 ukkujjiyâ[6] avaujjiyâ[7] ohariyâ[7] âhaṭṭu dalaejjâ; tahappagâraṃ
asaṇaṃ vâ 4 bhomâlohaḍam ti naccâ lâbhe saṃte no paḍigâhejjâ. ‖2‖

[14] A bhidaṃsu. [15] B ss. [16] A uvâremâṇe.
[1] A adds phalahaṃsi vâ. [2] B phalagaṃ. [3] A avahaṭṭu. [4] A uraṃ, C ûruṃ.
[5] B saṃghas.° [6] A uku°. [7] A °ya?

se bhikkhû vâ 2 *jâva* samâṇe, se jjaṃ puṇa jâṇejjâ: asaṇaṃ vâ 4 maṭṭiolittaṃ, taṃ tahappagâraṃ asaṇaṃ vâ 4 maṭṭiolittaṃ lâbhe saṃte no paḍigâhejjâ. kevalî bûyâ: âyâṇam eyaṃ; assaṃjae bhikkhupaḍiyâe maṭṭiolittaṃ asaṇaṃ vâ 4 ubbhiṃdamâṇe puḍhavikâyaṃ[7] samâraṃbhejjâ, tahâ[8] teuvâuvaṇassatitasakâyaṃ[9] samâraṃbhejjâ; puṇar avi olippamâṇe[10] pacchâkammaṃ karejjâ. a*h*a bhikkhûṇaṃ puvvovadiṭṭhâ 4, jaṃ tahappagâraṃ maṭṭiolittaṃ asaṇaṃ vâ 4 lâbhe saṃte no paḍigâhejjâ. ||3||

se bhikkhû vâ 2 *jâva* samâṇe, se jjaṃ puṇa jâṇejjâ: asaṇaṃ vâ 4 puḍhavikâyapatiṭṭhi*t*aṃ, tahappagâraṃ asaṇaṃ vâ 4 *jâva* no paḍigâhejjâ. se bhikkhû vâ 2, se jjaṃ puṇa jâṇejjâ: asaṇaṃ vâ 4 âukâyapatiṭṭhiyaṃ, *taha ceva.* evaṃ agaṇikâyapatiṭṭhi*t*aṃ *jâva* no paḍigâhejjâ. kevalî bûyâ: âyâṇam eyaṃ; assaṃjae bhikkhupaḍiyâe agaṇiṃ ussikkiyâ[11] 2 nissikkiyâ[11] 59
2 ohariyâ âhaṭṭu dalaejjâ. aha bhikkhûṇaṃ puvvovadiṭṭhâ 4 *jâva* no paḍigâhejjâ. ||4||

se bhikkhû vâ 2 *jâva* samâṇe, se jjaṃ puṇa jâṇejjâ: asaṇaṃ vâ 4 accusiṇaṃ assaṃjae bhikkhupaḍiyâe suppeṇa vâ vihuyaṇeṇa[12] vâ tâliyaṃṭeṇa vâ sâhâe vâ sâhâbhaṃgeṇa vâ pehuṇeṇa[13] vâ pehuṇahatthena[14] vâ celeṇa vâ celakaṇṇeṇa vâ hattheṇa vâ muheṇa vâ phumejja vâ vîejja vâ, se puvvâm eva âloejjâ: âuso ti[15] vâ, bhagiṇî ti[16] vâ, mâ evaṃ. tumaṃ 60
asaṇaṃ vâ 4 accusiṇaṃ suppeṇa vâ *jâva* phumâhi vâ, vîyâhi vâ; abhikaṃkhasi me dâtuṃ, em eva dalayâhi. se s'evaṃ vadaṃtassa paro suppeṇa vâ *jâva* vîittâ âhaṭṭu dalaejjâ; tahappagâraṃ asaṇaṃ vâ 4 aphâsuyaṃ *jâva* no paḍigâhejjâ. ||5||

se bhikkhû vâ 2 *jâva* samâṇe, se jjaṃ puṇa jâṇejjâ: asaṇaṃ vâ 4 vaṇassaikâyapatiṭṭhiyaṃ, tahappagâraṃ asaṇaṃ vâ 4 vaṇassatikâyapatiṭṭhiyaṃ[17] aphâsuyaṃ *jâva* no paḍigâhejjâ. evaṃ tasakâe vi. ||6|| 61

se bhikkhû vâ 2, se jjaṃ puṇa pâṇagajâyaṃ jâṇejja, taṃ jahâ: usseimaṃ vâ saṃseimaṃ vâ câulodagaṃ vâ anna*t*araṃ vâ tahappagâraṃ pâṇagajâ*t*aṃ a*dh*uṇâ dhotaṃ aṇaṃbilaṃ avvokkaṃtaṃ[18] apariṇa*t*aṃ aviddhatthaṃ, aphâsuyaṃ *javâ*

[7] A kk. [8] B om. [9] B teûvâû. [10] B olimp°. [11] B mk. [12] B vianeṇa. [13] B pihuṇeṇa. [14] AB pi°. [15] B tti. [16] B °ṇî tti. [17] B vaṇassaya. [18] A avvokaṃtaṃ.

no paḍigâhejjâ. aha puṇa evaṃ jâṇejjâ: cirâ dhoṭaṃ aṃbilaṃ vokkaṃtaṃ[19] pariṇataṃ viddhatthaṃ phâsuyaṃ *jâva* paḍigâhejjâ. ‖7‖

62 se bhikkhû vâ 2 *jâva* samâṇe, se jjaṃ puṇa pâṇagajâyaṃ jâṇejjâ, taṃ jahâ: tilodagaṃ vâ tusodagaṃ vâ javodagaṃ vâ âyâmaṃ vâ sovîraṃ vâ suddhaviyaḍaṃ vâ annataraṃ vâ tahappagâraṃ pâṇagajâtaṃ, puvvâm eva âloejjâ: âuso tti vâ, bhagiṇî ti[16] vâ, dâhisi me etto annaṭaraṃ pâṇagajâṭaṃ? se s' evaṃ vadaṃtaṃ paro vadejjâ: âusaṃto samaṇâ! tumaṃ ceve' daṃ pâṇagajâṭaṃ paḍiggaheṇa vâ ussiṃciyâ ṇaṃ oattiyâ ṇaṃ giṇhâhi! tahappagâraṃ pâṇagajâyaṃ sayaṃ vâ
63 gĕṇhĕjjâ paro vâ se dejjâ, phâsuyaṃ *jâva* paḍigâhejjâ. ‖8‖

se bhikkhû vâ 2 *jâva* samâṇe, se jjaṃ puṇa pâṇagaṃ jâṇejjâ: aṇaṃtarahiyâe puḍhavîe *jâva* saṃtâṇae uddhaṭṭu 2 nikkhitte, siyâ assaṃjae[20] bhikkhupaḍiyâe udaulleṇa vâ sasiṇiddheṇa[21] vâ sakasâeṇa vâ matteṇa sîṭodaeṇa vâ saṃbhoettâ âhaṭṭu dalaejjâ; tahappagâraṃ pâṇagajâṭaṃ aphâsuyaṃ *jâva* no paḍigâhejjâ.

eyaṃ[22] khalutassa bhikkhussa vâ 2 sâmaggiyaṃ. ‖9‖**7**‖

sattamo uddesao.

se bhikkhû vâ 2 *jâva* samâṇe, se jjaṃ puṇa jâṇejjâ, taṃ[1] jahâ[1]: aṃbapâṇagaṃ vâ aṃbâḍagapâṇagaṃ vâ kavitthapâṇagaṃ[1] vâ[1] mâtuluṃgapâṇagaṃ vâ muddiyâpâṇagaṃ vâ khajjûrapâṇagaṃ vâ dâlimapâṇagaṃ vâ nâlierapâṇagaṃ[2] vâ karîrapâṇagaṃ vâ kolapâṇagaṃ vâ âmalagapâṇagaṃ vâ ciṃcâpâṇagaṃ vâ annaṭaraṃ vâ tahappagâraṃ pâṇagajâtaṃ sayaṭṭhiyaṃ sakaṇuyaṃ sabîyagaṃ assaṃjae bhikkhupaḍiyâe
65 chavveṇa[3] vâ dûseṇa vâ vâlaeṇa vâ âvîliyâṇa[4] paripîliyâṇa parissâviyâṇa[5] âhaṭṭu dalaejjâ; tahappagâraṃ pâṇagajâyaṃ aphâsuyaṃ *jâva* no paḍigâhejjâ. ‖1‖

se bhikkhû vâ 2 *jâva* samâṇe se âgaṃtaresu vâ ârâmagâresu vâ gâhâvaṭikulesu vâ pariyâvasahesu vâ annagaṃdhâṇi vâ pâṇagaṃdhâṇi vâ âghâya, se tattha âsâyavaḍiyâe mucchie gaḍhie ajjhovavanne ahogaṃdho no gaṃdham âghâejjâ. ‖2‖

[19] A vâ°, B vu°. [20] B asaṃjae. [21] A sasaṇi°. [22] A evaṃ.

[1] A om, B i. marg. [2] A ṇâlaerap°. [3] A chappeṇa. [4] A °layâṇa. [5] B parisâiyaṇa.

se bhikkhû vâ 2 *jâva* samâṇe, se jjaṃ puṇa jâṇejjâ: sâluyaṃ vâ virâliyaṃ vâ sâsavaṇâliyaṃ vâ anna*t*araṃ vâ tahappagâraṃ âmagaṃ asatthapariṇataṃ aphâsuyaṃ *jâva* no paḍigâhejjâ. se bhikkhû vâ 2 *jâva* samâṇe, se jjaṃ puṇa jâṇejjâ: pippaliṃ vâ pippalicuṇṇaṃ vâ miriyaṃ vâ miriyacuṇṇaṃ[6] vâ siṃgaveraṃ vâ siṃgarevacuṇṇaṃ vâ anna*t*araṃ vâ tahappagâraṃ âmagaṃ asatthapariṇataṃ aphâsuyaṃ *jâva* no paḍigâhejjâ. ‖ 3 ‖

se bhikkhû vâ 2 *jâva* samâṇe, se jjaṃ puṇa palaṃbajâ*t*aṃ[7] 66
jâṇejjâ, taṃ jahâ: aṃbapalaṃbaṃ vâ aṃbâḍagapalaṃbaṃ vâ tâlapalaṃbaṃ[1] vâ[1] jhijjhiripalaṃbaṃ vâ surabhipalaṃbaṃ vâ sallaipalaṃbaṃ vâ anna*t*araṃ vâ tahappagâraṃ palaṃbajâ*t*aṃ âmagaṃ asatthapariṇataṃ aphâsuyaṃ *jâva* no paḍigâhejjâ. ‖ 4 ‖

se bhikkhû vâ 2 *jâva* samâṇe, se jjaṃ puṇa pavâlajâtaṃ jâṇejjâ, taṃ jahâ: âsotthapavâlaṃ vâ naggohapavâlaṃ vâ
pilaṃkhupavâlaṃ vâ nîûrapavâlaṃ vâ sallaipavâlaṃ vâ anna- 67
*t*araṃ vâ tahappagâraṃ pavâlajâ*t*aṃ âmagaṃ asatthapariṇataṃ aphâsuyaṃ *jâva* no paḍigâhejjâ. ‖ 5 ‖

se bhikkhû vâ 2 *jâva* samâṇe, se jjaṃ puṇa saraḍuyajâyaṃ jâṇejjâ, taṃ jahâ: aṃbasaraḍuyaṃ kavitthasaraḍuyaṃ[8] dâlimasaraḍuyaṃ pippalasaraḍuyaṃ anna*t*araṃ vâ tahappagâraṃ saraḍuyajâ*t*aṃ âmaṃ asatthapariṇataṃ aphâsuyaṃ *jâva* no paḍigâhejjâ. ‖ 6 ‖

se bhikkhû vâ 2 *jâva* samâṇe, se jjaṃ puṇa maṃthujâtaṃ[9] jâṇejjâ, taṃ jahâ: uṃbaramaṃthuṃ vâ pilaṃkhumaṃthuṃ[10] vâ[8] naggohamaṃthuṃ vâ âsothamaṃthuṃ vâ anna*t*araṃ vâ tahappagâraṃ maṃthujâ*t*aṃ âmayaṃ durukkaṃ[11] sâṇubîyaṃ aphâsuyaṃ *jâva* no paḍigâhejjâ. ‖ 7 ‖

se bhikkhû vâ 2 *jâva* samâṇe, se jjaṃ puṇa jâṇejjâ: âmaḍâgaṃ vâ pûtipinnâgaṃ[12] vâ ma*h*uṃ vâ majjaṃ vâ sappiṃ vâ kholaṃ vâ purâṇaṃ[13] ettha pâṇâ aṇuppasûtâ, ettha pâṇâ jâ*t*â, ettha pâṇâ saṃvuḍḍhâ, ettha pâṇâ avvukkaṃtâ,[14] ettha pâṇâ apariṇa*t*â,[15] ettha pâṇâ aviddhatthâ; no paḍigâhejjâ.[16] ‖ 8 ‖

se bhikkhû vâ 2 *jâva* samâṇe, se jjaṃ puṇa jâṇejjâ: 68

[6] A mirayac°. [7] A palaṃbagajâyam. [8] A om. [9] A maṃthuṃ. [10] B °kkh°, A om. [11] A durakkaṃ. [12] A ṇṇ. [13] B purâṇagaṃ. [14] A uva°, B va°. [15] A no pari°, B pari°. [16] B no viddh°.

ucchumeragaṃ vâ aṃkakareluyaṃ vâ kaserugaṃ vâ saṃghâḍagaṃ[17] vâ pûtiâlugaṃ vâ anna*t*araṃ vâ tahappagâraṃ âmagaṃ[18] asatthapariṇataṃ[8] *jâva* no paḍigâhejjâ. ‖ 9 ‖

se bhikkhû vâ 2 *jâva* samâṇe, se jjaṃ puṇa jâṇejjâ: uppalaṃ vâ uppalanâlaṃ vâ bhisaṃ vâ bhisamaṇâlaṃ[19] vâ pŏkkhalaṃ vâ pokkhalavibhaṃgaṃ vâ anna*t*araṃ vâ tahappagâraṃ *jâva* no paḍigâhejjâ. ‖ 10 ‖

se bhikkhû vâ 2 *jâva* samâṇe, se jjaṃ puṇa jâṇejjâ: agga-
69 bîyâṇi vâ mûlabîyâṇi vâ khaṃdhabîyâṇi vâ porabîyâṇi vâ, aggajâ*t*âṇi vâ mûlajâ*t*âṇi vâ khaṃdhajâ*t*âṇi vâ porajâ*t*âṇi vâ; nannattha takkalimatthaeṇa vâ takkalisîseṇa vâ nâlieramatthaeṇa vâ khajjûrimatthaeṇa vâ tâlamatthaeṇa vâ, anna*t*araṃ vâ tahappagâraṃ âmagaṃ[20] *jâva* no paḍigâhejjâ. ‖ 11 ‖

se bhikkhû vâ 2 *jâva* samâṇe, se jjaṃ puṇa jâṇejjâ: ucchuṃ vâ kâṇagaṃ[21] aṃgâriyaṃ sammissaṃ[18] samaṭṭhaṃ[8] vigadû-
70 si*t*aṃ[22] vettaggaṃ[23] kadalîûsugaṃ[24] vâ anna*t*araṃ vâ tahappagâraṃ âmagaṃ[25] *jâva* no paḍigâhejjâ. ‖ 12 ‖

se bhikkhû vâ 2 *jâva* samâṇe, se jjaṃ puṇa jâṇejjâ: lasuṇaṃ vâ lasuṇapattaṃ vâ lasuṇanâlaṃ vâ lasuṇakaṃdaṃ vâ lasuṇacoyagaṃ[26] vâ anna*t*araṃ vâ tahappagarâṃ âmagaṃ *jâva* no paḍigâhejjâ. ‖ 13 ‖

se bhikkhû vâ 2 *jâvâ* samâṇe, se jjaṃ puṇa jâṇejjâ: atthiyaṃ vâ kuṃbhipakkaṃ vâ tiṃdugaṃ vâ veluyaṃ[27] vâ kâsavanâliyaṃ vâ annataraṃ vâ tahappagâraṃ âmagaṃ *jâva* no paḍigâhejjâ ‖ 14 ‖

se bhikkhû vâ 2 *jâva* samâṇe, se jjaṃ puṇa jâṇejjâ: kaṇaṃ vâ kaṇakuṃḍagaṃ[28] vâ kaṇapûyaliyaṃ[29] vâ câulaṃ vâ câulapiṭṭhaṃ vâ[30] tilaṃ vâ tilapiṭṭhaṃ vâ tilapippaḍaṃ[31] vâ anna*t*araṃ vâ tahappagâraṃ âmagaṃ *jâva* no paḍigâhejjâ.

eyaṃ khalu tassa bhikkhussa vâ 2 sâmaggiyaṃ etc. ‖ 15 ‖ 8 ‖

aṭṭhamo uddesao.

iha khalu pâdîṇaṃ vâ paḍîṇaṃ vâ dâhiṇaṃ vâ udîṇaṃ vâ
72 saṃtegatiyâ saḍḍhâ bhavaṃti, gâhâva*t*î vâ *jâva* kammakarî

[17] B siṃgh°. [18] B om. [19] B mâṇ°, A muṇ 2. hd. [20] B âmaṃ. [21] B kâṇaṃ. [22] A vai°. [23] B °ggagaṃ. [24] A kâyali. [25] MSS. âmaṃ. [26] MSS. coyaṃ. [27] MSS. pelugaṃ. [28] A °ḍaṃ. [29] A pûliyaṃ, B pûyaliṃ. [30] A adds poliyaṃ vâ. [31] B pappaḍagaṃ.

vâ, tesiṃ ca ṇaṃ evaṃ vuttapuvvaṃ bhavati: je ime bhavaṃti
samaṇâ bhagavaṃto sîlamaṃto guṇamaṃto vaimaṃto[1] saṃjayâ
saṃvuḍâ baṃbhacârî uvarayâ mehuṇâo dhammâo, no khalu
etesiṃ kappai âhâkammie asaṇe vâ 4 bhottae vâ pâyae vâ;
se jjaṃ puṇa imaṃ amhaṃ appaṇo sayaṭṭhâe[2] niṭṭhitaṃ, taṃ
jahâ: asaṇaṃ vâ 4, savvam eyaṃ samaṇâṇaṃ nisirâmo. avi
yâiṃ vayaṃ pacchâ vi appaṇo sayaṭṭhâe asaṇaṃ vâ 4 ceteessâ-
mo. eyappagâraṃ nigghosaṃ soccâ nisamma tahappagâraṃ
asaṇaṃ vâ 4 aphâsuyaṃ *jâva* no paḍigâhejjâ. || 1 ||

se bhikkhû vâ 2 *jâva* samâṇe, vasamâṇe vâ gâmâṇugâmaṃ dûijjamâṇe, se jjaṃ puṇa jâṇejjâ: gâmaṃ vâ
jâva râyahâṇiṃ vâ, imaṃsi khalu gâmaṃsi vâ *jâva* râyahâṇiṃsi vâ saṃtegatiyassa bhikkhussa pure saṃthuyâ vâ
pacchâ saṃthuyâ vâ parivasaṃti, taṃ jahâ: gâhâvatî vâ
jâva kammakarî vâ, tahappagârâiṃ kulâiṃ no puvvâm eva
bhattâe vâ pâṇâe vâ nikkhamejja vâ pavisejja vâ. kevalî 73
bûyâ: âyâṇam eyaṃ; purâ pehâe tassa paro[3] aṭṭhâe asaṇaṃ
vâ 4 uvakarejja vâ uvakkhaḍejja vâ. aha bhikkhûṇaṃ puvvovadiṭṭhâ 4, jaṃ no[4] tahappagârâiṃ kulâiṃ etc. se ttam
âyâe egaṃtam[5] avakkamejjâ,[5] egaṃtam avakkamittâ aṇâvâyam asaṃloe ciṭṭhejjâ. se tattha kâleṇaṃ[6] aṇupavisejjâ, 2 ttâ
tatth' itarehiṃ kulehiṃ samudâṇiyaṃ esiyaṃ vesiyaṃ piṃḍa-
vâyam esittâ, âhâram âhârejjâ. se paro kâleṇa aṇupa- 74
viṭṭhassa âhâkammiyaṃ asaṇaṃ vâ 4 uvakarejja vâ uvakkhaḍejja vâ, taṃ c' egatio tusiṇîo uvehejjâ: âhaḍam evaṃ paccâ-
ikkhissâmi. mâiṭṭhaṇaṃ saṃphâse, no evaṃ karejjâ. se
puvvâm eva âloejjâ: âuso ti[7] vâ, bhagiṇî ti[8] vâ, no khalu me
kappati âhâkammiyaṃ vâ asaṇaṃ vâ 4 bhottae vâ pâyae[9]
vâ; mâ uvakarehi, mâ uvakkhaḍehi. se s' evaṃ vadaṃtassa
paro âhâkammiyaṃ asaṇaṃ vâ 4 uvakkhaḍettâ âhaṭṭu
dalaejjâ, tahappagâraṃ asaṇaṃ vâ 4 aphâsuyaṃ *jâva* no 75
paḍigâhejjâ. || 2 ||

se bhikkhû vâ 2 *jâva* samâṇe, se jjaṃ puṇa jâṇejjâ: maṃsaṃ
vâ macchaṃ vâ bhajjijjamâṇaṃ pehâe, tellapûyaṃ[10] vâ âesâe
uvakkhaḍijjamâṇaṃ pehâe, no khaddhaṃ 2 uvasaṃkamittu
obhâsejjâ, nannattha gilâṇanîsâe.[11] || 3 ||

[1] B vai°. [2] B atthâe. [3] A puro. [4] B jaṇṇo. [5] B om. [6] A kâle. [7] B tti.
[8] B °ṇi tti. [9] B pâittae. [10] A vibhajjamâṇaṃ p. tela°. [11] A milâṇâe.

se bhikkhû vâ 2 *jâva* samâṇe anna*t*araṃ bhoyaṇajâ*t*aṃ
paḍigâhettâ subbhiṃ subbhiṃ bhoccâ dubbhiṃ dubbhiṃ
pariṭṭhave*t*i. mâ*t*iṭṭhâṇaṃ saṃphâse, no evaṃ karejjâ.
subbhiṃ ti[5] vâ dubbhiṃ ti[5] vâ, savvam eva bhuṃjejjâ, no
kiṃci vi pariṭṭhavejjâ.[12] ||4||
76 se bhikkhû vâ 2 *jâva* samâṇe annataraṃ[13] pâṇagajâyaṃ
paḍigâhettâ pupphaṃ pupphaṃ âviittâ kasâyaṃ kasâyaṃ
pariṭṭhaveti. mâiṭṭhâṇaṃ saṃphâse, no evaṃ karejjâ.
pupphaṃ pupphe ti vâ, kasâyaṃ kasâe ti vâ, savvam eva
bhuṃjejjâ, no kiṃci vi pariṭṭhavejjâ. ||5||
se bhikkhû vâ 2 bahupariyâvannaṃ bhoyaṇajâyaṃ paḍigâhettâ, sâhammiyâ tattha vasaṃti saṃbhoiyâ samaṇunnâ aparihâriyâ adûragа*t*â, tesiṃ aṇâloiyâ aṇâmaṃtiyâ[14] pariṭṭhave*t*i.
77 mâiṭṭhâṇaṃ saṃphâse, no evaṃ karejjâ. se ttam âyâe tattha
gacchejjâ, 2 ttâ puvvâm eva âloejjâ : âusaṃto samaṇâ! ime
bhe asaṇe[15] vâ 4 bahupariyâvanne,[15] taṃ bhuṃja*h*a va[5] ṇaṃ.
se s' evaṃ vadaṃtaṃ paro vadejjâ : âusaṃto samaṇâ! âhâram
e*t*aṃ asaṇaṃ vâ 4 jâvatiyaṃ 2 parisaḍai,[16] tâvatiyaṃ
bhokkhâmo vâ pâhâmo vâ; savvam eyaṃ parisaḍai,
savvam eyaṃ bhokkhâmo vâ pâhâmo vâ.[17] ||6||
se bhikkhû vâ 2, se jjaṃ puṇa jâṇejjâ : asaṇaṃ vâ 4
paraṃ samuddissa bahiyâ nîhaḍaṃ taṃ parehiṃ asama-
78 ṇunnâ*t*aṃ aṇisaṭṭhaṃ aphâsuyaṃ *jâva* no paḍigâhejjâ. taṃ
parehiṃ samaṇunnâ*t*aṃ samaṇisaṭṭhaṃ phâsuyaṃ *jâva* paḍigâhejjâ.
e*t*aṃ khalu tassa bhikkhussa vâ 2 sâmaggiyaṃ, etc. ||7||**9**||

navamo uddesao.

se egatio sâhâraṇaṃ piṃḍavâyaṃ paḍigâhettâ te sâhammie
aṇâpucchittâ, jassa 2 iccha*t*i, tassa khaddhaṃ 2 dalayati.[1]
mâiṭṭhâṇaṃ saṃphâse, no evaṃ karejjâ. se ttam âyâe tattha
gacchejjâ, gacchittâ puvvâm evaṃ vadejjâ : âusaṃto samaṇâ!
79 saṃti mama pure saṃthuyâ vâ pacchâ saṃthuyâ vâ, taṃ
jahâ : âyarie vâ uvajjhâe vâ pavattî vâ there vâ gaṇî vâ
gaṇahare vâ gaṇâvaccheie vâ, avi yâiṃ etesiṃ khaddhaṃ 2

[12] BC savvaṃ bhuṃje na chaḍḍae. [13] B adds vâ. [14] B °te. [15] A °aṃ.
[16] B sarati. [17] B om. this clause.

[1] B dalâti.

dâhâmi. se ṇ' evaṃ vadaṃtaṃ paro vaejjâ: kâmaṃ khalu
âuso ahâpajjattaṃ nisirâhi[2] jâva*t*iyaṃ[3] 2 paro vadati, tâva*ti*-
yaṃ 2 nisirejjâ; savvam eyaṃ paro vadati, savvam eyaṃ
nisirejjâ. ||1||

se egatio maṇunnaṃ bhoyaṇajâyaṃ paḍigâhettâ paṃteṇa
bhoyaṇeṇa palicchâeti: mâ m' etaṃ dâtiyaṃ saṃtaṃ
daṭṭhûṇa sayam âtie, taṃ jahâ: âyarie vâ *jâva* gaṇâvaccheie
vâ, no khalu me kassai[5] kiṃci vi dâyavvaṃ siyâ. mâiṭṭhâṇaṃ saṃphâse, no evaṃ karejjâ. se ttam âyâe tattha
gacchejjâ, puvvâm eva uttâṇae hatthe paḍiggahaṃ kaṭṭu:
imaṃ khalu, imaṃ khalu tti âloejjâ, no kiṃci vi vigû-
hejjâ. ||2||

se ega*t*io anna*t*araṃ bhoyaṇajâyaṃ[6] paḍigâhettâ bhaddayaṃ[6] 2 bhoccâ, vivaṇṇaṃ virasam âharati. mâiṭṭhâṇaṃ
saṃphâse, no evaṃ karejjâ. ||3||

se bhikkhû vâ 2, se jjaṃ puṇa jâṇejjâ: aṃtarucchuyaṃ vâ
ucchugaṃḍiyaṃ vâ ucchucoyagaṃ vâ ucchumeragaṃ vâ
ucchusâlagaṃ vâ ucchuḍâlagaṃ vâ saṃpaliṃ[7] vâ saṃpalithâ- 80
la*g*aṃ[7] vâ, assiṃ khalu paḍigâhi*t*aṃsi appe siyâ bhoyaṇajâe
bahuujjhiyadhammie, tahappagâraṃ aṃtarucchuyaṃ *jâva*
saṃpalithâla*g*aṃ aphâsuyaṃ *jâva* no paḍigahejjâ. ||4||

se bhikkhû vâ 2, se jjaṃ puṇa jâṇejjâ: bahuyaṭṭhiyaṃ vâ
maṃsaṃ, macchaṃ[8] vâ bahukaṃṭagaṃ, assiṃ khalu paḍigâhi*t*aṃsi[9] appe siyâ bhoyaṇajâe bahuujjhiyadhammie, tahappagâraṃ bahuyaṭṭhiyaṃ vâ maṃsaṃ, macchaṃ vâ bahukaṃṭa-
gaṃ aphâsuyaṃ *jâva* no paḍigâhejjâ. ||5|| 81

se bhikkhû vâ 2 *jâva* samâṇe, siyâ ṇaṃ paro bahuaṭṭhieṇa
maṃseṇa vâ maccheṇa vâ uvanimaṃtejjâ: âusaṃto samaṇâ!
abhikaṃkhasi bahuaṭṭhiyaṃ maṃsaṃ paḍigâhĕttae? etappagâraṃ nighosaṃ soccâ nisamma se puvvâm eva âloejjâ: âuso
ti vâ bhaiṇî ti vâ, no khalu kappai me bahuaṭṭhiyaṃ maṃsaṃ
paḍigâhettae; abhikaṃkhasi me dâuṃ, jâvatiyaṃ tâvatiyaṃ
poggalaṃ dalayâhi, mâ aṭṭhiyâiṃ. se s' evaṃ vadaṃtassa
paro âhaṭṭu aṃto paḍiggahaṃsi bahuaṭṭhiyaṃ maṃsaṃ
paḍibhâettâ nîhaṭṭu dalaejjâ, tahappagâraṃ paḍiggahaṃ
parahatthaṃsi vâ parapâyaṃsi vâ aphâsuyaṃ *jâva* no paḍigâ-

[2] B om. [3] B jâvatidaṃ. [4] B tâvadiyaṃ. [5] AB kassati. [6] A °iṃ.
[7] A saṃva°. [8] A macchagaṃ. [9] B gg.

hejjâ. se ya âhacca paḍigâhie siyâ, taṃ no[10] tti vaejjâ, no
ha[11] tti, no haṃdaha tti vaejjâ. se ttam â*d*âya egaṃtam
avakkamejjâ, 2 ttâ ahe ârâmaṃsi vâ ahe uvassayaṃsi vâ
appaṃḍe *jâva* saṃtâṇae maṃsagaṃ macchagaṃ bhoccâ
aṭṭhiyâiṃ kaṃṭa*g*e gahâya se ttam âyâe egaṃtam avakka-
82 mejjâ ahe jhâmathaṃḍilaṃsi[12] vâ *jâva* pamajjiya 2 pariṭṭhavejjâ. ‖6‖

se bhikkhû vâ 2 *jâva* samâṇe, siyâ se paro abhihaṭṭu aṃto
paḍiggahae bilaṃ vâ loṇaṃ, ubbhiyaṃ vâ loṇaṃ paribhâettâ[13]
nîhaṭṭu dalaejjâ, tahappagâraṃ paḍiggahagaṃ parahatthaṃsi
vâ parapâyaṃsi vâ aphâsuyaṃ *jâva* no paḍigâhejjâ. âhacca
paḍigâhie siyâ, taṃ ca nâ' tidûragate jâṇejjâ, se ttam âyâe
tattha gacchejjâ, 2 ttâ puvvâm eva âloejjâ : âuso tti vâ,
83 bhaiṇî ti vâ, imaṃ te kiṃ jâṇa*t*â dinnaṃ, udâhu ajâṇayâ ?
se ya bhaṇejjâ : no khalu me jâṇa*t*â dinnaṃ, ajâṇa*t*â ; kâmaṃ
khalu âuso idâṇiṃ nisirâmi ; taṃ bhuṃjaha va ṇaṃ pari-
bhâeha[14] va ṇaṃ. taṃ parehiṃ samaṇunnâyaṃ samaṇu-
saṭṭhaṃ tato saṃjayâm eva bhuṃjejja vâ piejja vâ, jaṃ ca no
saṃcâeti bhottae vâ pâyae vâ, sâhammiyâ tattha vasaṃti
saṃbhoiyâ samaṇunnâ aparihâriyâ, tesiṃ aṇuppadâ*t*avvaṃ
siyâ ; no jattha sâhammiyâ, jah' eva bahupariyâvanne kîrati,
84 tah' eva kâyavvaṃ siyâ.

e*t*aṃ khalu tassa bhikkhussa vâ 2 sâmaggiyaṃ, etc. ‖7‖**10**‖

dasamo uddesao.

bhikkhâgâṇâm ege evam âhaṃsu : samâṇe vâ vasamâṇe vâ
gâmâṇugâmaṃ vâ dûijjamâṇe[1] maṇunnaṃ bhoyaṇajâyaṃ
labhittâ, se ya bhikkhû gilâti, se haṃdaha ṇaṃ tass' âharaha.
se ya bhikkhû no bhuṃjejjâ, tumaṃ c' eva ṇaṃ bhuṃjijjâsi.
se egatio bhokkhâmî ti[2] kaṭṭu paliuṃciya 2 âloejjâ, taṃ
jahâ : ime piṃḍe, ime loe, ime tittae, ime kaḍuyae, ime kasâe,
85 ime aṃbile, ime mahure ; no khalu etto kiṃci gilâṇassa sa*d*ati
tti.[3] mâiṭṭhâṇaṃ saṃphâse, no evaṃ karejjâ. tah'eva[4] taṃ
âloejjâ, jah' eva taṃ gilâṇassa sa*d*ati tti[3] ; taṃ tittayaṃ tittae
ti vâ, kaḍuyaṃ 2 kasâyaṃ 2 aṃbilaṃ 2 mahuraṃ 2. ‖1‖

[10] B taṇṇo. [11] B aṇaha. [12] B ll. [13] B pariyâe bhâettâe. [14] A pariyâ°, AB °dha.

[1] B dûti°. [2] B °i tti. [3] A om. [4] B tahâvi-jahâvi.

bhikkhâgâṇâm ege evam âhaṃsu, samâṇe vâ vasamâṇe vâ gâmâṇugâmaṃ[1] vâ dûijjamâṇo maṇunnaṃ bhoyaṇajâyaṃ labhittâ se ya bhikkhû gilâ*ti*: se haṃdaha ṇaṃ tass âharaha; se ya bhikkhû no bhuṃjejjâ, âharejjâsi ṇaṃ, no khalu ime aṃtarâe âharissâmi. ||2||

icc eyâiṃ âya*t*aṇâiṃ uvâtikkamma aha bhikkhû jâṇejjâ 86
satta piṃḍesaṇâo satta pâṇesaṇâo.

tattha khalu imâ paḍhamâ piṃḍesaṇâ. asaṃsaṭṭhe hatthe, asaṃsaṭṭhe matte; tahappagâreṇaṃ hattheṇa vâ matteṇa vâ asaṇaṃ vâ 4 sayaṃ vâ ṇaṃ jâejjâ, paro vâ se dejjâ, phâsuyaṃ paḍigâhejjâ.[5] paḍhamâ piṃḍesaṇâ. ||3||

ahâ 'varâ doccâ piṃḍesaṇâ. saṃsaṭṭhe hatthe saṃsaṭṭhe matte; *tah' eva*. doccâ piṃḍesaṇâ. ||4||

ahâ 'varâ taccâ piṃḍesaṇâ. iha khalu pâ*t*îṇaṃ vâ 4 saṃtegaṭiyâ saḍḍhâ bhavaṃti, gâhâvatî vâ *jâva* kammakarî 87
vâ, tesiṃ ca ṇaṃ annayaresu virûvarûvesu bhoyaṇajâ*t*esu uvanikkhittapuvve siyâ, taṃ jahâ: ṭhâlaṃsi vâ piḍharagaṃsi vâ saragaṃsi vâ paragaṃsi vâ varagaṃsi vâ, aha puṇa[6] evaṃ jâṇejjâ: asaṃsaṭṭhe hatthe saṃsaṭṭhe matte, saṃsaṭṭhe vâ hatthe asaṃsaṭṭhe matte, se ya paḍiggahadhârî siyâ pâṇipaḍiggahie vâ, se puvvâm eva âloejjâ: âuso ti vâ, bhagiṇî ti vâ, asaṃsaṭṭheṇaṃ hattheṇaṃ saṃsaṭṭheṇaṃ matteṇaṃ, saṃsaṭṭheṇa vâ hattheṇaṃ asaṃsaṭṭheṇaṃ matteṇaṃ. assiṃ 88
paḍiggahagaṃsi vâ pâṇiṃsi vâ nihaṭṭu uvittu dalayâhi. tahappagâraṃ bhoyaṇajâyaṃ sayaṃ vâ ṇaṃ jâejjâ, paro vâ se dejjâ, phâsuyaṃ *jâva* paḍigâhejjâ.[5] taccâ piṃḍesaṇâ. ||5||

ahâ 'varâ cautthâ piṃḍesaṇâ. se bhikkhû vâ 2, se jjaṃ puṇa jâṇejjâ: pihuyaṃ vâ *jâva* câulapalaṃbaṃ vâ, assiṃ khalu paḍigâhi*t*aṃsi[5] appe pacchâkamme appe pajjavajâe, tahappagâraṃ pihuyaṃ vâ sayaṃ vâ ṇaṃ jâejjâ *jâva* paḍigâhejjâ. cautthâ piṃḍesaṇâ.[5] ||6||

a*h*â 'varâ paṃcamâ piṃḍesaṇâ: se bhikkhû vâ 2 *jâva* samâṇe ogâhitam[7] eva bhoyaṇajâyaṃ jâṇejjâ, taṃ jahâ: sarâvaṃsi vâ diṃḍimaṃsi vâ kosagaṃsi vâ, aha puṇa evaṃ jâṇejjâ: bahupariyâvanne pâṇis' udagaleve, tahappagâraṃ asaṇaṃ vâ 4 sayaṃ vâ ṇaṃ jâejjâ *jâva* paḍigâhejjâ. paṃcamâ piṃḍesaṇâ. ||7||

[5] B gg. [6] A puṇ. [7] A uvahiyam.

ahâ 'varâ chaṭṭhâ piṃḍesaṇâ: se bhikkhû vâ 2 paggahiyaṃ[8] eva bhoyaṇajâyaṃ jâṇejjâ: jaṃ ca saaṭṭhâe paggahi-
89 yaṃ,[8] jaṃ ca paraṭṭhâe paggahiyaṃ,[8] taṃ pâdapariyâvannaṃ, taṃ pâṇipariyâvannaṃ phâsuyaṃ *jâva* paḍigâhejjâ. chaṭṭhâ piṃḍesaṇâ. ‖ 8 ‖

ahâ 'varâ sattamâ piṃḍesaṇâ. se bhikkhû vâ 2 *jâva* samâṇe bahuujjhiyadhammiyaṃ bhoyaṇajâyaṃ jâṇejjâ: jaṃ c' anne bahave dupayacaupayasamaṇamâhaṇaatihikivaṇavaṇîmagâ nâ 'vakaṃkhaṃti, taṃ tahappagâraṃ ujjhiyadhammiyaṃ bhoyaṇajâyaṃ sayaṃ vâ ṇaṃ jâejjâ, paro vâ se dejjâ *jâva* phâsuyaṃ paḍigâhejjâ. sattamâ piṃḍesaṇâ. ‖ 9 ‖

icc eyâo satta piṃḍesaṇâo. ahâ' varâo satta pâṇesaṇâo.
90 tattha khalu imâ paḍhamâ pâṇesaṇâ: asaṃsaṭṭhe hatthe, *taṃ ceva bhâṇiyavvaṃ navaraṃ.* cautthen' âṇattaṃ: se bhikkhû vâ 2 *jâva* samâṇe, se jjaṃ puṇa pâṇagajâyaṃ jâṇejjâ, taṃ jahâ: tilodagaṃ vâ tusodagaṃ vâ javodagaṃ vâ âyâmaṃ vâ sovîraṃ vâ suddhaviyaḍaṃ vâ; assiṃ khalu paḍigâhi*t*aṃsi[9] appe pacchâkamme, *tah' eva jâva* paḍigâhejjâ. ‖ 10 ‖

icc e*t*âsiṃ sattaṇhaṃ piṃḍesaṇâṇaṃ sattaṇhaṃ pâṇesaṇâṇaṃ annayaraṃ paḍimaṃ paḍivajjamâṇe no evaṃ vadejjâ:
91 micchâ paḍivannâ khalu ete bhayaṃtâro, ahaṃ ege sammâ paḍivanne; je ete bhayaṃtâro[10] eyâo paḍimâo paḍivajjittâ ṇaṃ viharaṃti, jo ya[11] ahaṃ aṃsi eyaṃ paḍimaṃ paḍivajjittâ ṇaṃ viharâmi, savve v[12] ete jiṇâṇâe uvaṭṭhitâ, annonnasamâhîe[13] evaṃ ca ṇaṃ viharaṃti.

evaṃ khalu tassa bhikkhussa vâ 2 sâmaggiyaṃ, etc. ‖ 11 ‖ **11** ‖

egâdaso uddesao.

padhamam ajjhayaṇaṃ.

piṃḍesaṇâ samattâ.

[8] AB uggahiyaṃ. [9] MSS. gg. [10] B bhayavaṃtâro. [11] A jaṃ ca. [12] A p. [13] A °hite, B °hîte.

BIIYAM AJJHAYAṆAṂ.

SEJJÂ.

se[1] bhikkhû vâ 2 abhikaṃkhejjâ uvassayaṃ esittae, se aṇupavisittâ gâmaṃ vâ nagaraṃ vâ *jâva* râyahâṇiṃ vâ, se 93
jjaṃ puṇa uvassayaṃ jâṇejjâ: saaṃḍaṃ sapâṇaṃ *jâva* saṃtâṇagaṃ, tahappagâre uvassae[2] no ṭhâṇaṃ vâ sejjaṃ vâ nisîhiyaṃ vâ cetejjâ. ‖1‖

se bhikkhû vâ 2, se jjaṃ puṇa uvassayaṃ jâṇejjâ: appaṃḍaṃ appapâṇaṃ *jâva* saṃtâṇagaṃ, tahappagâre uvassae paḍilehittâ[3] pamajjittâ[3] tato saṃjayâm eva ṭhâṇaṃ vâ 3 cetejjâ. se jjaṃ puṇa uvassayaṃ jâṇejjâ: assiṃ paḍiyâe egaṃ sâhammiyaṃ samuddissa pâṇâiṃ 4 samârabbha[4] samuddissa kîyaṃ pâmiccaṃ acchejjaṃ aṇisaṭṭhaṃ abhihaḍaṃ âhaṭṭu 94
ceteti, tahappagâre uvassae purisaṃtarakaḍe[5] vâ apurisaṃtarakaḍe[5] vâ *jâva* âsevie vâ no ṭhâṇaṃ vâ 3 cetejjâ; evaṃ bahave sâhammiyâ, egaṃ sâhammiṇiṃ,[6] bahave sâhammiṇîo. se bhikkhû vâ 2, se jjaṃ puṇa uvassayaṃ jâṇejjâ: bahave samaṇamâhaṇaatiʰikivaṇavaṇîmae pagaṇiyâ[7] samuddissa pâṇâiṃ 4 *jâva* ceteti, tahappagâre uvassae apurisaṃtarakaḍe[5] *jâva* aṇâsevi*t*e no ṭhâṇaṃ vâ 3 cetejjâ.
a*h*a puṇa evaṃ jâṇejjâ: purisaṃtarakaḍe[5] *jâva* âsevi*t*e 95
paḍilehittâ[3] pamajjittâ ta*t*o saṃjayâm eva ṭhâṇaṃ vâ 3 cetejjâ. ‖2‖

se bhikkhû vâ 2, se jjaṃ puṇa uvassayaṃ jâṇejjâ: assaṃjate bhikkhupaḍiyâe kaḍie vâ ukkaṃbie[8] vâ channe vâ litte vâ ghaṭṭhe vâ maṭṭhe vâ saṃmaṭṭhe vâ saṃpadhûmi*t*e vâ, tahappagâre uvassae apurisaṃtarakaḍe[5] vâ *jâva* aṇâsevie vâ no ṭhâṇaṃ vâ 3 cetejjâ. a*h*a puṇa evaṃ jâṇejjâ: purisaṃtarakaḍe *jâva* âsevite paḍilehittâ[3] pamajjittâ tato saṃja*t*âm eva *jâva* cetejjâ. ‖3‖ 96

[1] B je. [2] A uvassayae. [3] B °ettâ. [4] A °rambha. [5] B °gaḍe. [6] A °ṇî. [7] A om. [8] B okaṃbie, A ukkaṃpie.

se bhikkhû vâ 2, se jjaṃ puṇa uvassayaṃ jâṇejjâ: assaṃjae bhikkhupaḍiyâe[9] khuḍḍiyâo duvâriyâo mahalliyâo kujjâ — *jahâ piṃḍesaṇâe jâva* saṃthâragaṃ saṃthârejjâ, bahiyâ vâ niṇṇakkhu, tahappagâre uvassae apurisaṃtaragaḍe *jâva* aṇâsevi*t*e no ṭhâṇaṃ vâ 3 cetejjâ. aha puṇa evaṃ jâṇejjâ etc. (*rest of* § 3). ||4||

se bhikkhû vâ 2, se jjaṃ puṇa uvassayaṃ jâṇejjâ: assaṃjae bhikkhupaḍiyâe udagapasû*t*âṇi kaṃdâṇi vâ mûlâṇi vâ puttâṇi vâ pupphâṇi vâ phalâṇi vâ bîyâṇi vâ hariyâṇi vâ ṭhâṇâo ṭhâṇaṃ sâhara*t*i, bahiyâ vâ niṇṇakkhu etc. (*rest of* § 4). ||5||

se bhikkhû vâ 2, se jjaṃ puṇa uvassayaṃ jâṇejjâ: assaṃjae bhikkhupaḍiyâe pîḍhaṃ vâ phalagaṃ vâ nisseṇiṃ
97 vâ udûhalaṃ[10] vâ ṭhâṇâo ṭhâṇaṃ sâharati, bahiyâ vâ niṇṇakkhu etc. ||6||

se bhikkhû vâ 2, se jjaṃ puṇa uvassayaṃ jâṇejjâ, taṃ jahâ: khaṃdhaṃsi vâ maṃcaṃsi vâ mâlaṃsi vâ pâsâyaṃsi vâ hammiyatalaṃsi vâ annataraṃsi vâ tahappagâraṃsi aṃtalikkhajâyaṃsi, nannattha âgâḍhâgâḍhehiṃ kâraṇehiṃ ṭhâṇaṃ vâ 3 cetejjâ. se ya âhacca cetie siyâ, no tattha sîtodagavi-
98 yaḍeṇa vâ usiṇodagaviyaḍeṇa vâ hatthâṇi vâ pâ*d*âṇi vâ acchîṇi vâ daṃtâṇi vâ muhaṃ vâ uccholejja vâ pa*dh*oejja vâ, no tattha annaṃ ûsaḍhaṃ pagarejjâ, taṃ jahâ: uccâraṃ vâ pâsavaṇaṃ vâ khelaṃ vâ siṃghâṇiyaṃ[11] vâ pittaṃ vâ pûtiṃ vâ soṇiyaṃ vâ anna*t*araṃ vâ sarîrâvayavaṃ. kevalî bûyâ: âyâṇam eyaṃ; se tattha ûsaḍhaṃ pagaremâṇe payalejja vâ pavaḍejja vâ; se tattha payalemâṇe vâ pavaḍemâne vâ hatthaṃ vâ *jâva* sîsaṃ vâ anna*t*araṃ vâ kâyaṃsi iṃdiyajâyaṃ lûsejjâ, pâṇâṇi vâ 4 abhihaṇejja vâ *jâva* vavarovejja vâ. aha bhikkhûṇaṃ puvvovadiṭṭhâ 4, jaṃ tahappagâre uvassae aṃtalikkhajâ*t*e no ṭhâṇaṃ vâ 3 cetejjâ. ||7||

se, bhikkhû vâ 2, se jjaṃ puṇa uvassayaṃ jâṇejjâ: saitthiyaṃ sakhuḍḍaṃ sapasubhattapâṇaṃ, tahappagâre uvassae sâgârie no ṭhâṇaṃ vâ 3 cetejjâ. âyâṇam eyaṃ: bhikkhussa gâhâvatikuleṇaṃ saddhiṃ saṃvasamâṇassa alasa*g*e vâ visûie[12] vâ chaḍḍî vâ ṇaṃ uvvâhĕjjâ, anna*t*are

[9] A adds kaḍiyâe vâ. [10] A uṭṭahalaṃ. [11] B siṃghâṇaṃ. [12] B visûiâ.

vâ se dukkharo*g*âtaṃke samuppajjejjâ, assaṃjae karuṇa- 99
paḍiyâe[13] taṃ bhikkhussa gâ*t*uṃ tellena vâ ghaeṇa vâ
navaṇî*t*eṇa vâ vasâo vâ abbhaṃgĕjja vâ makkhijja[14] vâ[14]
siṇâṇeṇa vâ kakkeṇa vâ loddheṇa vâ vaṇṇeṇa vâ cuṇṇeṇa vâ
paumeṇa vâ âghaṃsejju vâ paghaṃsejja vâ uvvalejja vâ
uvvaṭṭejja[7] vâ[7] sîodagaviyaḍeṇa vâ usiṇodagaviyaḍeṇa vâ
uccholejja vâ pahoejja vâ siṃcejja vâ dâruṇâ vâ dârupari-
ṇâmaṃ[15] kaṭṭu agaṇikâyaṃ ujjâlejja vâ pajjâlejja vâ, ujjâlittâ
pajjâlittâ kâyaṃ âyâvejja vâ payâvejja vâ. aha bhikkhû- 100
ṇaṃ puvvovadiṭṭhâ 4, jaṃ tahappagâre sâgârie uvassae no
ṭhâṇaṃ vâ 3 cetejjâ. ||8|| âyâṇam eyaṃ: bhikkhussa sâgârie
uvassae vasamâṇassa iha khalu gâhâvaî vâ *jâva* kammakarî
vâ annamannaṃ akkosaṃti vâ vahaṃti[15] vâ ruṃbhaṃti vâ
uddavemti vâ; aha bhikkhû ṇaṃ uccâvayaṃ maṇaṃ
niyacchejjâ: ete khalu annamannam akkosaṃtu vâ, mâ vâ
akkosaṃtu, *jâva* mâ vâ uddavemtu. aha bhikkhûṇaṃ
puvvovadiṭṭhâ 4, jaṃ tahappagâre sâgârie uvassae no ṭhâ- 101
ṇaṃ vâ 3 cetejjâ. ||9|| âyâṇam eyaṃ: bhikkhussa gâhâvaî-
hiṃ saddhiṃ saṃvasamâṇassa iha khalu gâhâva*t*î appaṇo
sayaṭṭhâe agaṇikâyaṃ ujjâlejja vâ pajjâlejja vâ vijjhavejja
vâ. aha bhikkhû uccâvayaṃ maṇaṃ niyacchejjâ: ete khalu
agaṇikâyaṃ ujjâlemtu[17] vâ, mâ vâ ujjâlemtu[17] *jâva*[18] mâ
vâ vijjhavemtu. a*h*a bhikkhûṇaṃ puvvovadiṭṭhâ 4, jaṃ
tahappagâre uvassae no ṭhâṇaṃ vâ 3 cetejjâ. ||*10*|| âyâṇam
eyaṃ: bhikkhussa gâhâvaîhiṃ saddhiṃ saṃvasamâṇassa iha
khalu gâhâvatissa kŏṃḍale vâ guṇe vâ maṇî vâ mottie vâ
hiraṇṇe vâ suvaṇṇe vâ kaḍagâṇi vâ tuḍi*g*âṇi vâ tisaragâṇi vâ
pâlaṃbâṇi[19] vâ hâre vâ addhahâre vâ egâvalî vâ muttâvalî
vâ kaṇagâvalî vâ rayaṇâvalî vâ taruṇiyaṃ vâ kumâriṃ
alaṃkiyavi*bh*ûsiyaṃ pehâe, aha bhikkhû uccâvayaṃ maṇaṃ
niyacchejjâ: erisiyâ vâ, sâ na vâ erisiyâ,[14] iti vâ ṇaṃ bûyâ,[14] 102
iti vâ ṇaṃ maṇaṃsâejjâ. a*h*a bhikkhûṇaṃ puvvovadiṭṭhâ 4,
jaṃ etc. ||11|| âyâṇam eyaṃ bhikkhussa gâhâvaîhiṃ
saddhiṃ saṃvasamâṇassa iha khalu gâhâva*t*iṇîo vâ gâhâva*t*i-
dhûyâo vâ gâhâva*t*isuṇhâo vâ gâhâva*t*idhâîo vâ gâhâva*t*idâsîo
vâ gâhâva*t*ikammakarîo vâ—tâsiṃ ca ṇaṃ evaṃ vuttapuvvaṃ

[13] B kaluṇayâe. [14] B om. [15] A dâruṇaṃ pariṇâmaṃ. [16] B baṃdhaṃti.
[17] A °eṃsu. [18] B full phrase. [91] A pă°.

bhavati: je ime bhavaṃti samaṇâ.bhagavaṃto *jâva* uvaratâ
103 me*h*uṇâo dhammâo, no khalu eesiṃ kappai me*h*uṇaṃ[20] dhammaṃ paḍiyâraṇâe âuṭṭittae, jâ ya eesiṃ saddhiṃ me*h*uṇaṃ[20] dhammaṃ paḍiyâraṇâe âuṭṭejjâ, puttaṃ khalu sâ labhĕjjâ oyassiṃ teyassiṃ vaccassiṃ jasassiṃ saṃparâiyaṃ aloyadarisaṇijjaṃ[21]; etappagâraṃ nigghosaṃ soccâ nisamma tâsiṃ ca ṇaṃ anna*t*arî sahiyaṃ[22] taṃ tavassiṃ bhikkhuṃ mehuṇaṃ[20] dhammaṃ paḍiyâraṇâe âuṭṭâvejjâ. aha bhikkhûṇaṃ puvvovadiṭṭhâ 4, jaṃ tahappagâre uvassae no ṭhâṇaṃ vâ 3 cetejjâ.

eyaṃ khalu tassa bhikkhussa vâ 2 sâmaggiyaṃ, etc. || 12 || 1 ||

padhamo uddesao.

gâhâvatîṇâm ege suisamâyârâ bhavaṃti, bhikkhû ya asiṇâṇâe[1] moyasamâyâro, se taggaṃdhe duggaṃdhe paḍikûle paḍilome yâvi bhavati. jaṃ puvvakammaṃ, taṃ pacchâkammaṃ; jaṃ pacchâkammaṃ, taṃ puvvakammaṃ; te bhikkhupaḍiyâe vaṭṭamâṇâ karejja vâ no karejja vâ. aha bhikkhûṇaṃ puvvovadiṭṭhâ 4, jaṃ tahappagâre uvassae no ṭhâṇaṃ vâ 3 cetejjâ. || 1 || âyâṇam eyaṃ: bhikkhussa gâhâvatîhiṃ saddhiṃ saṃvasamâṇassa iha khalu gâhâvatissa
105 appaṇo sayaṭṭhâe[2] virûvarûve bhoyaṇajâ*t*e uvakkhaḍie siyâ; aha pacchâ bhikkhûpaḍiyâe asaṇaṃ vâ 4 uvakkhaḍejja vâ uvakarejja vâ, taṃ ca bhikkhû abhikaṃkhejjâ bhottae vâ pâyae[3] vâ viyaṭṭittae vâ. aha bhikkhûṇaṃ puvvovadiṭṭhâ 4, jaṃ etc. || 2 || âyâṇam eyaṃ: [4]bhikkhussa gâhâva*t*iṇâ saddhiṃ saṃvasamâṇassa iha khalu gâhâva*t*issa appaṇo sayaṭṭhâe virûvarûvâiṃ dâruyâiṃ bhinnapuvvâiṃ bhavaṃti. aha pacchâ bhikkhûpaḍiyâe virûvarûvâiṃ dâruyâiṃ bhiṃdejja vâ kiṇejja vâ pamiccejja[5] vâ dâruṇâ vâ dârupariṇâmaṃ kaṭṭu agaṇikâyaṃ ujjâlejja vâ pajjâlejja vâ. tattha bhikkhû abhikaṃkhejjâ âtâvettae vâ payâvettae vâ viyaṭṭittae vâ. aha bhikkhûṇaṃ puvvovadiṭṭhâ 4, jaṃ etc. || 3 ||

se bhikkhû vâ 2 uccârapâsavaṇeṇaṃ ubbâhijjamâṇe râo vâ viyâle vâ gâhâva*t*ikulassa duvâravâhaṃ avaguṇejjâ,[6] teṇo vâ

[20] A mehuṇa. [21] B âl°. [22] B saddhiṃ.

[1] B °ṇae. [2] B saaṭṭhâe. [3] B pattae. [4] A adds se. [5] B pametthejja. [6] A uva°

tassaṃdhicârî aṇupavisejjâ; tassa bhikkhussa no kappati 106
evaṃ vadittae: ayaṃ teṇo pavisati no vâ pavisati, uvalliyati vâ 2, âyati[7] vâ 2, vadati vâ no vâ vadati, teṇa haḍaṃ anneṇa haḍaṃ, tassa haḍaṃ annassa haḍaṃ, ayaṃ teṇe, ayaṃ uvacarae, ayaṃ haṃtâ, ayaṃ ettham akâsî. taṃ tavassiṃ bhikkhuyaṃ ateṇaṃ teṇam iti saṃkati. aha bhikkhûṇaṃ puvvovadiṭṭhâ 4, jaṃ etc. ||4||

se bhikkhû vâ 2, se jjaṃ puṇa uvassayaṃ jâṇejjâ, taṃ
jahâ: taṇapuṃjesu vâ palâlapuṃjesu vâ sayaṃḍe *jâva* 107
saṃtâṇae, tahappagâre uvassae no ṭhâṇaṃ vâ 3 cetejjâ. se bhikkhû vâ 2, se jjaṃ puṇa uvassayaṃ jâṇejjâ: taṇapuṃjesu vâ palâlapuṃjesu vâ appaṃḍehiṃ *jâva* cetejjâ. ||5||

se âgaṃtâresu vâ ârâmâgâresu vâ gâhâva*t*ikulesu vâ pariyâvasahesu vâ abhikkhaṇaṃ 2 sâhammiehiṃ ova*t*amâṇehiṃ no 'va*t*ejjâ. se âgaṃtâresu vâ 4, je bhayaṃtâro udubaddhiyaṃ[8] vâ vâsâvâsiyaṃ vâ kappaṃ uvâtiṇittâ tatth' eva bhujjo 2 saṃvasaṃti: ayam âuso kâlâtikkaṃtakiriyâ bhavati 1. ||6||

se âgaṃtâresu vâ 4, je bhayaṃtâro udubaddhiyaṃ[8] vâ vâsâvâsiyaṃ vâ kappaṃ uvâtiṇâvettâ taṃ duguṇâ duguṇeṇa apariharittâ tatth' eva bhujjo 2 saṃvasaṃti: ayam âuso uvaṭṭhâṇakiriyâ yâvi[9] bhavati 2. ||7||

iha khalu pâîṇaṃ vâ 4 saṃtegatiyâ saḍḍhâ bhavaṃti, gâhâva*t*îo vâ *jâva* kammakarîo vâ, tesiṃ ca ṇaṃ âyâragoyare no suṇisaṃte bhavati; taṃ saddahamâṇehiṃ pattiyamâṇehiṃ
royamâṇehiṃ bahave samaṇamâhaṇaati*h*ikivaṇavaṇîma*g*e[10] 109
samuddissa tattha 2 agârîhiṃ agârâiṃ cetitâiṃ, taṃ jahâ: âesaṇâṇi vâ âyataṇâṇi vâ devakulâṇi vâ sabhâo[11] vâ pavâkaraṇâṇi[12] vâ paṇiyagihâṇi vâ jâṇasâlâo vâ su*dh*âkammaṃtâṇi vâ dabbhakammaṃtâṇi vâ vaddhakammaṃtâṇi[13] vâ pappakammaṃtâṇi[14] vâ iṃgâlakammaṃtâṇi vâ kaṭṭhakammaṃtâṇi vâ susâṇakammaṃtâṇi vâ saṃtisunnâgâragirikaṃdarâsaṃtiselovaṭṭhâṇakammaṃtâṇi[15] vâ bhavaṇagihâṇi vâ, je bhayaṃtâro tahappagârâiṃ âesaṇâṇi vâ *jâva* bhavaṇagihâṇi vâ, tehiṃ ovayamâṇehiṃ ovayaṃti: ayam âuso abhikkaṃtakiriyâ yâvi bhavati 3. ||8||

[7] B âyavati. [8] B uḍu°. C uuvahiyaṃ. [9] Sometimes vi, sometimes omitted. [10] B vaṇimage. [11] B sahâṇi. [12] BC pavâṇi. [13] A vabbha. [14] A puvva, C vaṇa. [15] B kammaṃtâṇi after each of these words, but om. the second saṃti, and has kaṃdara.

iha khalu pâîṇaṃ vâ 4 *jâva* taṃ royamâṇehiṃ bahave
samaṇamâhaṇaatihikivaṇavaṇîmae samuddissa tattha 2 agârîhiṃ agârâiṃ ce*t*i*t*âiṃ bhavaṃti, taṃ jahâ : âesaṇâṇi vâ *jâva*
110 gihâṇi vâ, je bhayaṃtâro tahappagârâiṃ âesaṇâṇi vâ *jâva*
gihâṇi vâ tesiṃ aṇovayamâṇehiṃ ovayaṃti : ayam âuso
aṇabhikkaṃtakiriyâ yâvi bhavati 4. ‖9‖

iha khalu pâîṇaṃ vâ 4 saṃtegatiyâ saḍḍhâ bhavaṃti, taṃ
jahâ : gâhâvaî vâ *jâva* kammakarî vâ, tesiṃ ca ṇaṃ vuttapuvvaṃ bhavati : je ime bhavaṃti samaṇâ bhagavaṃto
sîlamaṃtâ *jâva* uvarayâ mehuṇâo dhammâo, no khalu eesiṃ
bhayaṃtârâṇaṃ kappa*t*i â*h*âkammie uvassae vatthae ; se jjâṇ'
111 imâṇi ambaṃ appaṇo aṭṭhâe ce*t*i*t*âiṃ bhavaṃti, âesaṇâṇi vâ
jâva gihâṇi vâ, savvâṇi tâṇi samaṇâṇaṃ nisirâmo, aviyâiṃ
vayaṃ pacchâ appaṇo sayaṭṭhâe cetessâmo, taṃ jahâ : âesaṇâṇi vâ *jâva* gihâṇi vâ. e*t*appagâraṃ nigghosaṃ soccâ
nisamma je bhayaṃtâro tahappagârâiṃ âesaṇâṇi vâ *jâva*
gihâṇi vâ uvâgacchaṃti, 2 ttâ i*t*arâ*t*arehiṃ[16] pâhuḍehiṃ
vaṭṭaṃti[17] : ayam âuso vajjakiriyâ yâvi bhavati 5. ‖10‖

iha khalu pâîṇaṃ vâ 4 *jâva*[18] vaṇîmae pagaṇiya 2
samuddissa tattha 2 agârîhiṃ agârâiṃ ce*t*i*t*âiṃ bhavaṃti,
taṃ jahâ : âesaṇâṇi vâ *jâva* gihâṇi vâ, je bhayaṃtâro
tahappagârâiṃ âesaṇâṇi vâ *jâva* gihâṇi vâ uvâgacchaṃti,
2 ttâ i*t*arâtarehiṃ pâhuḍehiṃ vaṭṭaṃti : ayam âuso mahâ-
vajjakiriyâ yâvi bhavati 6. ‖11‖

iha khalu pâîṇaṃ vâ 4 *jâva*[18] taṃ royamâṇehiṃ bahave
samaṇajâe samuddissa tattha 2 agârîhiṃ agârâiṃ ce*t*iyâiṃ
112 bhavaṃti, âesaṇâṇi vâ *jâva* gihâṇi ; je bhayaṃtâro tahappagârâiṃ âesaṇâṇi vâ *jâva* gihâṇi vâ uvâgacchaṃti 2, ttâ iyarâyarehiṃ pâhuḍehiṃ vaṭṭaṃti[19] : ayam âuso sâvajjakiriyâ
yâvi bhavati 7. ‖12‖

iha khalu pâîṇaṃ vâ 4 *jâva*[18] taṃ royamâṇehiṃ ekkaṃ
samaṇajâyaṃ samuddissa tattha 2 agârîhiṃ agârâiṃ ceiyâiṃ
bhavaṃti, âesaṇâṇi vâ *jâva* gihâṇi vâ mahayâ puḍhavikâyasamârambheṇaṃ, evaṃ âo teo vâu vaṇassai, mahayâ tasakâyasamârambheṇaṃ maha*t*â ârambheṇaṃ maha*t*â
samârambheṇaṃ mahayâ virûvarûvehiṃ pâvakamma-

[16] A itaretarehiṃ. [17] A viṭṭanti. [18] The MSS. have some more words of the above passage, § 8. [19] MSS. om.

kiccehiṃ, taṃ: châyaṇa*t*o levaṇa*t*o saṃthâraduvârapihaṇa*t*o sîtodae vâ pariṭṭhavi*t*apuvve[20] bhavati, agaṇikâe vâ ujjâli*t*apuvve bhavati; je bhayaṃtâro tahappagârâiṃ âesaṇâṇi vâ *jâva* gihâṇi vâ uvâgacchaṃti, 2 ttâ itarâtarehiṃ pâhuḍehiṃ dupakkhaṃ te kamma sevaṃti: ayam âuso mahâsâvajja- 113
kiriyâ yâvi bhavati 8. ||13||

iha khalu pâîṇaṃ vâ 4 *jâva* taṃ royamâṇehiṃ appaṇo sayaṭṭhâe tattha 2 agârîhiṃ agârâiṃ ce*ti*tâiṃ bhavaṃti, taṃ jahâ: âesaṇâṇi vâ *jâva* gihâṇi vâ mahatâ puḍhavikâyasamârambheṇaṃ *jâva* agaṇikâe ujjâlitapuvve bhavati; je bhayaṃtâro tahappagârâiṃ âesaṇâṇi vâ *jâva* gihâṇi vâ uvâgacchaṃti, 2 ttâ iyarâyarehiṃ pâhuḍehiṃ egapakkhaṃ te kamma sevaṃti: ayam âuso appasâvajjakiriyâ yâvi bhavati 9.

eyaṃ khalu tassa bhikkhussa vâ 2 sâmaggiyaṃ, etc. ||14||**2**||

biio uddesao.

se u[1] ṇo sulabhe phâsue uṃche ahesaṇijje no ya[2] khalu suddhe[3] imehiṃ pâhuḍehiṃ, taṃ: châyaṇa*t*o levaṇa*t*o saṃthâraduvârapihaṇa*t*o, se ya bhikkhucariyârae ṭhâṇarae nisîhiyâra*t*e sejjâsaṃthârapiṃḍesaṇârate. saṃti bhikkhuṇo evam akkhâiṇo ujjuyakaḍâ[4] niyâgapaḍivannâ amâyaṃ kuvvamâṇâ viyâhiyâ. saṃtega*t*iyâpâhuḍiyâ ukkhittapuvvâ bhavati, evaṃ 116
nikkhittapuvvâ bhavati, paribhâiyapuvvâ bhavati, paribhuttapuvvâ bhavati, pariṭṭhaviyapuvvâ[5] bhavati. evaṃ viyâgaremâṇe samiyâe viyâgareti, haṃtâ bhavati. ||1||

se bhikkhû vâ 2, se jjaṃ puṇa uvassayaṃ jâṇejjâ: khuḍḍiyâo khuḍḍaduvâriyâo nîyâo[6] saṃniruddhiyâo bhavaṃti, tahappagâre uvassae râo vâ viyâle vâ nikkhamamâṇe vâ pavisamâṇe vâ purâ hattheṇa[7] pacchâ pâena, tao[8] saṃjayâm eva nikkhamejja vâ pavisejja vâ. kevalî bûyâ: âyâṇam 117
eyaṃ; je tattha samaṇâṇa[9] vâ mâhaṇâṇa[9] vâ chattae vâ mattae vâ daṃḍae[10] vâ laṭṭhiyâ vâ bhisiyâ vâ cele[11] vâ cilimilî[12] cammae vâ cammakosae vâ cammachedaṇae vâ dubbaddhe vâ dunnikkhitte aṇikaṃpe calâcale, bhikkhû ya râo vâ viyâle

[20] B pariddhaviya.
[1] B ya. [2] A nâi. [3] A saṭṭhe. [4] B ujjuyaḍâ. [5] A °ṭṭhâ°. [6] AC nîiyâo. [7] A hatthaeṇa. [8] A tate. [9] A °ṇeṇa. [10] B ḍaṃḍae. [11] B celaṃ. [12] B °miṇiṃ.

vâ nikkhamamâṇe vâ pavisamâṇe vâ payalejja vâ pavaḍĕjja
118 vâ, se tattha payalemâṇe pavaḍemâṇe hatthaṃ vâ pâyaṃ vâ
jâva iṃdiyajâ*t*aṃ vâ lûsejja vâ pâṇâṇi vâ 4 abhihaṇejja vâ
jâva vavarovejja vâ. aha bhikkhûṇaṃ puvvovadiṭṭhâ 4, jaṃ
tahappagâre uvassae purâ hattheṇa pacchâ pâeṇa, tato saṃja-
yâm eva nikkhamejja vâ pavisejja vâ. ||2||

se âgaṃtâresu vâ 4 aṇuvîi [13] uvassayaṃ jâejjâ; je tattha
îsaro, je tattha samâhiṭṭhae, uvassayaṃ aṇunnavejjâ: âmaṃ
khalu âuso, a*h*âlaṃdaṃ ahâparinnâtaṃ vasissâmo, jâva
âusaṃtassa uvassae, jâva sâhammiyâ etâvatâ [14] uvassayaṃ
119 giṇhissâmo, teṇa paraṃ viharissâmo. ||3||

se bhikkhû vâ 2, jass' uvassae saṃvasejjâ, tassa puvvâṃ
eva nâmagoyaṃ jâṇejjâ, tao pacchâ tassa gihe nimaṃtemâ-
ṇassa aṇimaṃtemâṇassa vâ asaṇaṃ vâ 4 *jâva* no paḍigâ-
hejjâ. ||4||

se bhikkhû vâ 2, se jjaṃ puṇa uvassayaṃ jâṇejjâ: sasâga-
riyaṃ sâgaṇiyaṃ saudayaṃ, no pannassa nikkhamaṇapave-
saṇâe, no pannassa vâyaṇâ *jâva* ciṃtâe [15]; tahappagâre
uvassae no ṭhâṇaṃ vâ 3 cetejjâ. ||5||

se bhikkhû vâ 2, se jjaṃ puṇa uvassayaṃ jâṇejjâ: gâ-
120 hâvaikulassa majjhaṃ majjheṇaṃ gaṃtuṃ paṃthapaḍi-
baddhaṃ [16] vâ, no pannassa nikkhamaṇa *jâva* ciṃtâe;
tahappagâre uvassae no ṭhâṇaṃ vâ 3 cetejjâ. ||6||

se bhikkhû vâ 2 se jjaṃ puṇa uvassayaṃ jâṇejjâ: iha khalu gâhâva*t*î vâ *jâva* kammakarî vâ annamannam akkosaṃti *jâva* uddaveṃti, no pannassa *jâva* ciṃtâe; sa evaṃ naccâ tahappagâre uvassae no ṭhâṇaṃ vâ 3 cetejjâ. ||7||

se bhikkhû vâ 2, se jjaṃ puṇa uvassayaṃ jâṇejjâ: iha khalu gâhâvatî vâ *jâva* kammakarî vâ annamannassa gâ*t*aṃ telleṇa vâ ghaeṇa vâ navaṇîeṇa vâ vasâe [17] vâ abbhaṃge*t*i vâ makkhe*t*i [18] vâ, no pannassa *jâva* ciṃtâe; tahappagâre uvassae no ṭhâṇaṃ vâ 3 cetejjâ. ||8||

se bhikkhû vâ 2, se jjaṃ puṇa uvassayaṃ jâṇejjâ: iha khalu gâhâvatî vâ *jâva* kammakarîo vâ annamannassa gâ*t*aṃ siṇâṇeṇa vâ kakkeṇa vâ loddheṇa vâ vaṇṇeṇa vâ cuṇṇeṇa

[13] MSS. aṇuvîyî. [14] B itâva. [15] A vijjhâe. [16] A pattha°, C pahe pae paḍibaddhaṃ. [17] B kakkhae. [18] A maṃkheti. B me°.

vâ paumeṇa vâ âghaṃsaṃti vâ uvvalenti vâ uvvaṭṭeṃti vâ, no pannassa . . . (§ 8) . . . cetejjâ. ‖9‖

se bhikkhû vâ 2 etc. (§ 9 *to*) gâ*t*aṃ sî*t*oda*g*aviyaḍeṇa vâ 121
usiṇodagaviyaḍeṇa vâ uccholĕṃti vâ padhoveṃti[19] vâ siṃcaṃti vâ siṇâventi vâ, no pannassa etc. ‖10‖

se bhikkhû vâ 2 . . . (§ 9) . . . kammakarîo vâ nigiṇâ ṭhitâ nigiṇâ uvallîṇâ mehuṇadhammaṃ vinnaveṃti rahassiyaṃ vâ maṃtaṃ maṃteṃti, no pannassa etc. ‖11‖

se bhikkhû vâ 2, se jjaṃ puṇa uvassayaṃ jâṇejjâ: âiṇṇasaṃlekkhaṃ *jâva* pannassa no ṭhâṇaṃ vâ 3 cetejjâ. ‖12‖

se bhikkhû vâ 2 abhikaṃkhejjâ saṃthâragaṃ esittae, se jjaṃ puṇa saṃthâragaṃ jâṇejjâ: saaṃḍaṃ *jâva* saṃtâṇagaṃ, tahappagâraṃ saṃthâragaṃ lâbhe saṃte no paḍigâhejjâ. ‖13‖

se bhikkhû vâ 2, se jjaṃ puṇa saṃthâragaṃ jâṇejjâ: appaṃḍaṃ *jâva* saṃtâṇagaṃ garuyaṃ, tahappagâraṃ saṃthâragaṃ lâbhe saṃte no paḍigâhejjâ. ‖14‖

se bhikkhû vâ 2 . . . (§ 14) . . . saṃtâṇagaṃ lahuyaṃ 122
appaḍihâriyaṃ,[20] tahappagâraṃ etc. ‖15‖

se bhikkhû vâ 2 . . . (§ 15) . . . lahuyaṃ paḍihâriyaṃ[20] no ahâbaddhaṃ, tahappagâraṃ etc. ‖16‖

se bhikkhû vâ 2 . . . (§ 16) . . . paḍihâriyaṃ ahâbaddhaṃ, tahappagâraṃ saṃthâragaṃ *jâva* lâbhe saṃti paḍigâhejjâ. ‖17‖

icc e*t*âiṃ âya*t*aṇâiṃ uvâ*t*ikkamma â*h*a bhikkhû jâṇejjâ imâhiṃ cauhiṃ paḍimâhiṃ saṃthâragaṃ esittae. 123

tattha khalu imâ paḍhamâ paḍimâ. se bhikkhû vâ 2 uddisiya 2 saṃthâragaṃ jâejjâ, taṃ jahâ: ikkaḍaṃ vâ kaḍhiṇaṃ vâ jaṃtuyaṃ vâ paragaṃ vâ moragaṃ vâ taṇagaṃ vâ kusaṃ vâ kuccagaṃ vâ paccagaṃ vâ pippalagaṃ[21] vâ[21] palâlagaṃ vâ, se puvvâm eva âloejjâ: âuso ti vâ, bhagiṇî ti vâ, dâhisi me etto annataraṃ vâ saṃthâragaṃ? tahappagâraṃ saṃthâragaṃ sayaṃ vâ ya ṇaṃ jâejjâ paro vâ se dejjâ, phâsuyaṃ esaṇijjaṃ lâbhe saṃte paḍigâhejjâ. paḍhamâ paḍimâ. ‖18‖

ahâ 'varâ doccâ paḍimâ. se bhikkhû vâ 2 pehâe 2 saṃthâ- 124
ragaṃ jâejjâ, taṃ jahâ: gâhâva*t*iṃ[22] vâ *jâva* kammakariyaṃ[23]

[19] B pahoaṃti. [20] B °pâḍi°. [21] A om. [22] A °vaî. [23] A °rîu..

vâ, se puvvâm eva âloejjâ etc. (cf. § 18). doccâ paḍimâ. ‖19‖

ahâ 'varâ taccâ paḍimâ. se bhikkhû vâ 2 jass' uvassae
saṃvasejjâ, je tattha ahâsamannâgate, taṃ jahâ: ikkaḍe vâ
jâva palâle vâ, tassa lâbhe saṃvasejjâ, tassa alâbhe ukkuḍue
vâ nesajjie[24] vâ viharejjâ. taccâ paḍimâ. ‖20‖

ahâ 'varâ cautthâ paḍimâ. se bhikkhû vâ 2 ahâsaṃthaḍam eva saṃthâragaṃ jâejjâ, taṃ jahâ: puḍhavisilaṃ vâ
kaṭṭhasilaṃ vâ, ahâsaṃthaḍam eva, tassa lâbhe saṃvasejjâ,
125 tassa alâbhe ukkuḍue vâ nesajjie vâ viharejjâ. cautthâ
paḍimâ.

icc e*t*âṇaṃ cauṇhaṃ paḍimâṇaṃ anna*t*araṃ paḍimaṃ paḍivajjamâṇe, *taṃ ceva jâva* annonnasamâhîe evaṃ ca ṇaṃ
viharaṃti. ‖21‖

se bhikkhû vâ 2 abhikaṃkhejjâ saṃthâragaṃ paccappi-
ṇittae, se jjaṃ puṇa saṃthâragaṃ jâṇejjâ: saaṃḍaṃ *jâva*
saṃtâṇagaṃ, tahappagâraṃ saṃthâragaṃ no paccappiṇijjâ.
se bhikkhû vâ etc. appaṃḍaṃ *jâva* saṃtâṇagaṃ, ta*h*appagâraṃ saṃthâragaṃ paḍilehiya 2 pamajjiya 2 â*t*âviya 2
viṇiṭṭhuṇiya 2 tao saṃjayâm eva paccappiṇijjâ. ‖22‖

se bhikkhû vâ 2 samâṇe vâ vasamâṇe vâ gâmâṇugâmaṃ
dûtijjamâṇe puvvâm eva pannassa uccârapâsavaṇabhûmiṃ
paḍilehijjâ. kevalî bûyâ: âyâṇam eyaṃ; apaḍilehiyâe
uccârapâsavaṇabhûmîe bhikkhû vâ 2 râo vâ viyâle uccârapâsavaṇaṃ pariṭṭhavemâṇe payalejja vâ pavaḍejja vâ, se tattha
payalamâṇe vâ pavaḍamâṇe vâ hatthaṃ vâ pâyaṃ vâ *jâva*
lûsejjâ, pâṇâṇi vâ 4 *jâva* vavarovejjâ.[25] aha bhikkhûṇaṃ
puvvovadiṭṭhâ 4, jaṃ puvvâm eva pannassa uccârapâsavaṇabhûmiṃ paḍilehĕjjâ. ‖23‖

se bhikkhû vâ 2 abhikaṃkhejjâ saṃthâragabhûmiṃ paḍi-
127 lehittae, nannattha âyarieṇa vâ *jâva* gaṇâvaccheieṇa vâ
bâleṇa vâ vuḍḍheṇa vâ seheṇa vâ gilâṇeṇa vâ âeseṇa vâ
aṃteṇa vâ majjheṇa vâ sameṇa vâ visameṇa vâ pavâeṇa vâ
nivâ*t*eṇa vâ, tao saṃjayâm eva paḍilehiya 2 pamajjiya 2
bahuphâsuyaṃ sejjâsaṃthâragaṃ saṃtharejjâ. ‖24‖

se bhikkhû vâ 2 bahuphâsuyaṃ sejjâsaṃthâragaṃ saṃtha-

[24] B nesijjie. [25] MSS. vavaroejjâ.

rittâ abhikaṃkhejjâ bahuphâsue sejjâsaṃthârae duruhittae. se bhikkhû vâ 2 bahuphâsuyaṃ sejjâsaṃthâragaṃ duruhamâṇe se puvvâm eva sasîsovariyaṃ kâyaṃ pâe ya pamajjiya, tao saṃjayâm eva bahuphâsue sejjâsaṃthârae duruhejjâ, duruhittâ tato saṃjayâm eva bahuphâsue sejjâsaṃthârae saejjâ. ||25||

se bhikkhû vâ 2 bahuphâsue sejjâsaṃthârae sayamâṇe no annamannassa hatthenaṃ hatthaṃ pâeṇaṃ[26] pâyaṃ kâeṇaṃ[27] kâyaṃ âsâejjâ, aṇâsâyamîṇe[28] tao saṃjayâm eva bahuphâsue sejjâsaṃthârae saejjâ. ||26||

se bhikkhû vâ 2 ûsasamâṇe[29] vâ nîsasamâṇe[29] vâ kâsamâṇe
vâ chîyamâṇe vâ jaṃbhâyamâṇe vâ uḍḍoe vâ vâtanisaggaṃ[30] 128
vâ karemâṇe, puvvâm eva âsayaṃ[31] vâ[32] posayaṃ[33] vâ[32] pâṇiṇâ paripihettâ, tato saṃjayâm eva ûsasejja[29] vâ *jâva* vâyanisaggaṃ karejjâ. ||27||

se bhikkhû vâ 2 samâ v' egayâ sejjâ bhavejjâ, visamâ v' egayâ sejjâ bhavejjâ, pavâyâ v. e. s. bh., nivâyâ v. e. s. bh., sasarakkhâ v. e. s. bh., appasasarakkhâ v. e. s. bh.,[21] sadaṃsamasagâ v. e. s. bh., appadaṃsamasagâ v. e. s. bh., saparisâḍâ v. e. s. bh., aparisâḍâ v. e. s. bh., sauvasaggâ v. e. s. bh., niruvasaggâ v. e. s. bh.; tahappagârâhiṃ sejjâhiṃ saṃvijjamâṇâhiṃ paggahitatarâgaṃ vihâraṃ viharejjâ, no kiṃci vigilâejjâ.

eyaṃ khalu tassa bhikkhussa vâ 2 sâmaggiyaṃ, jaṃ savvaṭṭhehiṃ sahite sadâ jaejjâ si tti bemi. ||28|| **3** ||

taio uddesao.

sejjâ samattâ.

biiyam ajjhayaṇaṃ.

26 A pâeṇa. 27 AB kâeṇa. 28 A °mâṇe. 29 B °sâs°. 30 AC nissagge. 31 BC âsataṃ. 32 A ca. 33 A posataṃ.

TAIYAM AJJHAYAṆAṂ.

IRIYÂ.

abbhuvagate khalu vâsâvâse, abhipavuṭṭhe bahave pâṇâ abhisaṃbhûyâ, bahave bîyâ ahuṇâ[1] bhinnâ, aṃtarâ se maggâ
130 bahupâṇâ bahubîyâ *jâva* saṃtâṇagâ aṇannokkaṃtâ[2] paṃthâ, no vinnâyâ maggâ; s' evaṃ naccâ no gâmâṇugâmaṃ dûijjejjâ, ta*t*o saṃjayâm eva vâsâvâsaṃ uvalliejjâ. || 1 ||

se bhikkhû vâ 2, se jjaṃ puṇa jâṇejjâ: gâmaṃ vâ *jâva* râyahâṇiṃ vâ, imaṃsi khalu gâmaṃsi vâ *jâva* râyahâṇiṃsi vâ no mahatî vihârabhûmî, no mahatî viyârabhûmî, no sulabhe pîḍhaphalagasejjâsaṃthâra*g*e, no sulabhe phâsue uṃche ahesaṇijje, bahave jattha samaṇamâhaṇaatihikivaṇavaṇîmagâ
131 uvâga*t*â, uvâgamissaṃti, accâiṇṇâ vittî, no pannassa nikkhamaṇapavesaṇa *jâva* dhammâṇuogaciṃtâe; s' evaṃ naccâ tahappagâraṃ gâmaṃ vâ nagaraṃ vâ *jâva* râyahâṇiṃ vâ no vâsâvâsaṃ uvalliejjâ. || 2 ||

se bhikkhû vâ 2 . . . (§ 2) . . . râyahâṇiṃsi vâ mahatî vihârabhûmî, mahatî viyârabhûmî, sulabhe jattha pîḍhe 4,
132 no jattha bahave samaṇâ *jâva* uvâgamissaṃti, appâiṇṇâ vittî *jâva* râyahâṇiṃ vâ, tato saṃjayâm eva vâsâvâsaṃ uvalliejjâ. || 3 ||

aha puṇa evaṃ jâṇejjâ: cattâri mâsâ vâsâṇaṃ vîtikkaṃtâ hemaṃtâṇa ya paṃcadasarâyakappe parivusite, aṃtarâ se maggâ bahupâṇâ *jâva* saṃtâṇagâ, no jattha bahave samaṇa *jâva* uvâgamissaṃti ya,[3] s' evaṃ naccâ no gâmâṇugâmaṃ dûijjejjâ.[4] || 4 ||

aha puṇa evaṃ jâṇejjâ . . . (§ 4) . . . aṃtarâ se maggâ appaṃḍâ *jâva* saṃtâṇagâ, bahave jattha samaṇa *jâva* uvâgamissaṃti ya, s' evaṃ naccâ ta*t*o saṃjayâm eva gâmâṇugâmaṃ dûijjejjâ.[4] || 5 ||

[1] A ahaṇu. [2] B aṇannokaṃta. [3] A om. [4] MSS. dûti°.

se bhikkhû vâ 2 gâmâṇugâmaṃ dûijjamâṇe[5] pura*t*o juga-
mâyaṃ pehamâṇe daṭṭhûṇa, tase pâṇe uddhaṭṭu pâdaṃ
rîejjâ, sâhaṭṭu pâdaṃ rîejjâ, vitiricchaṃ vâ kaṭṭu pâdaṃ
rîejjâ, sati parakkame saṃja*t*âm eva parakkamejjâ, no
ujjuyaṃ gacchejjâ, ta*t*o saṃjayâm eva gâmâṇugâmaṃ
dûijjejjâ.[5] ‖6‖

se bhikkhû vâ 2 gâmâṇugâmaṃ dûijjamâṇe[5] aṃtarâ se 133
pâṇâṇi vâ bîyâṇi vâ hariyâṇi vâ udae vâ maṭṭiyâ vâ
aviddhatthe sa*t*i parakkame *jâva* no ujjuyaṃ gacchejjâ, ta*t*o
saṃjayâm eva gâmâṇugâmaṃ dûijjejjâ.[6] ‖7‖

se bhikkhû vâ 2 gâmâṇugâmaṃ dûijjamâṇe[5] aṃtarâ se
virûvarûvâṇi paccaṃtikâṇi dasugâya*t*aṇâṇi milakkhûṇi aṇâri-
yâṇi dussamappâṇi duppannavaṇijjâṇi akâlapaḍibohîṇi akâla-
paḍibhoîṇí sa*t*i lâḍhe vihârâe saṃtharamâṇehiṃ jaṇavaehiṃ,
no vihâravattiyâe pavajjejjâ gamaṇâe. ‖8‖ 134

kevalî bûyâ: âyâṇam eyaṃ; te ṇaṃ bâlâ: ayaṃ teṇe,
ayaṃ upacarae, ayaṃ ta*t*o âga*t*e tti kaṭṭu taṃ bhikkhuṃ
akkosejja vâ *jâva* uddavejja vâ vatthaṃ paḍiggahaṃ kaṃbalaṃ pâyapuṃchaṇaṃ acchiṃdejja bhiṃdejja vâ avaharejja vâ
pariṭṭhavejja vâ; aha bhikkhûṇaṃ puvvovadiṭṭhâ 4, jaṃ no
tahappagârâṇi[7] virûvarûvâṇi paccaṃtiyâṇi dasugâyataṇâṇi
jâva vihâravattiyâe no pavajjejjâ gamaṇâe, ta*t*o saṃjayâm eva
gâmâṇugâmaṃ dûijjejjâ.[5] ‖9‖

se bhikkhû vâ 2 gâmâṇugâmaṃ dûijjamâṇe[5] aṃtarâ se 135
arâyâṇi vâ gaṇarâyâṇi vâ juvarâyâṇi vâ dorajjâṇi vâ verajjâ-
ṇi vâ viruddharajjâṇi vâ, sati lâḍhe vihârâe saṃtharamâṇehiṃ[8] jaṇavaehiṃ,[8] no vihâravattiyâe pavajjejjâ gamaṇâe.
kevalî bûyâ: âyâṇam eyaṃ; te ṇaṃ bâlâ: ayaṃ teṇe *taṃ
ceva jâva* gamaṇâe, ta*t*o saṃjayâm eva gâmâṇugâmaṃ
dûijjejjâ.[5] ‖10‖

se bhikkhû vâ 2 gâmâṇugâmaṃ dûijjamâṇe aṃtarâ se
vihaṃ siyâ, se jjaṃ puṇa vihaṃ jâṇejjâ: egâheṇa vâ duyâheṇa vâ tiyâheṇa vâ cauyâheṇa vâ paṃcâheṇa vâ pâuṇejja 136
vâ no vâ pâuṇejjâ, tahappagâraṃ vihaṃ aṇegâhagamaṇijjaṃ
sati lâḍhe *jâva* gamaṇâe. ‖11‖

kevalî bûyâ: âyâṇam eyaṃ; aṃtarâ se vâsaṃsi vâ pâṇesu

[5] B dûti°. [6] B gacchejjâ. [7] B °âiṃ. [8] A °esu vâ.

vâ paṇaesu vâ vîesu vâ hariesu vâ udaesu vâ maṭṭiyâe[9] vâ aviddhatthae.[10] aha bhikkhûṇaṃ puvvovadiṭṭhâ 4, jaṃ tahappagâraṃ vihaṃ aṇegâhagamaṇijjaṃ *jâva* no gamaṇâe; tato saṃjayâm eva gâmâṇugâmaṃ dûijjejjû.[5] ‖12‖

se bhikkhû vâ 2 gâmâṇugâmaṃ dûijjamâṇe aṃtarâ se nâvâsaṃtârimaṃ udayaṃ siyâ, se jjaṃ puṇa nâvaṃ jâṇejjâ: assaṃjae[11] bhikkhupaḍiyâe kiṇejja vâ pâmiccejja vâ nâvâe vâ nâvaṃ pariṇâmaṃ kaṭṭu thalâo vâ nâvaṃ jalaṃsi ogâhejjâ,[12] jalâo vâ nâvaṃ thalaṃsi ukkasejjâ,[13] puṇṇaṃ vâ nâvaṃ ussiṃcejjâ, sannaṃ vâ nâvaṃ uppîlavejjâ; tahappagâraṃ nâvaṃ uḍḍhagâmiṇiṃ vâ ahegâmiṇiṃ vâ tiriyagâmiṇiṃ vâ paraṃ joyaṇamerâe addhajoyaṇamerâe vâ appataro[14] vâ bhujjataro[14] vâ no duruhejjâ gamaṇâe. ‖13‖

137 se bhikkhû vâ 2 puvvâm eva tiricchasaṃpâtimaṃ nâvaṃ jâṇejjâ, jâṇittâ se ttam âyâe egaṃtam avakkaṃejjâ, 2 ttâ bhaṃḍagaṃ paḍilehejjâ,[15] 2 ttâ egao[16] bhoyaṇabhaṃḍagaṃ karejjâ, 2 ttâ sasîsovariyaṃ[17] kâyaṃ pâe pamajjejjâ, 2 ttâ sâgâraṃ bhattaṃ paccakkhâejjâ, 2 ttâ egaṃ pâyaṃ jale kiccâ, egaṃ pâyaṃ thale kiccâ, tato saṃjayâm eva nâvaṃ duruhejjâ. ‖14‖

se bhikkhû vâ 2 nâvaṃ duruhamâṇe vâ no nâvâe purao
duruhejjâ, no nâvâe aggao duruhejjâ, no nâvâe majjhato[17]
138 duruhejjâ, no vâhâo pagijjhiya 2 aṃguliyâe uddisiya[18] 2
oṇamiya 2 unnamiya 2 nijjhâejjâ. ‖15‖

s' evaṃ nâvâgato nâvâgayaṃ vadejjâ: âusaṃto samaṇâ! eyaṃ tumaṃ nâvaṃ ukkasâhi vâ vokkasâhi vâ khivâhi vâ rajjûe vâ gahâya âkasâhi.[19] no s' eyaṃ parinnaṃ parijâṇĕjjâ,[20] tusiṇîo uvehejjâ. ‖16‖

se ṇaṃ paro nâvâgato nâvâgayaṃ vaejjâ: âusaṃto samaṇâ! no saṃcâesi tumaṃ nâvaṃ ukkasittae vâ vokkasittae vâ khivittae vâ rajjuyâe vâ gahâya âkasittae; âhara etaṃ nâvâe rajjuyaṃ, sayaṃ ceva ṇaṃ vayaṃ nâvaṃ ukkasissâmo vâ *jâva* rajjuyâe gahâya âkasissâmo, no s' eyaṃ parinnaṃ parijâṇejjâ, tusiṇîo uvehejjâ. ‖17‖

se ṇaṃ paro nâvâgao nâvâgayaṃ vaejjâ: âusaṃto samaṇâ!

[9] A °yâsu. [10] B °âe. [11] B asaṃjae. [12] A uggahejjâ. [13] B ogâhejjâ. [14] B °re. [15] B paḍigâhejjâ. [16] MSS. egâ. [17] B °ovari. [17] A majjhâ. [18] A uvadaṃsiya. [19] B rajjuyâi vâ jâva rajjûe vâ gahâya âkasissâmo. A âgasâhi, i. marg. jâva rajjûe vâ gahâya âgasissâmo. [20] B jâṇejjâ.

saṃcâesi taṃ tumaṃ nâvaṃ âlitteṇa vâ pîḍheṇa[21] vâ vaṃseṇa vâ valaeṇa vâ avallaeṇa vâ vâhehi. no s' etaṃ parinnaṃ parijâṇejjâ, tusiṇîo uvehejjâ. ||18||

se ṇaṃ paro nâvâga*t*o nâvâga*t*aṃ va*d*ejjâ: âusaṃto samaṇâ! etaṃ tâ tumaṃ nâvâe udayaṃ hattheṇa vâ pâeṇa 139
vâ matteṇa vâ paḍiggaheṇa vâ nâvâussiṃcaeṇa vâ ussiṃcâhi. no s' etaṃ etc. ||19||

se ṇaṃ paro nâvâga*t*o nâvâga*t*aṃ vadejjâ: âusaṃto samaṇâ! etaṃ tâ tumaṃ nâvâe uttiṃgaṃ hattheṇa vâ pâeṇa[22] vâ bâhuṇâ vâ ûruṇâ vâ udareṇa vâ sîseṇa vâ kâeṇa vâ nâvâussiṃcaeṇa vâ celeṇa vâ maṭṭiyâe vâ kusapattaeṇa vâ kuruviṃdeṇa vâ pihehi. no s' e*t*aṃ etc. ||20||

se bhikkhû vâ 2 nâvâe uttiṃgeṇa udayaṃ âsavamâṇaṃ pehâe uvaruvariṃ nâvaṃ kajjalâvemâṇaṃ pehâe, no paraṃ uvasaṃkamittu evaṃ bûyâ: âusaṃto gâhâvaî! eyaṃ te nâvâe udayaṃ uttiṃgeṇa âsavati, uvaruvari vâ[3] nâvâ kajjalâveti. etappagâraṃ maṇaṃ vâ vaiṃ[23] vâ no para*t*o kaṭṭu viharejjâ; appussue abahilese egaṃtigeṇa appâṇaṃ viosejja[24] samâ*h*îe, ta*t*o saṃjayâm eva nâvâsaṃtârime udae a*h*âriyaṃ rîejjâ. 140

eyaṃ khalu tassa bhikkhussa vâ sâmaggiyaṃ, etc. ||21||**1**||

paḍhamo uddesao.

se ṇaṃ paro nâvâgato nâvâgayaṃ vaejjâ: âusaṃto samaṇâ! eyaṃ tâ tumaṃ chattayaṃ vâ *jâva* cammache*d*aṇagaṃ vâ gĕṇhâhi, e*t*âṇi tumaṃ virûvarûvâṇi satthajâyâṇi dhârehi, eyaṃ tâ tumaṃ dâragaṃ vâ dârigaṃ vâ pajjehi. no se taṃ parinnaṃ parijâṇejjâ, tusiṇîo uvehejjâ. ||1||

se ṇaṃ paro nâvâga*t*o nâvâgayaṃ vaejjâ: âusaṃto! esa ṇaṃ samaṇe bhaṃḍabhârie bhava*t*i, se ṇaṃ bâhâe gahâya 141
nâvâo udagaṃsi pakkhivaha. etappagâraṃ nigghosaṃ soccâ nisamma se ya cîvaradhârî siyâ, khippâm eva cîvarâṇi uvveḍhejja vâ nivveḍhejja[1] vâ upphesaṃ vâ karejjâ.[2] ||2|| aha puṇa evaṃ jâṇejjâ: abhikaṃtakûrakammâ khalu bâlâ bâhâhiṃ gahâya nâvâo udagaṃsi pakkhivejjâ; se puvvâm eva va*d*ejjâ: âusaṃto gâhâvatî! mâ m' etto bâhâe gahâya

[21] B pîḍhaeṇa vâ. [22] A pâdeṇa. [23] A vaiṃ, B vâyaṃ. [24] C viposejja.
[1] B niveḍejja, A veḍhejja. [2] Com. upposaṃ vâ kujjâ.

nâvâ*t*o udagamsi pakkhivaha; sayam ceva nam nâvâo uda-
142 gamsi ogâhissâmi.[3] se n' evam vadamtam paro sahasâ
balasâ[4] bâhâhim gahâya udagamsi pakkhivejjâ, tam no
sumane siyâ, no dummane siyâ, no uccâvayam manam
niyacchejjâ, no tesim bâlânam ghâtâe bahâe[5] samutthejjâ,
appussue *jâva* samâhîe, ta*t*o samjayâm eva udagamsi
pavejjâ. ‖3‖

se bhikkhû vâ 2 udagamsi pavamâne no hatthena hattham,
pâena pâyam, kâena kâyam âsâdejjâ. se anâsâdae anâsâ*d*a-
mîne[6] tato samjayâm eva pavejjâ. ‖4‖

143 se bhikkhû vâ 2 udagamsi pavamâne no omagganimaggi-
yam[7] karejjâ, mâ m' eyam udagam kannesu vâ acchîsu vâ
nakkamsi vâ muhamsi vâ pariyâvajjejjâ, ta*t*o samjayâm eva
uda*g*amsi pavejjâ. ‖5‖

se bhikkhû vâ 2 udagamsi pavamâne dovvaliyam pâunejjâ,
khippâm eva uvahim vigimcejja[8] vâ visohejja vâ, no ceva
nam sâtijjejjâ. aha puna evam jânejjâ: pârae siyâ udagâo
tîram pâunittae, tato samjayâm eva udaullena vâ sasiniddhena
vâ kâena udagatîre citthejjâ. ‖6‖

se bhikkhû vâ 2 udaullam vâ sasiniddham vâ kâyam no
âmajjejja vâ pamajjejja vâ samlihejja vâ nillihejja vâ uvvalejja vâ uvvattejja vâ âyâvejja vâ payâvejja vâ. aha puna
evam jânejjâ: vigatodae me kâe, vŏcchinnasinehe, tahappa-
gâram kâyam âmajjejja vâ *jâva* payâvejja vâ, tato samjayâm
eva gâmânugâmam dûijjejjâ.[9] ‖7‖

144 se bhikkhû vâ 2 gâmânugâmam dûijjamâne no parehim
saddhim parijaviya gâmânugâmam dûijjejjâ[9]; tato samjayâm
eva gâmanugâmam dûijjejja.[9] ‖8‖

se bhikkhû vâ 2 gâmânugâmam dûijjamâne[9] amtarâ se
jamghâsamtârime udae siyâ, se puvvâm eva sasîsovariyam
kâyam pâ*d*e pamajjejjâ, se puvvâm eva pamajjittâ *jâva* egam
pâdam jale kiccâ, egam pâdam thale kiccâ, tato samjayâm eva
jamghâsamtârime udae ahâriyam[10] rîejjâ. ‖9‖

145 se bhikkhû vâ 2 jamghâsamtârime udae ahâriyam[10]
rîyamâne no hatthena hattham *jâva*[11] anâsâdamîne, tato
samjayâm eva jamghâsamtârime udae a*h*âriyam[10] rîejjâ. ‖10‖

se bhikkhû vâ 2 jamghâsamtârime udae ahâriyam[10]

[3] B uggâhissâmi. [4] B palasâ. [5] B ghâtae vâhâe. [6] A °mâne. [7] B °mugg°, A °ayam. [8] A vik°. [9] B dûti°. [10] B âhârîyam. [11] A full phrase.

rîyamâṇe no sâyâvaḍiyâe[12] no paridâhapaḍiyâe mahatimahâlayaṃsi udagaṃsi kâyaṃ viosejjâ, *tato* etc. aha puṇa evaṃ jâṇejjâ: pârae siyâ udagâo tîraṃ pâuṇittae, tao saṃjayâm eva 146
udaullena vâ sasiṇiddheṇa vâ kâeṇa udagatîre ciṭṭhejjâ. ‖ 11 ‖

se bhikkhû vâ 2 udaullaṃ vâ kâyaṃ sasiṇiddhaṃ vâ kâyaṃ no âmajjejja vâ pamajjejja[13] vâ.[13] aha puṇa evaṃ jâṇejjâ: vigatodae me kâe vocchinnasiṇehe; tahappagâraṃ kâyaṃ âmajjejja vâ *jâva*[14] payâvejja[14] vâ,[14] tato saṃjayâm eva gâmâṇugâmaṃ dûijjejjâ.[9] ‖ 12 ‖

se bhikkhû vâ 2 gâmâṇugâmaṃ dûijjamâṇe no maṭṭiyâgaehiṃ pâehiṃ hariyâṇi chiṃdiya 2 vikujjiya 2 viphâliya ummaggeṇa hariyavadhâe gacchejjâ, jam etaṃ[15] pâehiṃ maṭṭiyaṃ khippâm eva hari*tâ*ṇi avaharantu. mâtiṭṭhâṇaṃ saṃphâse, no evaṃ karejjâ. se puvvaṃ eva appahariyaṃ maggaṃ paḍilehejjâ, *tato* saṃjayâm eva gâmâṇugâmaṃ dûijjejjâ.[9] ‖ 13 ‖

se bhikkhû vâ 2 gâmâṇugâmaṃ dûijjamâṇe[9] aṃtarâ se vappâṇi vâ phalihâṇi vâ pâgârâṇi vâ toraṇâṇi vâ aggalâṇi vâ aggalapâsagâṇi vâ gaḍḍâo vâ darîo vâ, sati parakkame 147
saṃjayâm eva parakkamejjâ, no ujjuyaṃ gacchejjâ. ‖ 14 ‖

kevalî bûyâ: âyâṇam eyaṃ; se tattha parakkamamâṇe payalejja vâ pavaḍejja vâ, se tattha payalemâṇe vâ pavaḍamâṇe vâ rukkhâṇi vâ gummâṇi vâ layâo vâ vallîo vâ taṇâṇi vâ gahaṇâṇi vâ hariyâṇi vâ avalaṃbiya 2 uttarejjâ. je tattha pâḍipahiyâ uvâgacchaṃti, te pâṇî jâejjâ; tao saṃjayam eva avalaṃbiya uttarejjâ, tao saṃjayâm eva gâmâṇugâmaṃ dûijjejjâ.[9] ‖ 15 ‖

se bhikkhû vâ 2 gâmâṇugâmaṃ dûijjamâṇe[9] aṃtarâ se javasâṇi vâ sagaḍâṇi vâ rahâṇi vâ sacakkâṇi vâ paracakkâṇi vâ seṇaṃ vâ virûvarûvaṃ saṃniviṭṭhaṃ pehâe, sati parakkame saṃjayâm eva parakkamejjâ, no ujjuyaṃ gacchejjâ. se ṇaṃ paro seṇâgato[16] vadejjâ: âusaṃto! esa ṇaṃ samaṇe seṇâe abhiṇivâriyaṃ kare*ti*, se ṇaṃ vâhâe gahâya âgasaha! se ṇaṃ paro vâhâhiṃ gahâya âgasĕjjâ;[17] taṃ no sumaṇe siyâ *jâva* samâhîe, tao saṃjayâm eva gâmâṇugâmaṃ 148
dûijjejjâ.[7] ‖ 16 ‖

[12] B sâya°. [13] B om., A i. marg. [14] om. [15] A jam eehiṃ. [16] A °gate.
[17] B âkasijjâ.

aṃtarâ se pâḍipahiyâ uvâgacchejjâ, te ṇaṃ pâḍipahiyâ evaṃ vadejjâ: âusaṃtâ samaṇâ! kevatie se gâme vâ *jâva* râyahâṇiṃ vâ? kevatiyâ ettha âsâ hatthî gâmapiṃḍolagâ maṇussâ parivasaṃti? se bahubhatte bahuudae bahujaṇe[18] bahujavase? se appabhatte appaudae appajaṇe appajavase? eyappagârâṇi pasiṇâṇi puṭṭho no vâgarejjâ,[19] eyappagârâṇi pasiṇâṇi no pucchejjâ.[20]

149 eyaṃ khalu tassa bhikkhussa vâ 2 sâmaggiyaṃ, etc. ‖17‖2‖

biio uddesao.

se bhikkhû vâ 2 gâmâṇugâmaṃ dûijjamâṇe,[1] aṃtarâ se vappâṇi vâ phalihâṇi vâ pâgârâṇi vâ *jâva* darîo vâ kûḍâgârâṇi vâ pâsâdâṇi vâ nûmagihâṇi vâ rukkhagihâṇi vâ pavvayagihâṇi vâ rukkhaṃ vâ cetiyakaḍaṃ, thûbhaṃ vâ cetiyakaḍaṃ, âesaṇâṇi vâ *jâva* bhavaṇagihâṇi vâ, no bâhâo pagijjhiya 2 aṃguliyâe uddisiya 2 oṇamiya 2 unnamiya 2
150 nijjhâejjâ; ta*t*o saṃjayâm eva gâmâṇugâmaṃ dûijjejjâ.[1] ‖1‖

se bhikkhû vâ 2 gâmâṇugâmaṃ dûijjamâṇe,[1] aṃtarâ se kacchâṇi vâ daviyâṇi vâ nûmâṇi vâ valayâṇi vâ gahaṇâṇi vâ gahaṇaviduggâṇi vâ vaṇâṇi vâ pavvayâṇi vâ pavva*t*aviduggâṇi vâ pavvatagihâṇi[2] vâ[2] agaḍâṇi vâ talâgâṇi vâ dahâṇi vâ vadîo vâ nâvîo vâ pŏkkharaṇîo vâ dîhiyâo vâ
151 guṃjâliyâo vâ sarâṇi vâ sarapaṃtiyâṇi vâ sarasarapaṃtiyâṇi vâ, no vâhâo pagijjhiya 2 *jâva* nijjhâejjâ. ‖2‖

kevalî bûyâ: âyâṇam eyaṃ; je tattha migâ vâ pasû[3] vâ pakkhî vâ sarîsivâ vâ jalacarâ[4] vâ thalacarâ[4] vâ khahacarâ[4] vâ sattâ, te uttasejja vâ vittasejja vâ vâḍaṃ vâ saraṇaṃ vâ kaṃkhejjâ: vâreti me ayaṃ samaṇe. aha bhikkhûṇaṃ puvvovadiṭṭhâ, 4 jaṃ no[5] bâhâo pagijjhiya 2 *jâva* nijjhâejjâ, tao saṃjayâm eva âyariovajjhâehiṃ saddhiṃ gâmâṇugâmaṃ dûijjejjâ.[1] ‖3‖

se bhikkhû vâ 2 âyariovajjhâehiṃ saddhiṃ gâmâṇugâmaṃ dûijjamâṇe[1] no âyariovajjhâyassa hattheṇa vâ hatthaṃ *jâva* aṇâsâyamîṇe, tao saṃjayâm eva âyariovajjhâehiṃ *jâva* dûijjejjâ. ‖4‖

[18] A °jâṇe. [19] Calc. âikkhejjâ. [20] B reads: e. p. no pucchejjâ, e. p. puṭṭho vâ apuṭṭho vâ no vâgarejjâ.

[1] B dûti°. [2] B om. [3] B pasuyâ. [4] A °raṃ. [5] A janno.

se bhikkhû vâ 2 âyariovajjhâehiṃ saddhiṃ gâmâṇugâmaṃ dûijjamâṇe,[1] aṃtarâ se pâḍipahiyâ[6] uvâgacchejjâ, te ṇaṃ pâḍipahiyâ[6] evaṃ vadejjâ: âusaṃto samaṇâ! ke tubbhe,[7] kao vâ eha, kahiṃ vâ gacchihi*h*a? je tattha âyarie vâ uvajjhâe vâ, se bhâsejja vâ viyâgarejja vâ; âyariovajjhâyassa bhâsamâ- 152
ṇassa vâ viyâgaremâṇassa vâ no aṃtarâ bhâsaṃ karejjâ; tao a*h*ârâtiṇiyâe[8] dûijjejjâ.[1] ‖5‖

se bhikkhû vâ 2 ahârâtiṇiyaṃ[9] gâmâṇugâmaṃ dûijjamâṇe, no râ*t*iṇiyassa hatthena hatthaṃ *jâva* aṇâsâyamâṇe, tao saṃjayâm eva ahârâ*t*iṇiyaṃ[10] gâmâṇugâmaṃ dûijjejjâ.[1] ‖6‖

se bhikkhû vâ 2 ahârâtiṇiyaṃ dûijjamâṇe, aṃtarâ se pâḍipahiyâ uvâgacchejjâ, te ṇaṃ pâḍipa*h*iyâ evaṃ vadejjâ: âusaṃto samaṇâ! ke tubbhe? je tattha savvarâtiṇie, se bhâsejja vâ 2, râtiṇiyassa bhâsamâṇassa viyâgaremâṇassa no aṃtarâ bhâsaṃ bhâsejjâ, tato saṃjayâm eva gâmâṇugâmaṃ dûijjejjâ.[1] ‖7‖

se bhikkhû vâ 2 gâmâṇugâmaṃ dûijjamâṇe,[1] aṃtarâ se pâḍipahiyâ uvâgacchejjâ, te ṇaṃ pâḍipahiyâ evaṃ vadejjâ:[11] âusaṃto samaṇâ! aviyâiṃ etto paḍipahe pâsaha, taṃ jahâ: maṇussaṃ vâ goṇaṃ vâ mahisaṃ vâ pasuṃ[12] vâ pakkhiṃ vâ sirîsivaṃ va jalayaraṃ vâ, âikkhaha, daṃseha! taṃ no 153
âikkhejjâ, no daṃsejjâ; no tassa taṃ parinnaṃ parijâṇejjâ, tusiṇîe uvehejjâ, jâṇaṃ vâ no jâṇaṃ ti vadejjâ, tao saṃjayâm eva gâmâṇugâmaṃ dûijjejjâ.[1] ‖8‖

se bhikkhû vâ 2 . . . (§ 8) . . . paḍipahe pâsaha: udagapasûyâṇi kaṃdâṇi vâ mûlâṇi vâ tayâ pattâ pupphâ phalâ bîyâ, udagaṃ vâ saṃnihiyaṃ agaṇiṃ vâ saṃnikkhittaṃ? 154
sesaṃ taṃ ceva. âikkhaha *jâva* dûijjejjâ.[1] ‖9‖

se bhikkhû vâ 2 . . . (§ 8) . . . paḍipahe pâsaha: javasâṇi vâ *jâva* virûvarûvaṃ saṃniviṭṭhaṃ se âikkhaha *jâva* dûijjejjâ.[1] ‖10‖

se bhikkhû vâ 2 . . . (§ 8) . . . âusaṃto samaṇâ! kevatie etto gâme vâ *jâva* râyahâṇiṃ vâ? se âikkhaha *jâva* dûijjejjâ.[1] ‖11‖

se bhikkhû vâ 2 . . . (§ 8) . . . âusaṃto samaṇâ! kevatie

[6] A paḍi°, B °bahiyâ. [7] A tujjhe. [8] A âhâ°, B °ṇie. [9] A âhâ°. [10] A âhârâtiṇiyâe. [11] B vayâsî. [12] A pasû. [13] B om.

etto gâmassa vâ nagarassa vâ *jâva* râyahâṇîe vâ magge? se
âikkhaha *tah'eva jâva* dûijjejjâ.[1] ‖12‖

se bhikkhû vâ 2 gâmâṇugâmaṃ dûijjamâṇe, aṃtarâ se
goṇaṃ viyâlaṃ paḍipa*h*e pehâe *jâva* cittavillaḍaṃ[14] viyâlaṃ
paḍipa*h*e pehâe, no tesiṃ bhîto[15] ummaggeṇaṃ gacchejjâ, no
maggâo maggaṃ saṃkamejjâ, no gahaṇaṃ vâ vaṇaṃ vâ
155 duggaṃ vâ aṇupavisejjâ, no rukkhaṃsi duruhejjâ, no mahatimahâlayaṃsi udagaṃsi kâyaṃ viosejjâ, no vâḍaṃ vâ saraṇaṃ vâ seṇaṃ vâ satthaṃ vâ kaṃkhejjâ, appussue *jâva*
samâhîe, tato saṃjayâm eva gâmâṇugâmaṃ dûijjejjâ.[1] ‖13‖

se bhikkhû vâ 2 gâmâṇugâmaṃ dûijjamâṇe,[1] aṃtarâ se
vihaṃ siyâ, se jjaṃ puṇa vihaṃ jâṇejjâ: imaṃsi khalu
vihaṃsi bahave âmosagâ uvagaraṇapaḍiyâe[16] saṃpiṃḍiyâ[17]
gacchejjâ, no tesiṃ bhîo ummaggaṃ *ceva jâva* samâhîe, tato
saṃjayâm eva gâmâṇugâmaṃ dûijjejjâ.[1] ‖14‖

se bhikkhû vâ 2 gâmâṇugâmaṃ dûijjamâṇe, aṃtarâ se
âmosagâ gacchejjâ, te ṇaṃ âmosagâ evaṃ vadejjâ: âusaṃto
samaṇâ! âhara[18] evaṃ vatthaṃ vâ 4, dehi, vikkhivâhi! taṃ
no se[2] dejjâ, nikkhivejjâ; no vaṃdiya 2 jâejjâ, no aṃjaliṃ
kaṭṭu jâejjâ, no kaluṇapaḍiyâe jâejjâ, dhammiyâe jâyaṇâe[19]
jâejjâ tusiṇîyabhâveṇa vâ. ‖15‖

te ṇaṃ âmosagâ sayaṃ karaṇijjaṃ ti kaṭṭu akkosaṃti
vâ *jâva* uddaveṃti vâ vatthaṃ vâ 4 acchiṃdejja vâ *jâva*
156 pariṭṭhavejja vâ, taṃ no gâmasaṃsâriyaṃ kujjâ, no râya-
saṃsâriyaṃ kujjâ, no paraṃ uvasaṃkamittu bûyâ: âusaṃto
gâhâvaî! ete khalu me âmosagâ uvagaraṇapaḍiyâe sayaṃ
karaṇijjaṃ ti kaṭṭu akkosaṃti vâ *jâva* pariṭṭhaveṃti vâ.
etappagâraṃ maṇaṃ vâ vaiṃ vâ no pura*to* kaṭṭu viharejjâ;
appussue *jâva* samâhîe, tato saṃjayâm eva gâmâṇugâmaṃ
dûijjejjâ.[1]

eyaṃ khalu tassa bhikkhussa vâ 2 sâmaggiyaṃ, etc. ‖16‖**3**‖

157 taio uddesao.

iriyâ samattâ.

taiyam ajjhayaṇaṃ.

[14] A cittacillaya, B °villaḍaṃ. [15] B bhitto. [16] MSS. uvakaraṇa. [17] A om.
[18] MSS. âhâra. [19] B jay°.

CAUTTHAM AJJHAYAṆAM.

BHÂSÂJÂYÂ.

se bhikkhû vâ 2 vaiyâyârâiṃ soccâ nisamma imâiṃ aṇâyârâiṃ aṇâyariyapuvvâiṃ jâṇejjâ: je kohâ vâ vâyaṃ viuṃjaṃti, je mâṇâ vâ, je[1] mâyâe vâ, je lobhâ vâ vâyaṃ viuṃjaṃti, jâṇa*t*o vâ pharusaṃ vadaṃti, ajâṇa*t*o vâ pharusaṃ va*d*aṃti; savvam etaṃ sâvajjaṃ vajjejjâ; vivegam âyâe dhuvaṃ ce'daṃ jâṇejjâ adhuvaṃ vâ. ‖ 1 ‖

asaṇaṃ vâ 4 labhiya no labhiya, bhuṃjiya no bhuṃjiya, 159
aduvâ âgate[2] aduvâ no âgate,[2] aduvâ eti aduvâ no eti, aduvâ ehiti aduvâ no ehiti, tattha[3] vi âgate[2] tattha[3] vi no âgate,[2] tattha[4] vi eti tattha[4] vi no eti, tattha[4] vi ehiti tattha vi no ehiti. ‖ 2 ‖

aṇuvîi niṭṭhâbhâsîsami*t*âe saṃjae bhâsaṃ bhâsejja, taṃ jahâ: egavayaṇaṃ duvayaṇaṃ bahuvayaṇaṃ itthîvayaṇaṃ purisavayaṇaṃ napuṃsagavayaṇaṃ ajjhatthavayaṇaṃ uvaṇîyavayaṇaṃ avaṇîyavayaṇaṃ uvaṇîyaavaṇîyavayaṇaṃ avaṇî-
yauvaṇîyavayaṇaṃ tîyavayaṇaṃ paḍuppannavayaṇaṃ aṇâga- 161
tavayaṇaṃ paccakkhavayaṇaṃ parokkhavayaṇaṃ. se egavayaṇaṃ va*d*issâmi, egavayaṇaṃ vaejjâ, *jâva* parokkhavayaṇaṃ vadissâmi, parokkhavayaṇaṃ vadejjâ. itthî v' esaṃ purisa v' esaṃ napuṃsaga v'esaṃ, evaṃ vâ c'eyaṃ annahâ vâ c' eyaṃ, aṇuvîi niṭṭhâbhâsî samiyâe saṃjae bhâsaṃ bhâsejjâ. ‖ 3 ‖

icc eyâiṃ âya*t*aṇâiṃ uvâtikamma aha bhikkhû jâṇejjâ cattâri bhâsâjâyâiṃ, taṃ jahâ: saccam egaṃ paḍhamaṃ
bhâsâjâyaṃ, bîyaṃ mosaṃ, taiyaṃ saccâmosaṃ, jaṃ n'eva 162
saccaṃ n'eva mosaṃ n'eva saccâmosaṃ asaccâmosaṃ taṃ cauttham bhâsâjâtaṃ, se bemi. je ya atîtâ, je ya paḍuppannâ, je ya aṇâga*t*â arahaṃtâ bhagavaṃtâ,[5] savva te eyâṇi cattâri bhâsâjâyâiṃ bhâsiṃsu vâ bhâsaṃti vâ bhâsissaṃti vâ, pannaviṃsu vâ 3, savvâiṃ ca ṇaṃ eyâṇi acittâṇi vaṇṇamaṃtâṇi

[1] B om. [2] B âgato. [3] B ettha. [4] BC ettha. [5] A °to.

gaṃdhamaṃtâṇi rasamaṃtâṇi[6] phâsamaṃtâṇi[6] caovacaiṭâiṃ
vippariṇâmadhammâiṃ[7] bhavaṃtî 'ti samakkhâṭâiṃ. ‖4‖
163 se bhikkhû vâ 2 puvvaṃ bhâsâ abhâsâ, bhâsijjamâṇî bhâsâ
bhâsâ, bhâsâsamayavitikkaṃtâ[8] bhâsiyâ bhâsâ abhâsâ. ‖5‖

se bhikkhû vâ 2 jâyabhâsâ saccâ, jâyabhâsâ mosâ, jâyabhâsâ saccâmosâ; tahappagâraṃ bhâsaṃ sâvajjaṃ sakiriyaṃ kakkasaṃ sakaḍuyaṃ niṭṭhuraṃ pharusaṃ aṇhayakariṃ chedakariṃ bhedakariṃ pariṭâvaṇakariṃ uddavaṇakariṃ bhûtovaghâṭiyaṃ abhikaṃkha no bhâsaṃ[1] bhâsejjâ. ‖6‖

se bhikkhû vâ 2 jâyabhâsâ suhumâ, jâyabhâsâ asaccâmosâ,
164 tahappagâraṃ bhâsaṃ asâvajjaṃ akiriyaṃ *jâva* abhûṭovaghâtiyaṃ abhikaṃkha bhâsaṃ bhâsejjâ. ‖7‖

se bhikkhû vâ 2 pumaṃ âmaṃtemâṇe âmaṃtite vâ apaḍisuṇemâṇe no evaṃ vadejjâ: hole ti[9] vâ, ghole ti[9] vâ, vasule[10] ti[9] vâ, kupakkhe ti[9] vâ, ghaḍadâse ti[9] vâ, sâṇe ti[9] vâ, teṇe ti[9] vâ, cârie[11] tti[9] vâ, mâî ti vâ, musâvâdî ti vâ, iti yâiṃ tumâiṃ ti yâiṃ[1] te jaṇagâ; etappagâraṃ bhâsaṃ sâvajjaṃ *jâva* abhikaṃkha no bhâsejjâ. ‖8‖

se bhikkhû vâ pumaṃ âmaṃtemâṇe âmaṃtite vâ apaḍi-
165 suṇemâṇe[12] evaṃ vadejjâ: amuge *ti* vâ, âuso ti vâ, âusaṃtâro ti vâ, sâvage[13] ti vâ, uvâsage ti vâ, dhammie ti vâ, dhammappie ti vâ, eyappagâraṃ bhâsaṃ asâvajjaṃ *jâva* abhûtovaghâtiyaṃ abhikaṃkha bhâsejjâ. ‖9‖

se bhikkhû vâ 2 itthiṃ âmaṃtemâṇe âmaṃtite vâ apaḍisuṇemâṇî[14] no evaṃ vadejjâ: holî ti vâ, gholî ti vâ; *itthigameṇaṃ netavvaṃ.* ‖10‖

se bhikkhû vâ 2 itthiṃ[15] âmaṃtemâṇe âmaṃtite vâ apaḍisuṇemâṇî evaṃ vadejjâ: âuso ti vâ, bhagiṇî ti vâ, bhotî ti vâ, bhagavatî ti vâ, sâvige ti vâ, uvâsie ti vâ, dhammie ti vâ, dhammappie ti vâ, eyappagâraṃ bhâsaṃ asâvajjaṃ *jâva* abhikaṃkha bhâsejjâ. ‖11‖

se bhikkhû vâ 2 no evaṃ vadejjâ: nabhedeve[16] ti vâ, gajjadeve ti vâ, vijjudeve ti vâ, pavuṭṭhadeve ti vâ, paḍaṭu vâ vâsaṃ mâ vâ paḍaṭu, nippajjaṭu vâ sâsaṃ mâ vâ nippajjaṭu, vibhâvau[17] vâ rayaṇî mâ vâ vibhâvau,[17] udeu[18] vâ sûrie mâ

[6] A °vaṃtâṇi. [7] A vivihadhammâiṃ. [8] B °viikkaṃtaṃ ca ṇaṃ. [9] B tti. [10] B °li. [11] A core. [12] MSS. ss. [13] MSS. sâvako. [14] A °mîṇe. [15] A itthiyaṃ, B itthî. [16] A nabhaṃ, C nabho. [17] B vibhâtu, C vibhâyatu. [18] A uveu, B udao, C udau.

vâ udeu,[19] se vâ râyâ jaya*t*u mâ vâ jaya*t*u, no etappagâraṃ bhâsaṃ bhâsejjâ. || 12 || 166

pannavaṃ se bhikkhû vâ 2 aṃtalikkhe ti vâ, gujjhâṇucarie ti vâ, sammucchie ti vâ, nivaie vâ paoe vadejja vâ: vuṭṭhavalâhage[20] tti.

eyaṃ khalu tassa bhikkhussa vâ 2 sâmaggiyaṃ, etc. || 13 || **1** ||

paḍhamo uddesao.

se bhikkhû vâ 2 jahâ v' egaiyâiṃ rûvâiṃ pâsejjâ, tahâ vi tâiṃ no evaṃ vadejjâ, taṃ jahâ: gaṃḍî gaṃḍî ti vâ, kuṭṭhî 2 ti vâ *jâva* mahumehiṇi tti[1] vâ hatthacchinne hatthacchinne ti vâ; *evaṃ* pâda nakka kaṇṇa utthâ; je yâv' anne tahappagârâ eyappagârâhiṃ[2] bhâsâhiṃ buiyâ[3] buiyâ[3] kuppaṃti 167
mâṇavâ, te yâvi tahappagârâ eyappagârâhiṃ[4] bhâsâhiṃ abhikaṃkha no bhâsejjâ.[5] || 1 ||

se bhikkhû vâ 2 jahâ v' egaiyâiṃ rûvâiṃ pâsejjâ, tahâ vi evaṃ vadejjâ: oyaṃsî oyaṃsî ti vâ, teyaṃsî 2 ti vâ,[6] abhirûvaṃ 2, paḍirûvaṃ 2, pâsâdiyaṃ 2, darisaṇijjaṃ darisiṇîe ti vâ, je yâv' anne tahappagârâ eyappagârâhiṃ bhâsâhiṃ buiyâ[3] 2 no kuppaṃti mâṇavâ, te yâvi tahappagârâ eyappagârâhiṃ bhâsâhiṃ abhikaṃkha bhâsaṃ bhâsejjâ. tahappa- 168
gâraṃ bhâsaṃ asâvajjaṃ *jâva* bhâsejjâ. || 2 ||

se bhikkhû vâ 2 jahâ v' egatiyâiṃ rûvâiṃ pâsejjâ, taṃ jahâ: vappâṇi vâ *jâva* bhavaṇagihâṇi vâ, tahâ vi tâiṃ no evaṃ vadejjâ: sukaḍe vâ, suṭṭhu kaḍe *ti* vâ, sâhukallâṇaṃ ti vâ karaṇijje[7] i vâ. eyappagâraṃ bhâsaṃ sâvajjaṃ *jâva* no bhâsejjâ. || 3 ||

se bhikkhû vâ 2 . . . (§ 3) . . . tahâ vi tâiṃ evaṃ vadejjâ, taṃ jahâ: âraṃbhakaḍe ti vâ, sâvajjakaḍe ti vâ, payattakaḍe ti vâ, pâsâdiyaṃ pâsâdie ti vâ, darisaṇîyaṃ 2, abhirûvaṃ 2, paḍirûvaṃ 2, eyappagâraṃ bhâsaṃ asâvajjaṃ *jâva* bhâsejjâ. || 4 ||

se bhikkhû vâ 2 asaṇaṃ vâ 2 uvakkhaḍiyaṃ[8] pehâe, tahâ vi taṃ no evaṃ vadejjâ, taṃ jahâ: sukaḍe ti vâ, suṭṭhu kaḍe ti vâ, sâhukaḍe ti vâ, kallâṇe ti vâ, karaṇijje ti vâ, eyappagâraṃ bhâsaṃ sâvajjaṃ *jâva* no bhâsejjâ. || 5 ||

[19] MSS. 2 [20] B °go.

[1] B °mehî ti. [2] B taha°. [3] A bûtiyâ. [4] B taha°, A etaha°. [5] B adds tahappagâraṃ asâvajjaṃ jâva bhâsejjâ. [6] B vaccaṃsî ti vâ. [7] B jjâ. [8] A kh.

se bhikkhû vâ 2 asaṇaṃ vâ 4 uvakkhaḍiyaṃ[8] pehâe evaṃ vadejjâ, taṃ jahâ: âraṃbhakaḍe ti vâ, sâvajjakaḍe ti vâ,
169 payattakaḍe ti vâ, bhaddayaṃ bhaddae ti vâ, ûsaḍhaṃ 2, rasiyaṃ 2, maṇunnaṃ 2, eyappagâraṃ bhâsaṃ asâvajjaṃ *jâva* bhâsejjâ. ‖ 6 ‖

se bhikkhû vâ 2 maṇussaṃ vâ goṇaṃ vâ mahisaṃ vâ migaṃ vâ pasuṃ vâ pakkhiṃ[9] vâ sirîsivaṃ[10] vâ jalayaraṃ vâ, se[11] ttaṃ parivûḍhakâyaṃ pehâe, no evaṃ vadejjâ: thulle ti vâ, pametile[12] ti vâ, vaṭṭe ti vâ, vajjhe ti vâ, pâime[13] ti vâ. eyappagâraṃ bhâsaṃ sâvajjaṃ *jâva* no bhâsejjâ. ‖ 7 ‖

se bhikkhû vâ 2 maṇussaṃ vâ *jâva* jalayaraṃ vâ, se ttaṃ parivûḍhakâyaṃ pehâe evaṃ vadejjâ: parivûḍhakâe ti vâ,
170 uvacittakâe ti vâ, thirasaṃghayaṇe[14] ti vâ, cittamaṃsasoṇie ti vâ, paḍipuṇṇaiṃdie ti vâ; eyappagâraṃ bhâsaṃ asâvajjaṃ *jâva* bhâsejjâ. ‖ 8 ‖

se bhikkhû vâ 2 virûvarûvâo gâo pehâe no evaṃ vadejjâ, taṃ jahâ: dojjhâ ti vâ, dammâ ti vâ, gorahâ ti vâ, vâhimâ ti vâ, rahajoggâ ti vâ; eyappagâraṃ bhâsaṃ sâvajjaṃ *jâva* no bhâsejjâ. ‖ 9 ‖

se bhikkhû vâ 2 virûvarûvâo gâo pehâe evaṃ vadejjâ, taṃ jahâ: juvaṃ gave ti vâ, dheṇû ti vâ, rasavatî ti vâ, hasse ti vâ, mahallae ti vâ, mahavvae[15] ti[15] vâ,[15] saṃvahaṇe[16] ti vâ, eyappagâraṃ bhâsaṃ asâvajjaṃ *jâva* bhâsejjâ. ‖ 10 ‖

se bhikkhû vâ 2 tah'eva gaṃtum[17] ujjâṇâiṃ pavva*t*âṇi[18] vaṇâṇi vâ rukkhâ mahallâ pehâe no evaṃ vadejjâ: pâsâyajoggâ ti vâ, toraṇajoggâ ti vâ, gihajoggâ ti vâ, phalihajoggâ ti vâ, aggalajoggâ ti vâ, nâvâjoggâ ti vâ, udagajoggâ ti vâ[19] doṇî-pîḍha-caṃgavera-naṃgalakuliya-jaṃta-laṭṭhî-nâbhigaṃdî-âsaṇa-sayaṇa-jâṇa-uvassaya-joggâ ti vâ; eyappagâraṃ bhâsaṃ sâvajjaṃ *jâva* no bhâsejjâ. ‖ 11 ‖

171 se bhikkhû vâ 2 tah' eva gaṃtum ujjâṇâiṃ pavva*t*âṇi vaṇâṇi vâ rukkhâ mahallâ pehâe evaṃ vadejjâ, taṃ jahâ: jâtimaṃtâ ti vâ, dîhavaṭṭâ ti vâ, mahâlayâ ti vâ, payâtasâlâ ti vâ, viḍimasâlâ ti vâ, pâsâdiyâ ti vâ 4; eyappagâraṃ bhâsaṃ asâvajjaṃ *jâva* abhikaṃkha bhâsejjâ. ‖ 12 ‖

[9] B pakkhî. [10] A siri°. [11] B sa. [12] B pamedale. [13] A pâyame, B pâdame. [14] A para°. [15] A om. [16] A °vâh°. [17] B gaṃt'. [18] A pavvayâiṃ. [19] A aggalanâvâudaga.

se bhikkhû vâ 2 bahusaṃbhûtâ vaṇaphalâ pehâe no evaṃ vadejjâ, taṃ jahâ: pakkâ ti vâ, pâtakhajjâ ti vâ, velociyâ[20] ti vâ, ṭâlâ ti vâ, pehâ ti vâ; eyappagâraṃ bhâsaṃ sâvajjaṃ *jâva* no vadejjâ. ‖13‖ se bhikkhû vâ 2 bahusaṃbhûtâ vaṇaphalâ pehâe[21] evaṃ vadejjâ, taṃ jahâ: asaṃthaḍâ ti vâ, 172
bahunivaṭṭimaphalâ ti vâ, bahusaṃbhûyâ ti vâ, bhûtarûvâ ti vâ; eyappagâraṃ bhâsaṃ asâvajjaṃ *jâva* bhâsejjâ. ‖14‖

se bhikkhû vâ 2 bahusaṃbhûyâo osahîo pehâe tahâ[15] vi tâo[15] no evaṃ vadejjâ, taṃ jahâ: pakkâ ti vâ, nîliyâ ti vâ, chavî ti vâ, lâimâ ti vâ, bhajjimâ ti vâ, bahukhajjimâ ti vâ; eyappagâraṃ bhâsaṃ sâvajjaṃ *jâva* no bhâsejjâ. ‖15‖ se bhikkhû vâ 2 bahusaṃbhûyâo osahîo pehâe tahâ[15] vi tâo[15]
evaṃ vadejjâ, taṃ jahâ: rûḍhâ ti vâ, bahusaṃbhû*t*â ti vâ, 173
thirâ ti vâ, ûsaḍhâ ti vâ, gabbhiyâ ti vâ, pasû*t*â ti vâ, sasârâ ti vâ, eyappagâraṃ bhâsaṃ asâvajjaṃ *jâva* bhâsejjâ. ‖16‖

se bhikkhû vâ 2, jahâ v' egatiyâiṃ saddâiṃ suṇejjâ, tahâ vi tâiṃ[22] no evaṃ vadejjâ, taṃ jahâ: susadde ti vâ 2, eyappagâraṃ bhâsaṃ sâvajjaṃ *jâva* no bhâsejjâ; tahâ vi tâiṃ evaṃ vadejjâ, taṃ jahâ: susaddaṃ susadde ti vâ, dusaddaṃ[15] dusadde[15] ti vâ;[15] eyappagâraṃ bhâsaṃ asâvajjaṃ *jâva* bhâsejjâ. ‖17‖ *evaṃ* rûvaiṃ: kaṇhe ti vâ 5; gaṃdhâiṃ: subbhigaṃdhe ti vâ 2; rasâiṃ: tittâṇi vâ 5; phâsâiṃ: kakkhaḍâṇi vâ. ‖18‖

se bhikkhû vâ 2 vaṃtâ kohaṃ ca mâṇaṃ ca mâyaṃ ca lobhaṃ ca aṇuvîi niṭṭhâbhâsî nisammabhâsî aturiyabhâsî vivegabhâsî samiyâe saṃjate bhâsaṃ bhâsejjâ.

eyaṃ khalu tassa bhikkhussa vâ 2 sâmaggiyaṃ, etc. ‖19‖**2**‖

biio uddesao.

bhâsâjâyâ samattâ.

cauttham ajjhayaṇaṃ.

[20] A velotimâ, B velotîyâ, C velovigâ. [21] B adds tahâ vi. [22] B eyâiṃ.

PAṂCAMAM AJJHAYAṆAM.

VATTHESAṆÂ.

se bhikkhû vâ 2 abhikaṃkhejjâ vatthaṃ esittae, se jjaṃ
puṇa vatthaṃ evaṃ jâṇejjâ, taṃ jahâ; jaṃgiyaṃ vâ bhaṃgiyaṃ vâ sâṇayaṃ vâ pottagaṃ vâ khomiyaṃ vâ tûlakaḍaṃ vâ,
175 tahappagâraṃ vatthaṃ; je niggaṃthe taruṇe juvaṃ bala-
vaṃ appâyaṃke thirasaṃghayaṇe, se egaṃ vatthaṃ dhârejjâ,
no bitiyaṃ; jâ niggaṃthî, sâ cattâri saṃghâḍîo dhârejjâ:
egaṃ duhatthavitthâraṃ, do tihatthavitthârâo, egaṃ cau-
hatthavitthâraṃ. tahappagârehiṃ[1] vatthehiṃ asaṃvijja-
mâṇehiṃ aha pacchâ egam egaṃ saṃsîvejjâ. ||1||
se bhikkhû vâ 2 paraṃ addhajoyaṇamerâe vatthapaḍiyâe
no abhisaṃdhârejjâ gamaṇâe. se bhikkhû vâ 2, se jjaṃ
176 puṇa vatthaṃ jâṇejjâ: assiṃ paḍiyâe egaṃ sahammiyaṃ
sammuddissa pâṇehiṃ *jahâ piṃḍesaṇâe*[2] *bhâṇiyavvaṃ*;[3]
evaṃ bahave sâhammiyâ, egaṃ sâhammiṇiṃ, bahave
sâhammiṇîo, bahave samaṇamâhaṇa; *tah' eva* purisaṃtara-
kaḍaṃ *jahâ piṃḍesaṇâe*. ||2||
se bhikkhû vâ 2, se jjaṃ puṇa vatthaṃ jâṇejjâ: assaṃjae
bhikkhupaḍiyâe kîtaṃ vâ dhoyaṃ vâ rattaṃ vâ ghaṭṭhaṃ[3]
vâ maṭṭhaṃ vâ sammaṭṭhaṃ vâ saṃpadhûvitaṃ vâ, tahappagâraṃ vatthaṃ apurisaṃtarakaḍaṃ *jâva* no paḍigâhejjâ.
aha puṇa evaṃ jâṇejjâ: purisaṃtarakaḍaṃ *jâva* paḍigâ-
hejjâ. ||3||
177 se bhikkhû vâ 2, se jjâiṃ puṇa vatthâiṃ jâṇejjâ: virûvarûvâiṃ mahaddhaṇamollâiṃ, taṃ jahâ: âiṇâṇi[4] vâ sahiṇâṇi[5]
vâ sahiṇakallâṇi vâ âyâṇi vâ kâyagâṇi vâ khomiyâṇi vâ
dugullâṇi vâ paṭṭâṇi vâ malayâṇi vâ pattuṇṇâṇi vâ aṃsuyâṇi
vâ cîṇaṃsuyâṇi vâ desaragâṇi vâ amilâṇi vâ gajjalâṇi vâ
vâ phâliyâṇi[6] vâ kâyahâṇi[7] vâ[3] kaṃbalagâṇi vâ pâvarâṇi

[1] AC eehiṃ. [2] cf. II. 1. 1 §§ 11, etc. [3] A om. [4] A âtiṇ°, B âyîṇagâṇi. [5] B sâh°. [6] B phal°. [7] B koy°, A om.

vâ anna*t*arâṇi vâ tahappagârâiṃ vatthâiṃ mahaddhaṇamollâiṃ lâbhe saṃte no paḍigâhejjâ. ‖4‖

se bhikkhû vâ 2, se jjâiṃ puṇa âîṇapâuraṇâṇi vatthâṇi
jâṇejjâ, taṃ jahâ: uddâṇi vâ pesâṇi vâ pesalesâṇi vâ kiṇha-
migâîṇagâṇi[8] vâ nîlamigâîṇagâṇi[8] vâ goramigâîṇagâṇi[8] vâ
kaṇagâṇi vâ kaṇagakaṃtâṇi vâ kaṇagapaṭṭâṇi vâ kaṇa-
gakhaiyâṇi vâ kaṇagaphusiyâṇi vâ vagghâṇi vâ âbha-
raṇâṇi vâ âbharaṇacittâṇi vâ anna*t*arâṇi vâ tahappagârâiṃ âîṇapâuraṇâṇi[9] vatthâṇi lâbhe saṃte no paḍigâ- 178
hejjâ. ‖5‖

icc etâiṃ âya*t*aṇâiṃ uvâtikamma aha bhikkhû jâṇejjâ
cauhiṃ paḍimâhiṃ vatthaṃ esittae. tattha khalu paḍhamâ
paḍimâ: se bhikkhû vâ 2 uddissiya vatthaṃ jâejjâ: jaṃgiyaṃ vâ bhaṃgiyaṃ vâ sâṇayaṃ vâ pottayaṃ vâ komiyaṃ vâ
tûlakaḍaṃ vâ, tahappagâraṃ vatthaṃ sayaṃ vâ ṇaṃ jâejjâ,
paro vâ se[10] dejjâ, phâsuyaṃ esaṇijjaṃ lâbhe saṃte *jâva*
paḍigâhejjâ. paḍhamâ paḍimâ. ‖6‖

ahâ 'varâ doccâ paḍimâ: se bhikkhû vâ 2 pehâe pehâe 179
vatthaṃ jâejjâ, gâhâvatî vâ *jâva* kammakarî vâ, se puvvâm
eva âloejjâ: âuso tti vâ, bhagiṇî ti vâ, dâhisi me etto annataraṃ vatthaṃ? tahappagâraṃ vatthaṃ sayaṃ vâ ṇaṃ
jâejjâ, paro vâ se dejjâ, phâsuyaṃ esaṇijjaṃ lâbhe saṃte
paḍigâhejjâ. doccâ paḍimâ. ‖7‖

ahâ 'varâ taccâ paḍimâ: se bhikkhû vâ 2, se jjaṃ puṇa
vatthaṃ jâṇejjâ, taṃ jahâ: aṃtarijjagaṃ vâ uttarijjagaṃ vâ,
tahappagâraṃ, etc. (cf. § 7) taccâ paḍimâ. ‖8‖ 180

ahâ 'varâ cautthâ paḍimâ: se bhikkhû vâ 2 ujjhiya-
dhammaṃ vatthaṃ jâejjâ, jaṃ c' anne bahave samaṇamâ-
haṇaatidhikivaṇavaṇîmagâ nâ 'vakaṃkhaṃti, tahappagâraṃ
ujjhiyadhammiyaṃ vatthaṃ, etc. (cf. § 7). cautthâ paḍimâ.
icc' etâṇaṃ cauṇhaṃ paḍimâṇaṃ *jahâ Piṃḍesaṇâe.* ‖9‖

siyâ ṇaṃ tâe esaṇâe esamâṇaṃ paro vadejjâ: âusaṃto
samaṇâ! ejjâhi tumaṃ mâseṇa vâ dasarâeṇa vâ paṃcarâeṇa
vâ sue vâ suyarâ*t*e vâ! to te vayaṃ, âuso! annataraṃ
vatthaṃ dâhâmo. etappagâraṃ nigghosaṃ soccâ nisamma
se puvvâm eva âloejja: âuso tti vâ, bhaiṇî ti vâ, no khalu me

[8] A °dîṇagâṇi, B °yîṇagâṇi. [9] A âdîṇa°. [10] B se vâ, A vâ ṇaṃ.

kappati e*t*appagâre[11] saṃgâre[3] paḍisuṇettae; abhikaṃkhasi me dâuṃ,[12] iyâṇim eva dalayâhi! se ṇ' evaṃ vadaṃtaṃ paro vadejjâ: âusaṃto samaṇâ! aṇugacchâhi! to te vayaṃ âuso annataraṃ vatthaṃ dâhâmo. se puvvâm eva âloejjâ:
181 no khalu me kappati saṃgâravayaṇe paḍisuṇettae, abhikaṃkhasi me dâuṃ, iyâṇim eva dalayâhi! se ṇ' evaṃ vadaṃtaṃ se ṇaṃ paro vadejjâ: âuso tti vâ, bha*g*iṇî ti vâ, âhara eyaṃ vatthaṃ, samaṇassa dâhâmo;[13] aviyâiṃ vayaṃ pacchâ vi appaṇo sayaṭṭhâe pâṇâiṃ bhûtâiṃ jîvâiṃ sattâiṃ samârabbha[14] samuddissa *jâva* cetissâmo. etappagâraṃ nigghosaṃ soccâ nisamma tahappagâraṃ vatthaṃ aphâsuyaṃ *jâva* no paḍigâhejjâ. ‖ 10 ‖

siyâ ṇaṃ paro ṇettâ vaejjâ: âuso tti vâ, bhaiṇî ti vâ, âhara eyaṃ vatthaṃ siṇâṇeṇa[5] vâ âghaṃsittâ[16] vâ paghaṃsettâ vâ samaṇass' imaṃ dâsâmo. etappagâraṃ nigghosaṃ soccâ nisamma se puvvâm eva âloejjâ: âuso tti vâ, bhaiṇî ti vâ, mâ eyaṃ vatthaṃ siṇâṇeṇa vâ *jâva* paghaṃsâhi vâ. abhikaṃkhasi me dâuṃ, em eva dalayâhi! se s'evaṃ vayaṃtassa paro siṇâṇeṇa vâ *jâva* paghaṃsittâ dalaejjâ; tahappagâraṃ vatthaṃ aphâsuyaṃ *jâva* no paḍigâhejjâ. ‖ 11 ‖

se ṇaṃ paro ṇettâ vadejjâ: âuso tti vâ, bhaiṇî ti vâ,
182 âhara eyaṃ vatthaṃ sîodagaviyaḍeṇa vâ usiṇodagaviyaḍeṇa vâ ucchulejja vâ paccholejja[17] vâ; abhikaṃkhasi me dâ*t*uṃ, *sesaṃ tah' eva jâva* no paḍigâhejjâ. ‖ 12 ‖

se ṇaṃ paro ṇettâ vadejjâ: âuso tti vâ, bhaiṇî ti vâ, âhara eyaṃ vatthaṃ, kaṃdâṇi vâ *jâva* hariyâṇi vâ visohĕttâ samaṇassa ṇaṃ dâsâmo. e*t*appagâraṃ nigghosaṃ soccâ
183 nisamma *jâva* bhaiṇî ti vâ, mâ e*t*âṇi tumaṃ kaṃdâṇi vâ *jâva* visohehi! no khalu me kappati eyappagâre vatthe paḍigâhettae. se s' evaṃ vadaṃtaṃ paro kaṃdâṇi vâ *jâva* visohettâ dalaejjâ; tahappagâraṃ vatthaṃ aphâsuyaṃ *jâva* no paḍigâhejjâ. ‖ 13 ‖

se paro ṇettâ vatthaṃ nisarejjâ; se puvvâm eva âloejjâ: âuso tti vâ, bhaiṇî ti vâ, tumaṃ c' eva ṇaṃ saṃtiyaṃ vatthaṃ aṃto aṃteṇa paḍilehissâmi. kevalî bûyâ: âyâṇam eyaṃ;

[11] A °raṃ. [12] A adds vâ. [13] A dâsâmo. [14] MSS. samârambha. [15] AB siṇâṇe. [16] A âlabhittâ. [17] A pacchoejjâ, C uccholettâ vâ padhovettâ vâ.

vatthaṃteṇa[18] obaddhaṃ siyâ kuṃḍale vâ guṇe vâ hiraṇṇe
vâ suvaṇṇe vâ maṇî vâ *jâva* rayaṇâvalî vâ pâṇe vâ bîe vâ
harie vâ. aha bhikkhûṇaṃ puvvovadiṭṭhâ 4 *jâva* puvvâm
eva vatthaṃ aṃto aṃteṇo paḍilehejjâ. ||14||

se bhikkhû vâ 2, se jjaṃ puṇa vatthaṃ jâṇejjâ: saaṃḍaṃ
jâva saṃtâṇaṃ vâ, tahappagâraṃ vatthaṃ aphâsuyaṃ *jâva*
no paḍigâhejjâ. se bhikkhû vâ 2, se jjaṃ puṇa vatthaṃ
jâṇejjâ: appaṃḍaṃ *jâva* saṃtâṇagaṃ aṇalaṃ athiraṃ
adhuvaṃ adhâraṇijjaṃ roijjaṃtaṃ no ruccai, tahappagâraṃ
vatthaṃ aphâsuyaṃ *jâva* no paḍigâhejjâ. ||15||

se bhikkhû vâ 2, se jjaṃ puṇa vatthaṃ jâṇejjâ: alaṃ 184
thiraṃ dhuvaṃ dhâraṇijjaṃ roijjaṃtaṃ ruccai,[19] tahappagâ-
raṃ vatthaṃ phâsuyaṃ *jâva* paḍigâhejjâ. ||16||

se bhikkhû vâ 2 no navae me vatthe ti khaṭṭu no bahudesieṇa siṇâṇeṇa vâ *jâva* paghaṃsejja vâ. se bhikkhû vâ 2
no navae me vatthe ti kaṭṭu no bahudesieṇa sîtodagaviyaḍeṇa
vâ usiṇodagaviyaḍeṇa vâ *jâva* padhoejja vâ. ||17||

se bhikkhû vâ 2 dubbhigaṃdhe me vatthe tti[3] kaṭṭu no
bahudesieṇa vâ siṇâṇeṇa vâ, *tah' eva* sîtodagaviyaḍeṇa vâ
usiṇodagaviyaḍeṇa vâ *âlâvao.* ||18|| 185

se bhikkhû vâ 2 abhikaṃkhejjâ vatthaṃ âyâvettae vâ
payâvettae vâ, tahappagâraṃ vatthaṃ no aṇaṃtarahiyâe
puḍhavîe no sasaṇiddhâe *jâva* saṃtâṇâe âyâvejja vâ payâvejja
vâ. ||19||

se bhikkhû vâ 2 abhikaṃkhejjâ vatthaṃ âyâvettae vâ
payâvettae vâ, tahappagâraṃ vatthaṃ thûṇaṃsi vâ gihelu-
gaṃsi vâ usuyâlaṃsi vâ kâmajalaṃsi[20] vâ annayare vâ
tahappagâre aṃtalikkhajâe dubbaddhe dunnikkhitte aṇi-
kaṃpe calâcale no âyâvejja vâ payâvejja vâ. ||20||

se bhikkhû vâ 2 . . . (§ 20) . . . vatthaṃ kuliyaṃsi vâ
bhittiṃsi vâ silaṃsi[22] vâ leluṃsi[23] vâ annatare vâ tahappa-
gâre aṃtalikkhajâe *jâva* no âyâvejja vâ payâvejja vâ. ||21||

se bhikkhû vâ 2 . . . (§ 20) . . . vatthaṃ khaṃdhaṃsi
vâ maṃcagaṃsi vâ mâlaṃsi vâ pâsâyaṃsi vâ hammiyatalaṃsi
vâ annatare vâ, etc. (cf. § 21). ||22||

se ttam âdâe egaṃtam avakkamejjâ, ahe jhâmathaṃḍillaṃsi 186

[18] A vattheṇa. [19] A adds me. [20] B °jâlaṃsi. [21] B duppa°, A duvi°.
[22] B seluṃsi. [23] B om.

jâva annayaraṃsi vâ tahappagâraṃsi thaṃḍillaṃsi paḍilehiya
2 pamajjiya 2, tato saṃjayâm eva vatthaṃ âyâvejja vâ payâvejja vâ.
eyaṃ khalu tassa bhikkhussa vâ 2 sâmaggiyaṃ, etc. ‖ 23 ‖ **1** ‖
paḍhamo uddesao.

se bhikkhû vâ 2 ahesaṇijjâiṃ vatthâiṃ jâejjâ, ahâpariggahiyâiṃ vatthâiṃ dhârejjâ, no dhoejjâ, no raĕjjâ, no dhoya-
rattâiṃ vatthâiṃ dhârejjâ apaliuṃcamâṇe gâmantaresu omacelie; etaṃ khalu vatthadhârissa bhikkhussa sâmaggiyaṃ.
187 se bhikkhû vâ 2 gâhâvaṭikulaṃ piṃḍavâyapaḍiyâe pavisiukâme savvacîvaram âyâe gâhâṭikulaṃ piṃḍavâyapaḍiyâe
nikkhamejja vâ pavisejja vâ; *evaṃ* bahiyâviyârabhûmî vâ
vihârabhûmî vâ gâmâṇugâmaṃ dûijjejjâ.[1] aha puṇa evaṃ
jâṇejjâ: tivvadesiyaṃ vâ vâsaṃ vâsamâṇaṃ pehae, *jahâ
Piṃḍesaṇâe navaraṃ* savvacîvaram âdâe. ‖ 1 ‖
se egaṭio muhuttagaṃ 2 paḍihâriyaṃ[2] vatthaṃ jâejjâ *jâva*
188 egâheṇa vâ duyâheṇa vâ tiyâheṇa vâ cauyâheṇa vâ paṃcâheṇa
vâ vippavasiya uvâgacchejjâ, tahappagâraṃ vatthaṃ no
appaṇâ giṇhejjâ, no annamannassa dejjâ, no pâmiccaṃ kujjâ,
no vattheṇa vatthaṃ pariṇâmaṃ karejjâ, no paraṃ uvasaṃkamittu evaṃ vadejjâ: âusaṃto samaṇâ! abhikaṃkhasi vatthaṃ
dhârettae vâ pariharittae vâ? thiraṃ vâ ṇaṃ saṃtaṃ[3] no
palicchiṃdiya 2 pariṭṭhavejjâ, tahappagâraṃ sasaṃdhiyaṃ
vatthaṃ tassa ceva nisirejjâ,[4] no attâ ṇaṃ sâijjejjâ. eyappa-
189 gâraṃ nigghosaṃ soccâ nisamma, je bhayaṃtâro tahappagârâṇi vatthâṇi sasaṃdhiyâṇi[5] muhuttagaṃ 2 se soccâ nisamma
jâittâ[6] *jâva* egâheṇa vâ duyâheṇa vâ tiyâheṇâ vâ cauyâheṇa
vâ paṃcâheṇa vâ vippavasiya 2 uvâgacchaṃti, tahappagârâṇi
vatthâṇi no appaṇâ giṇhaṃti, no annamannassa aṇuvayaṃti,
taṃ ceva jâva sâijjaṃti bahuvayaṇeṇa[8] bhâsiyavvaṃ. ‖ 3 ‖
se haṃtâ aham avi muhuttagaṃ paḍihâriyaṃ[9] vatthaṃ
jâittâ *jâva* egâheṇa vâ duyâheṇa vâ tiyâheṇa vâ cauyâheṇa
vâ paṃcâheṇa vâ vippavasiya 2 uvâgacchissâmi, aviyâiṃ

[1] B dûti°. [2] B pâḍi°, C adds vîyaṃ. [3] A sittaṃ. [4] A om. the rest.
[5] B om, A saṃdh°. [6] A om. se to jâittâ. [7] A appaṇo. [8] AC bahumâṇeṇa.
[9] B pâḍi°, AC pari°.

eyaṃ mam' evaṃ[10] siyâ. mâiṭṭhâṇaṃ saṃphâse, no evaṃ karejjâ. ||4||

se bhikkhû vâ 2 no vaṇṇamaṃtâiṃ vatthâiṃ vivaṇṇâiṃ karejjâ, no vivaṇṇâiṃ vaṇṇamaṃtâiṃ karejjâ; annaṃ vatthaṃ labhissâmi tti kaṭṭu no annamannassa dejjâ, no pâmiccaṃ kujjâ, no vattheṇa vatthaṃ pariṇâmaṃ karejjâ, no paraṃ uvasaṃkamittu[11] evaṃ vadejjâ: âusaṃto samaṇâ! abhikaṃkhasi me[12] vatthaṃ dhârittae vâ pariharittae vâ? thiraṃ vâ ṇaṃ saṃtaṃ no palicchiṃdiya 2 pariṭṭhavejjâ, jahâ v' eyaṃ vatthaṃ pâvagaṃ paro mannai. ||5||

paraṃ ca ṇaṃ adattahârî paḍipahe pehâe tassa vatthassa nidâṇâe no tesiṃ bhîo ummaggeṇa gacchejjâ *jâva* appussue *jâva* tato saṃjayâm eva gâmâṇugâmaṃ dûijjejjâ.[1] ||6||

se bhikkhû vâ 2 gâmâṇugâmaṃ dûijjamâṇe aṃtarâ se vihaṃ siyâ, se jjaṃ puṇa vihaṃ jâṇejjâ: imaṃsi khalu vihaṃsi bahave âmosagâ vatthapaḍiyâe saṃpiṃḍiyâ gacchejjâ, no tesiṃ bhîo ummaggeṇa gacchejjâ *jâva* gâmâṇugâmaṃ dûijjejjâ.[1] ||7||

se bhikkhû vâ 2 gâmâṇugâmaṃ dûijjamâṇe,[1] aṃtarâ se âmosagâ saṃpiṃḍiyâ gacchejjâ, te ṇaṃ âmosagâ evaṃ vadejjâ: âusaṃto samaṇâ! âhar' etaṃ[13] vatthaṃ dehi nikkhivâhi *jahâ''riyâe ṇ' âṇattaṃ*[14] *vatthapaḍiyâe.*

eyaṃ khalu tassa bhikkhussa vâ 2 sâmaggiyaṃ, etc. ||8||**2**||

biio uddesao.

vatthesaṇâ samattâ.

paṃcamam ajjhayaṇam.

[10] A eyaṃ. [11] B repeats § 4 from muhuttagaṃ to the end. [12] B om. [13] B ehi. [14] A natteṇaṃ.

CHAṬṬHAM AJJHAYAṆAṂ.

PÂESAṆÂ.

192 se bhikkhû vâ 2 abhikaṃkhejjâ pâyaṃ[7] esittae, se jjaṃ puṇa pâyaṃ jâṇejjâ, taṃ jahâ: lâupâyaṃ vâ dârupâyaṃ vâ maṭṭiyâpâyaṃ, vâ tahappagâraṃ pâyaṃ; je niggaṃthe taruṇe *jâva* thirasaṃghayaṇe, se egaṃ pâyaṃ dhârejjâ, no bîyaṃ.[2] se bhikkhû vâ 2 paraṃ addhajoyaṇamerâe no abhisaṃdhârejjâ gamaṇâe. se bhikkhû vâ 2, se jjaṃ puṇa pâyaṃ jâṇejjâ, assiṃ paḍiyâe egaṃ sâhammiyaṃ samuddissa pâṇâiṃ *jahâ Piṃḍesaṇâe cattâri âlâvagâ, paṃcamo* bahave samaṇamâhaṇâ pagaṇiya *tah' eva.* se bhikkhû vâ 2 assaṃjae bhikkhupaḍiyâe bahave samaṇamâhaṇa *Vatthesaṇâlâvao.* ‖ 1 ‖

se jjâiṃ puṇa pâyâiṃ jâṇejjâ virûvarûvâiṃ mahaddhaṇamollâiṃ, taṃ jahâ: ayapâyâṇi vâ taupâyâṇi[3] vâ sîsagahiraṇṇa-suvaṇṇa-rîriya-hârapuḍa-maṇi-kâya-kaṃsa-saṃkhasiṃga-daṃta-cela-sela-pâyâṇi[4] vâ cammapâyâṇi vâ, annaya-
193 râṇi vâ tahappagârâiṃ virûvarûvâiṃ mahaddhaṇamollâiṃ pâyâiṃ aphâsuyâiṃ *jâva* no paḍigâhejjâ. ‖ 2 ‖

se bhikkhû vâ 2, se jjâiṃ puṇa pâyâiṃ jâṇejjâ virûvarûvâiṃ mahaddhaṇabaṃdhaṇâiṃ, taṃ jahâ: ayabaṃdhaṇâṇi *jâva* cammabaṃdhaṇâṇi, tahappagârâiṃ mahaddhaṇabaṃdhaṇâiṃ aphâsuyâiṃ *jâva* no paḍigâhejjâ. ‖ 3 ‖

icc etâiṃ âyataṇâiṃ uvâtikamma aha bhikkhû jâṇejjâ cauhiṃ paḍimâhiṃ pâyaṃ esittae.

tattha khalu imâ paḍhamâ paḍimâ. se bhikkhû vâ 2 uddisiya 2 pâyaṃ jâejjâ, taṃ jahâ: lâuyapâyaṃ vâ dârupâyaṃ vâ[5] maṭṭiyâpâyaṃ vâ,[5] tahappagâraṃ pâyaṃ sayaṃ vâ ṇaṃ jâejjâ *jâva* paḍigâhejjâ. paḍhamâ paḍimâ. ‖ 4 ‖

[1] B has frequently pâda, A pâta and pâda. [2] B bitiyaṃ. [3] B taua°. [4] B repeats pâyâṇi vâ after each of these words. [5] A om. pâyaṃ vâ.

ahâ 'varâ doccâ padimâ. se bhikkhû vâ 2 pehâe pâyaṃ
jâejjâ, taṃ jahâ: gâhâvati vâ *jâva* kammakarî vâ, se puvvâm
eva âloejjâ: âuso tti[6] vâ, bhaiṇî ti vâ, dâhisi me etto annataraṃ pâyaṃ, taṃ jahâ: lâuyapâyaṃ vâ 3, tahappagâraṃ
pâyaṃ sayaṃ vâ ṇaṃ jâejjâ *jâva* paḍigâhejjâ. doccâ
paḍimâ. ||5||

ahâ 'varâ taccâ paḍimâ. se bhikkhû vâ 2, se jjaṃ puṇa
pâyaṃ jâṇejjâ: saṃgaiyaṃ ti vâ vejaiyaṃ ti vâ, tahappagâraṃ pâyaṃ sayaṃ vâ ṇaṃ jâejjâ *jâva* paḍigâhejjâ. taccâ
paḍimâ. ||6||

ahâ 'varâ cautthâ paḍimâ. se bhikkhû vâ 2 ujjhiya- 194
dhammiyaṃ pâyaṃ[7] jâejjâ, jaṃ c' anne bahave samaṇamâhaṇâ *jâva* vaṇîmagâ nâ 'vakaṃkhaṃti, tahappagâraṃ pâyaṃ[7]
sayaṃ vâ *jâva* paḍigâhejjâ. cautthâ paḍimâ. icc eyâṇaṃ
cauṇhaṃ paḍimâṇaṃ annayaraṃ paḍimaṃ *jahâ Piṃḍe-
sâṇae.* ||7||

se ṇaṃ etâe esaṇâe esamâṇaṃ paro pâsittâ vadejjâ: âusaṃto
samaṇâ! ejjâsi tumaṃ mâseṇa vâ *jahâ Vathesaṇâe.* ||8||

se ṇaṃ paro ṇettâ vadejjâ: âuso tti vâ, bhaiṇî ti vâ, âhar'
eyaṃ pâyaṃ telleṇa vâ ghaeṇa vâ navaṇîeṇa vâ vasâe vâ 195
abbhaṃgettâ vâ, *tah' evâ siṇâṇâdi, tah'eva sîtodagâdi,
kaṃdagâdi tah' eva.* ||9||

se ṇaṃ paro ṇettâ[8] vaejjâ:[9] âusaṃto samaṇâ; muhuttagaṃ 2 acchâhi jâva tâva amhe asaṇaṃ vâ 4 uvakaresu[10] vâ
uvakkhaḍesu[10] vâ, to te vayaṃ, âuso! sapâṇaṃ sabhoyaṇaṃ
paḍiggahaṃ dâsâmo, tucchae paḍiggahae dinne samaṇassa
no[7] suṭṭhu[7] no sâhu bhavati. se puvvâm evâ âloejjâ: âuso
tti vâ, bhaiṇî ti vâ, no khalu me kappai âdhâkammie asaṇe
vâ 4 bhottae vâ pâyae vâ, mâ uvakarehi vâ uvakkhaḍehi vâ,
abhikaṃkhasi me dâtuṃ, em eva dalayâhi! se s' evaṃ
vadaṃtassa paro asaṇaṃ vâ 4 uvakarettâ uvakkhaḍettâ
sapâṇaṃ sabhoyaṇaṃ paḍiggahagaṃ dalaejjâ, tahappagâraṃ
paḍiggahagaṃ[11] aphâsuyaṃ *jâva* no paḍigâhejjâ. ||10||

siyâ se paro uvaṇettâ[12] paḍiggahagaṃ nisirejjâ, se
puvvâm eva âloejjâ: âuso tti vâ, bhaiṇî ti vâ, tumaṃ ceva

[6] B ti. [7] B om. [8] B nettâ. [9] A om. [10] B °iṃsu. [11] A paḍiggahaṃ.
[12] A avaṇettâ.

ṇaṃ saṃtiyaṃ paḍiggahagaṃ aṃto aṃteṇa paḍilehissâmi.[13]
196 kevalî bûyâ : âyâṇam eyaṃ ; aṃto paḍiggahaṃsi pâṇâṇi vâ bîyâṇi vâ hariyâṇi vâ. aha bhikkhûṇaṃ puvvovadiṭṭhâ 4, jaṃ puvvâm eva paḍiggahagaṃ aṃtaṃ aṃteṇa paḍilehejjâ. ‖ 11 ‖

saaṃḍâdi *savve âlâvagâ jahâ Vatthesaṇâe n'âṇattaṃ* telleṇa vâ ghaeṇa vâ navaṇîeṇa vâ vasâe vâ siṇâṇâdi *jâva* annayaraṃsi vâ tahappagâraṃsi thaṃḍillaṃsi paḍilehiya 2 pamajjiya 2 tao saṃjayâm eva âmajjejja vâ.

eyaṃ khalu tassa bhikkhussa vâ 2 sâmaggiyaṃ, etc. ‖ 2 ‖ **1** ‖

paḍhamo uddesao.

197 se bhikkhû vâ 2 gâhâva*t*ikulaṃ piṃḍavâyapaḍiyâe pavisamâṇe puvvâm eva pehâe paḍiggahagaṃ avahaṭṭu pâṇe pamajjiya rayaṃ tato saṃjayâm eva gâhâva*t*ikulaṃ piṃḍavâyapaḍiyâe pavisejja vâ nikkhamejja vâ. kevalî bûyâ : âyâṇam eyaṃ ; aṃto paḍiggahagaṃsi pâṇe vâ bîe vâ rae vâ pariyâvajjejjâ. aha bhikkhûṇaṃ puvvovadiṭṭhâ 4, jaṃ puvvâm eva pehâe paḍiggahagaṃ avahaṭṭu pâṇe pamajjiya rayaṃ tato saṃjayâm eva gâhâva*t*ikulaṃ piṃḍavâyapaḍiyâe pavisejja vâ nikkhamejja vâ. ‖ 1 ‖

se bhikkhû vâ 2 gâhâvaî *jâva* samâṇe, siyâ se paro abhihaṭṭu anto[2] paḍiggahagaṃsi sîodagaṃ paribhâettâ nîhaṭṭu dalaejjâ, tahappagâraṃ paḍiggahagaṃ parahatthaṃsi vâ parapâyaṃsi[3] vâ aphâsuyaṃ jâva no paḍigâhejjâ. ‖ 2 ‖

se ya âhacca paḍigâhie siyâ, se khippâm eva udayaṃsi sâharejjâ, sapaḍiggaham âyâe evaṃ pariṭṭhavejjâ sasaṇiddhâe va naṃ bhûmîe niyamejjâ. ‖ 3 ‖

198 se bhikkhû vâ 2 udaullaṃ[4] vâ sasaṇiddhaṃ vâ paḍiggahaṃ no âmajjejja vâ *jâva* payâvejja vâ. aha puṇa evaṃ jâṇejjâ : vi*g*aḍodae[5] me paḍiggahae chinnasiṇehe, tahappagâraṃ paḍiggahagaṃ tato saṃjayâm eva âmajjejja vâ *jâva* payâvejja vâ. ‖ 4 ‖

se bhikkhû vâ 2 gâhâva*t*ikulaṃ pavisi*t*ukâme paḍiggaham âyâe gâhâva*t*ikulaṃ piṃḍavâyapaḍiyâe pavisejja vâ nikkha-

[13] B °hessâmi.

[1] A to. [2] B aṃto. [3] MSS. pâdaṃsi. [4] A ullaṃ. [5] read vigaodae. [6] B dûti°. [7] B bîtiyâe.

mejja vâ; evaṃ bahiyâ viyârabhûmî vâ vihârabhûmî vâ gâmâṇugâmaṃ dûijjejjâ;[6] tivvadesiyâdi *jahâ bîyâe*[7] *Vatthesaṇâe navaraṃ ettha* paḍiggahao. 199

eyaṃ khalu tassa bhikkhussa 2 sâmaggiyaṃ, etc. ||5||**2**||

biio uddesao.

pâesaṇâ samattâ.

chaṭṭham ajjhayaṇaṃ.

SATTAMAM AJJHAYAṆAṂ.

OGGAHAPAḌIMÂ.

samaṇe[1] bhavissâmi aṇagâre akiṃcaṇe aputte apasû paradattabhogî, pâvaṃ kammaṃ no karissâmî 'ti samuṭṭhâe, savvaṃ bhaṃte adinnâdâṇaṃ paccâikkhâmi. se aṇupavisittâ gâmaṃ vâ *jâva* râyahâṇiṃ vâ n' eva sayaṃ adinnaṃ giṇhejjâ, n' ev' anneṇaṃ[2] adinnaṃ giṇhâvejjâ, n' ev' annaṃ adinnaṃ giṇhaṃtaṃ pi[3] samaṇujâṇejjâ; jehi vi saddhiṃ saṃpavvaie, tesiṃ pi yâiṃ bhikkhû chattagaṃ vâ mattagaṃ vâ daṃḍa-
200 gaṃ[4] vâ[4] *jâva* cammacchedaṇagaṃ vâ tesiṃ puvvâm eva ŏggahaṃ aṇaṇunnaviya apaḍilehiya appamajjiya no giṇhejja vâ pagiṇhejja vâ; tesiṃ puvvâm eva ŏggahaṃ aṇunnaviya paḍilehiya pamajjiya *tato* saṃjayâm eva ogiṇhejja[5] vâ pagiṇhejja vâ. ||1||

se âgaṃtaresu vâ 4 aṇuvîi uggahaṃ jâejjâ, je tattha îsare,[6] je tattha samâhiṭṭhâe, te ŏggahaṃ aṇunnavejjâ: kâmaṃ khalu, âuso! ahâlaṃdaṃ ahâparinnâtaṃ vasâmo,
201 jâva âuso, jâva âusaṃtassa ŏggahe, jâva sâhammiyâ, etâva ŏggahaṃ ogiṇhissâmo,[7] teṇa paraṃ viharissâmo. ||2||

se kiṃ puṇa tatth' oggahaṃsi ev' oggahiyaṃsi, je tattha sâhammiyâ saṃbhoiyâ samaṇunnâ uvâgacchejjâ, je teṇa sayam esiyae[8] asaṇe vâ 4, teṇa te sâhammiyâ saṃbhoiyâ samaṇunnâ uvanimaṃtejjâ,[9] no ceva ṇaṃ parapaḍiyâe uggijjhiya uvanimaṃtejjâ. ||3||

se âgaṃtaresu vâ 4 *jâva* kiṃ puṇa tatth' oggahaṃsi ev' oggahiyaṃsi, je tattha sâhaṃmiyâ annasaṃbhoiyâ samaṇunnâ
202 uvâgacchejjâ, je teṇaṃ sayam esiyae[8] pîḍhe vâ phalae vâ sejjâ vâ saṃthârae vâ, teṇaṃ te sâhammie[10] annasaṃbhoie

[1] B samaṇo. [2] B annehiṃ. [3] B ginhaṃtam api. [4] B om. [5] B uvagiṇhejja. [6] B îsaro. [7] A uvaggahaṃ giṇhissamo. [7] B °ttae, C °yâe. [9] A uvanimaṃte, B uvaṇi° always. [10] A sâhammiyâe,

samaṇunne uvanimaṃtejjâ, no ceva ṇaṃ parapaḍiyâe ogiṇhiya ogiṇhiya [11] uvanimaṃtejjâ. ||4||

se âgaṃtaresu vâ 4 *jâva* se kiṃ puṇa tatth' oggahaṃsi ev' oggahiyaṃsi, je tattha gâhâva*t*îṇa vâ gâhâvaiputtâṇa vâ sûî [12] vâ pippalae vâ kaṇṇasohaṇae vâ na*h*acchedaṇae vâ, taṃ appaṇo egassa aṭṭhâe paḍihâriyaṃ jâittâ no annamannassa dejja vâ aṇupadĕjja vâ sayaṃ karaṇijjaṃ ti kaṭṭu, se ttam 203
âdâe tattha gacchejjâ, 2 ttâ puvvâm eva uttâṇae hatthe kaṭṭu bhûmîe vâ ṭhavettâ: imaṃ khalu imaṃ khalu tti âloejjâ, no ceva ṇaṃ sayaṃ pâṇiṇâ parapâṇiṃsi paccappiṇejjâ. ||5||

se bhikkhû vâ 2, se jjaṃ puṇa oggahaṃ jâṇejjâ: aṇaṃtarahi*t*âe puḍhavîe sasaṇiddhâe puḍhavîe *jâva* saṃtâṇâe, tahappagâraṃ oggahaṃ no ogiṇhejjâ vâ. ||6||

se bhikkhû vâ 2, se jjaṃ puṇa oggahaṃ jâṇejjâ: thûṇaṃsi vâ 4 tahappagâre aṃtalikkhajâe dubaddhe [13] *jâva* no oggahaṃ ogiṇhejjâ.[14] ||7||

se bhikkhû vâ 2, se jjaṃ puṇa oggahaṃ jâṇejjâ: kuliyaṃsi vâ *jâva* no ogiṇhejja vâ. se bhikkhû vâ 2 khaṃdaṃsi vâ anna*t*are vâ tahappagâre *jâva* no oggahaṃ ogiṇhejja vâ. ||8||

se bhikkhû vâ 2, se jjaṃ puṇa oggahaṃ jâṇejjâ: sasâgâriyaṃ sâgaṇiyaṃ saudayaṃ saitthiṃ sakhuḍḍaṃ sapasuṃ sabhattapâṇaṃ, no pannassa nikkhamaṇapavesa *jâva* dhammâṇujogaciṃtâe, s' evaṃ naccâ tahappagâre uvassae sasâgârie *jâva* sakhuḍḍapasubhattapâṇe no oggahaṃ ogiṇhejja 204
vâ. ||9||

se bhikkhû vâ 2, se jjaṃ puṇa oggahaṃ jâṇejjâ: gâhâva*t*ikulassa majjhaṃ majjheṇaṃ gaṃtuṃ paṃthe paḍibaddhaṃ vâ, no pannassa *jâva* se evaṃ naccâ tahappagâre uvassae no oggahaṃ ogiṇhejja vâ. ||10||

se bhikkhû vâ 2, se jjaṃ puṇa oggahaṃ jâṇejjâ: iha khalu gâhâvaî [15] vâ *jâva* kammakarîo vâ annamannaṃ akkosaṃti vâ, *tah' eva* tellâdi siṇâṇâdî sîodagaviyaḍâdi nigiṇâ ṭhi*t*â *jâha Sejjâe âlâvagâ navaraṃ oggahavattavvatâ.* ||11||

se bhikkhû vâ 2, se jjaṃ puṇa oggahaṃ jâṇejjâ: âiṇṇaṃ [17]

[11] B ogijjhiya 2, C ugijjhiya uginhiya. [12] A sûtî, B sûyî. [13] B orig. dubuddhe, corr. duppaddhe. [14] B sa khuḍḍapasubhattapâṇaṃ. [15] B °vati. [16] A °rî. [17] A âyannaṃ, B lekkhaṃ.

saṃlekkha no pannassa *jâva* ciṃtâe, tahappagâre uvassae no oggahaṃ ogiṇhejja vâ.

eyaṃ khalu tassa bhikkhussa vâ 2 sâmaggiyaṃ, etc. ‖ 12 ‖ **1** ‖

paḍhamo uddesao.

se âgaṃtâresu vâ 4 aṇuvîi oggahaṃ jâejjâ, je tattha îsare, je samâhiṭṭhâe, te oggahaṃ aṇunnavejjâ:[1] kâmaṃ khalu, âuso! ahâlaṃdaṃ ahâparinnâtaṃ vasâmo, jâva âuso, jâva
205 âusaṃtassa oggahe, jâva sâhammiyâ, ettâva[2] oggahaṃ ogiṇhissâmo, teṇa paraṃ viharissâmo.

se kiṃ puṇa tatth[3] oggahaṃsi ev' oggahiyaṃsi? je tattha samaṇâṇa vâ mâhaṇâṇa vâ daṃḍae vâ chattae vâ *jâva* cammacchedaṇae vâ, taṃ no aṃtohiṃto vâhiṃ nîṇejjâ, bahiyâo vâ ṇaṃ[4] anto no pavesejjâ, suttaṃ vâ no paḍibohejjâ, tesiṃ kiṃci vi appattiyaṃ paḍiṇîyaṃ karejjâ. ‖ 1 ‖

se bhikkhû vâ 2 abhikaṃkhejjâ aṃbavaṇaṃ uvâgacchittae, je tattha îsare, je tattha samâhiṭṭhâe, te oggahaṃ aṇujâ-
206 ṇâvejjâ: kâmaṃ khalu, auso! *jâva* viharissâmo. se kiṃ puṇa tatth' oggahaṃsi ev' oggahiyaṃsi? aha bhikkhû icchejjâ aṃbaṃ bhottae vâ, se jjaṃ puṇa aṃbaṃ jâṇejjâ saaṃḍaṃ *jâva* saṃtâṇagaṃ,[5] tahappagâraṃ aṃbaṃ aphâsuyaṃ *jâva* no paḍigâhejjâ. ‖ 2 ‖

se bhikkhû vâ 2, se jjaṃ puṇa aṃbaṃ jâṇejjâ: appaṃḍaṃ *jâva* saṃtâṇagaṃ atiricchachinnaṃ avvocchinnaṃ, aphâsuyaṃ *jâva* no paḍigâhejjâ. se bhikkhû vâ 2, se jjaṃ puṇa aṃbaṃ jâṇejjâ: appaṃḍaṃ *jâva* saṃtâṇagaṃ tiricchachinnaṃ
207 vocchinnaṃ phâsuyaṃ[6] *jâva* paḍigâhejjâ. ‖ 3 ‖

se bhikkhû vâ 2 abhikaṃkhejjâ aṃbabhittagaṃ vâ aṃbapesiyaṃ vâ aṃbacoyagaṃ vâ aṃbasâlagaṃ vâ aṃbaḍâlagaṃ[7] vâ bhottae vâ pâyae[8] vâ, se jjaṃ puṇa jâṇejjâ: aṃbabhittagaṃ[9] *jâva* aṃbaḍâlagaṃ vâ saaṃḍaṃ *jâva* saṃtâṇagaṃ aphâsuyaṃ *jâva* no paḍigâhejjâ. se bhikkhû vâ 2, se jjaṃ puṇa jâṇejjâ: aṃbabhittagaṃ *jâva* aṃbaḍâlagaṃ vâ appaṃḍaṃ *jâva* saṃtâṇagaṃ atiricchachinnaṃ avvocchinnaṃ aphâsuyaṃ *jâva* no paḍigâhejjâ. se bhikkhû vâ 2 . . . *jâva*

[1] B oijjâ, A °ittâ. [2] B etâva. [3] B tattha. [4] B om. [5] A saṃtâṇaṃ. [6] A om. [7] AC °dâla°, B corrects °ḍâla° by 2. hd. [8] B pâdae. [9] B *jâva* to end of § 4 i. marg. 2. hd.

saṃtâṇagaṃ tiricchachinnaṃ vocchinnaṃ phâsuyaṃ *jâva* paḍigâhejjâ. || 4 ||

se bhikkhû vâ 2 abhikaṃkhejjâ ucchuvaṇaṃ uvâgacchittae, je tattha îsare *jâva* oggahaṃsi. aha bhikkhû icchejjâ ucchuṃ bhottae vâ pâyae vâ, se jjaṃ puṇa jâṇejjâ : saaṃḍaṃ *jâva* no paḍigâhejjâ. atiricchachinnaṃ *tah' eva* tiricchachinnaṃ *tah' eva.* se bhikkhû vâ 2, se jjaṃ puṇa abhikaṃkhejjâ aṃtarucchuyaṃ vâ ucchugaṃḍiyaṃ vâ ucchucoyagaṃ vâ 208
ucchusâlagaṃ vâ ucchuḍâlagaṃ vâ bhottae vâ pâyae vâ, se jjaṃ puṇa jâṇejjâ aṃtarucchuyaṃ vâ *jâva* ḍâlagaṃ vâ saaṃḍaṃ *jâva* no paḍigâhejjâ. se bhikkhû vâ 2 . . . appaṃḍaṃ *jâva* no paḍigâhejjâ; tiricchachinnaṃ *tah' eva,* atiricchachinnaṃ *tah' eva.* || 5 ||

se bhikkhû vâ 2 abhikaṃkhejjâ lhasuṇavaṇaṃ uvâgacchittae, *tah' eva tinni âlâvagâ, navaraṃ* lhasuṇaṃ. se bhikkhû vâ 2 abhikaṃkhejjâ lhasuṇaṃ vâ lhasuṇakaṃdaṃ vâ lhasuṇacoyagaṃ vâ lhasuṇanâlagaṃ vâ bhottae vâ pâyae vâ, se jjaṃ puṇa jâṇejjâ : lhasuṇaṃ vâ *jâva* lhasuṇabîyaṃ vâ saaṃḍaṃ *jâva* no paḍigâhejjâ; *evaṃ* atiricchachinne vi, tiricchachinne *jâva* paḍigâhejjâ. || 6 ||

se bhikkhû vâ 2 âgaṃtâresu vâ 4 *jâv'* oggahiyaṃsi, je tattha gâhâvaîṇa vâ gâhâvaiputtâṇa vâ icc eyâiṃ âyataṇâiṃ uvâtikkamma aha bhikkhû jâṇejjâ imâhiṃ sattahiṃ paḍimâ- 209
hiṃ oggahaṃ ogiṇhittae. || 7 ||

tattha khalu imâ[6] paḍhamâ paḍimâ. se[6] âgaṃtâresu vâ 4 aṇuvîi[10] oggahaṃ jâejjâ *jâva* viharissâmo. paḍhamâ paḍimâ. || 8 ||

ahâ 'varâ doccâ paḍimâ. jassa ṇaṃ bhikkhussa evaṃ bhavati :[11] ahaṃ ca[12] khalu annesiṃ bhikkhûṇaṃ aṭṭhâe oggahaṃ ogiṇhissâmi,[13] annesiṃ bhikkhûṇaṃ oggahie oggahe uvallissâmi. doccâ paḍimâ. || 9 ||

ahâ 'varâ taccâ paḍimâ. jassa ṇaṃ . . . (cf. § 9) ogiṇ- 210
hissâmi,[13] annesiṃ ca bhikkhûṇaṃ[4] oggahie oggahe no uvallissâmi. taccâ paḍimâ. || 10 ||

ahâ 'varâ cautthâ paḍimâ. jassa ṇaṃ . . . (cf. § 9) no[4] ogiṇhissâmi,[13] annesiṃ ca oggahie oggahe uvallissâmi. cautthâ paḍimâ. || 11 ||

[10] A °vîti, B °vîyi. [11] A om. jassa to bhavati. [12] B âhacca. [13] B giṇh°.

ahâ 'varâ paṃcamâ paḍimâ. jassa ṇaṃ . . . (cf. § 9) appaṇo aṭṭhâe oggahaṃ giṇhissâmi,[14] no doṇhaṃ, no tiṇhaṃ, no cauṇhaṃ, no paṃcaṇhaṃ. paṃcamâ paḍimâ. ‖ 12 ‖

ahâ 'varâ chaṭṭhâ paḍimâ. se bhikkhû vâ 2, jass' ev' oggahe uvalliejjâ, je tattha ahâsamannâgate, taṃ jahâ: ikkaḍe vâ *jâva* palâle vâ; tassa lâbhe saṃvasejjâ, tassa alâbhe ukkuḍue[15] vâ nesajjie vâ viharejjâ. chaṭṭhâ paḍimâ. ‖ 13 ‖

ahâ 'varâ sattamâ paḍimâ. se bhikkhû vâ 2 ahâsaṃthaḍam eva oggahaṃ jâejjâ, taṃ jahâ: puḍhavisilaṃ vâ kaṭṭhasilaṃ vâ, ahâsaṃthaḍam eva; tassa lâbhe saṃvâsejjâ, tassa alâbhe ukkuḍuo vâ nesajjio vâ viharejjâ. sattamâ
211 paḍimâ.

icc etâsiṃ sattaṇhaṃ paḍimâṇaṃ annatariṃ *jahâ Piṃḍesaṇâe*. ‖ 14 ‖

suyaṃ me âusaṃ teṇa bhagavatâ evam akkhâyaṃ. iha khalu therehiṃ bhagavaṃtehiṃ paṃcavihe ŏggahe pannatte: devĕṃdoggahe, râoggahe,[16] gâhâvatiŏggahe, sâgâriyaoggahe, sâhammiyaoggahe.

eyaṃ khalu tassa bhikkhussa vâ 2 sâmaggiyaṃ, etc. ‖ 15 ‖ **2** ‖

biio uddesao.

oggahapaḍimâ samattâ.

sattamam ajjhayaṇaṃ.

[14] B ugg°. [15] B ukkuḍuo. [16] B râyâuggahe, A râyogg°.

BIIYÂ CÛLÂ.

SATTIKKAIO.

aṭṭhamam ajjhayaṇaṃ.

se bhikkhû vâ 2 abhikaṃkhati ṭhâṇaṃ[1] ṭhâittae,[1] se
aṇupavisejjâ gâmaṃ vâ nagaraṃ vâ *jâva* saṃnivesaṃ vâ, se
aṇupavisittâ gâmaṃ vâ *jâva* saṃnivesaṃ vâ, se jjaṃ puṇa 212
ṭhâṇaṃ jâṇejjâ : sayaṃḍaṃ *jâva* samakkaḍâsaṃtâṇayaṃ, taṃ
tahappagâraṃ ṭhâṇaṃ aphâsuyaṃ aṇesaṇijjaṃ lâbhe saṃte
no paḍigâhejjâ. *evaṃ Sejjâgamenaṃ neyavvaṃ jâva* udaya-
pasûe[2] tti. ‖ 1 ‖

icc etâiṃ[3] âyataṇâiṃ uvâtikkamma aha bhikkhû icchejjâ
cauhiṃ paḍimâhiṃ ṭhâṇaṃ ṭhâittae.

tatth' imâ paḍhamâ paḍimâ. acittaṃ khalu uvasajjejjâ
avalaṃbĕjjâ kâeṇa vipparikammâdî, saviyâraṃ ṭhâṇaṃ
ṭhâissâmi tti paḍhamâ paḍimâ. ‖ 2 ‖

ahâ 'varâ doccâ paḍimâ. acittam . . . (cf. § 2) no saviyâraṃ 213
ṭhâṇaṃ ṭhâissâmi tti doccâ paḍimâ. ‖ 3 ‖

ahâ 'varâ taccâ paḍimâ. acittaṃ[4] . . . (cf. § 3) no kâeṇa
vipparikammâdî, no saviyâraṃ ṭhâṇaṃ ṭhâissâmi tti taccâ
paḍimâ. ‖ 4 ‖

ahâ 'varâ cautthâ paḍimâ. acittaṃ[5] khalu uvasajjejjâ
no avalaṃbejjâ kâeṇa no vipparikammâdî no saviyâraṃ
ṭhâṇaṃ ṭhâissâmi ; vosaṭṭhakesamaṃsulomanahe saṃṇi- 214
ruddhaṃ vâ ṭhâṇaṃ vâ ṭhâissâmi tti cautthâ paḍimâ. ‖ 5 ‖

icc eyâsiṃ cauṇhaṃ paḍimâṇaṃ *jâva* paggahiyatarâyaṃ[6]
viharejjâ n' eva kiṃci vi vadejjâ.

eyaṃ khalu tassa bhikkhussa vâ 2 sâmaggiyaṃ, etc. ‖ 6 ‖

ṭhâṇasattikkayaṃ samattaṃ.

[1] MSS. frequently ṭṭh. [2] BC pasuyâe (cf. 2. 1. § 5). [3] A eiyâiṃ. [4] B accittaṃ. [5] MSS. accittaṃ. [6] A °âiṃ.

navamam ajjhayaṇaṃ.

se bhikkhû vâ 2 abhikaṃkhati nisîhiyaṃ phâsuyaṃ gamaṇâe; se puṇa nisîhiyaṃ jâṇejjâ:[1] saaṃḍaṃ sapâṇaṃ *jâva* makkaḍâsaṃtâṇayaṃ, tahappagâraṃ nisîhiyaṃ aphâsu-
215 yaṃ aṇesaṇijjaṃ lâbhe saṃte no cetĕssâmi. se bhikkhû vâ 2 abhikaṃkhati nisîhiyaṃ gamaṇâe, se jjaṃ puṇa nisîhiyaṃ jâṇejjâ: appapâṇaṃ appabîyaṃ *jâva* makkaḍâsaṃtâṇayaṃ,[2] tahappagâraṃ nisîhiyaṃ phâsuyaṃ esaṇijjaṃ lâbhe saṃte cetĕssâmi. *evaṃ Sejjâgameṇaṃ neyavvaṃ jâva* udayapasuyâe tti. ‖1‖

je tattha duvaggâ vâ tivaggâ vâ cauvaggâ vâ paṃcavaggâ vâ abhisaṃdhârenti[3] nisîhiyam gamaṇâe, te no annamannassa kâyaṃ âliṃgĕjja[4] vâ viliṃgejja[4] vâ cuṃbejja[4] vâ daṃtehi
216 vâ nahehi[5] vâ[5] acchiṃdejja vâ.

eyaṃ[6] khalu tassa bhikkhussa vâ bhikkhuṇîe vâ sâmaggiyaṃ, jaṃ savvaṭṭhehiṃ sahie samie sadâ jâejjâ s'eyam iṇaṃ mannejjâ si tti bemi. ‖2‖

nisîhiyasattikkayaṃ samattaṃ.

dasamam ajjhayaṇaṃ.

se bhikkhû vâ 2 uccârapâsavaṇakiriyâe ubbâhijjamâṇe[1] sayassa pâyapuṃchaṇassa asatîe tato pacchâ sâhammiyaṃ jâejjâ. se bhikkhû vâ 2, se jjaṃ puṇa thaṃḍilaṃ jâṇejjâ: saaṃḍaṃ sapâṇaṃ *jâva* makkaḍâsaṃtâṇayaṃ,[2] tahappa-
217 gâraṃsi thaṃḍilaṃsi no uccârapâsavaṇaṃ vosirejjâ. se bhikkhû vâ 2, se jjaṃ puṇa thaṃḍilaṃ jâṇejjâ: appapâṇaṃ appabîyaṃ *jâva* makkaḍâsaṃtâṇayaṃ,[2] tahappagâraṃsi thaṃḍilaṃsi uccârapâsavaṇe vosirejjâ. ‖1‖

se bhikkhû vâ 2, se jjaṃ puṇa thaṃḍilaṃ jâṇejjâ: assiṃ paḍiyâe egaṃ sâhammiyaṃ samuddissa, assiṃ paḍiyâe bahave sâhammiyâ sammuddissa, assiṃ paḍiyâe egaṃ sâhammiṇiṃ samuddissa, assiṃ paḍiyâe bahave sâhammiṇîo 3 samuddissa, assiṃ paḍiyâe bahave samaṇamâhaṇavaṇîmaga pagaṇiya 2 pâṇâiṃ 4 *jâva* uddesiyaṃ ceteti, tahappagâraṃ thaṃḍilaṃ purisaṃtarakaḍaṃ[4] vâ *jâva* bahiyâ nîhaḍaṃ vâ,[5] annataraṃsi

[1] B jâṇiyâ. [2] MSS. °yaṃsi. [3] A °eti, C °ei. [4] AC °jjâ. [5] B om. [6] AC evaṃ.

[1] B uppâh°, A uvvâh°. [2] MSS. °yaṃsi. [3] B °ṇiyâo, A ṇio. [4] B adds apurisaṃtarakaḍaṃ. [5] B adds aṇîhaḍaṃ.

vâ tahappagâraṃsi thaṃḍilaṃsi no uccârapâsavaṇaṃ vosirejjâ. ‖2‖
se bhikkhû vâ 2, se jjaṃ puṇa thaṃḍilaṃ jâṇejjâ: bahave
samaṇamâhaṇakivaṇavaṇîmagaati*h*î samuddissa pâṇâiṃ 4
jâva uddesiyaṃ ceteti, apurisaṃtara*k*aḍaṃ[6] *jâva* bahiyâ
aṇîhaḍaṃ,[7] anna*t*araṃsi vâ tahappagâraṃsi thaṃḍilaṃsi no
uccârapâsavaṇaṃ vosirejjâ. aha puṇa evaṃ jâṇejjâ: puri- 218
saṃtara*k*aḍaṃ *jâva* bahiyâ nîhaḍaṃ vâ, anna*t*araṃsi vâ
tahappagâraṃsi thaṃḍilaṃsi uccârapâsavaṇaṃ vosirejjâ. ‖4‖
se bhikkhû vâ 2, se jjaṃ puṇa thaṃḍilaṃ jâṇejjâ: assiṃ
paḍiyâe kayaṃ vâ kâriyaṃ vâ pâmicciyaṃ vâ channaṃ vâ
ghaṭṭhaṃ vâ maṭṭhaṃ vâ littaṃ vâ samaṭṭhaṃ vâ saṃpadhû-
vi*t*aṃ[8] vâ anna*t*araṃsi tahappagâraṃsi thaṃḍilaṃsi no uccârapâsavaṇaṃ vosirejjâ. ‖5‖
se bhikkhû vâ 2, se jjaṃ puṇa thaṃḍilaṃ jâṇejjâ: iha
khalu gâhâva*t*î vâ gâhâva*t*iputtâ vâ kaṃdâṇi vâ mûlâṇi vâ 219
jâva hariyâṇi vâ aṃtâto vâ bâhiṃ nîharanti,[9] bâhîo[10] vâ
aṃtaṃ sâharaṃti, annayaraṃsi vâ tahappagâraṃsi thaṃḍilaṃsi no uccârapâsavaṇaṃ vosirejjâ. ‖6‖
se bhikkhû vâ 2, se jjaṃ puṇa thaṃḍilaṃ jâṇejjâ: khaṃdhaṃsi vâ pîḍhaṃsi vâ maṃcaṃsi vâ mâlaṃsi vâ aṭṭaṃsi[11]
vâ pâsâyaṃsi vâ annayaraṃsi[12] vâ tahappagâraṃsi[13] thaṃḍilaṃsi no uccârapâsavaṇaṃ vosirejjâ. ‖7‖
se bhikkhû vâ 2, se jjaṃ puṇa thaṃḍilaṃ jâṇejjâ:
aṇaṃtarahiyâe puḍhavîe sasaṇiddhâe puḍhavîe sasarakkhâe
puḍhavîe maṭṭiyâmakkaḍâe cittamaṃtâe silâe cittamaṃtâe
lelue[14] kolâvâsaṃsi vâ dâruyaṃsi vâ jîvapa*t*iṭṭhiyaṃsi vâ
jâva makkaḍâsaṃtâṇayaṃsi annayaraṃsi vâ tahappagâraṃsi
thaṃḍilaṃsi no uccârapâsavaṇaṃ vosirejjâ. ‖8‖
se bhikkhû vâ 2, se jjaṃ puṇa thaṃḍilaṃ jâṇejjâ: iha
khalu gâhâva*t*î vâ gâhâvatiputtâ vâ kaṃdâṇi vâ *jâva* bîyâṇi
vâ parisâḍeṃsu vâ parisâḍeṃti vâ parisâḍessaṃti vâ, annaya- 220
raṃsi vâ tahappagâraṃsi thaṃḍilaṃsi no uccârapâsavaṇaṃ
vosirejjâ. ‖9‖
se bhikkhû vâ 2, . . . (§ 9) . . . gâhâvatiputtâ vâ sâlîṇi
vâ vîhîṇi vâ muggâṇi vâ mâsâṇi vâ[15] tilâṇi vâ kulatthâṇi vâ

[6] A puris°. [7] AB nîhaḍaṃ. [8] B saṃpadhuviyaṃ. [9] B °ṃti. [10] B pâhîto
[11] A ahaṃsi, B aṭṭhaṃsi. [12] B om. [13] AB om. [14] B loluyâe. [15] A adds vilâṇi vâ.

javâṇi vâ javajavâṇi vâ pa*t*iriṃsu vâ pa*t*iriṃti[16] vâ pa*t*irissaṃti vâ, anna*t*araṃsi vâ etc. ||10||

se bhikkhû vâ 2, se jjaṃ puṇa thaṃḍilaṃ jâṇejjâ: âmoyâṇi vâ ghasâṇi vâ bhiluyâṇi vâ vijjalâṇi vâ khâṇuyâṇi vâ kaḍavâṇi[17] vâ pagaḍâṇi vâ darîṇi vâ paduggâṇi vâ samâṇi vâ visamâṇi vâ anna*t*araṃsi vâ etc. ||11||

se bhikkhû vâ 2, se jjaṃ puṇa thaṃḍilaṃ jâṇejjâ: mâṇusaraṃdhaṇâṇi vâ mahisakaraṇâṇi vâ vasabhakaraṇâṇi vâ assakaraṇâṇi vâ hatthikaraṇâṇi[12] vâ kukkuḍakaraṇâṇi vâ makkaḍakaraṇâṇi vâ lâvayakaraṇâṇi vâ vaṭṭayakaraṇâṇi vâ
221 tittirikaraṇâṇi vâ kavo*t*akaraṇâṇi vâ kapiṃjalakaraṇâṇi vâ anna*t*araṃsi vâ etc. ||12||

se bhikkhû vâ 2, se jjaṃ puṇa thaṃḍilaṃ jâṇejjâ: vehâṇasaṭṭhâṇesu vâ gaddhapaṭṭhaṭṭhâṇesu vâ merupavaḍaṇaṭṭhâṇesu vâ tarupavaḍaṇaṭṭhâṇesu vâ agaṇiphaṃḍayaṭṭhâṇesu vâ anna*t*araṃsi vâ etc. ||13||

se bhikkhû vâ 2, se jjaṃ puṇa thaṃḍilaṃ jâṇejjâ: ârâmâṇi
222 vâ ujjâṇâṇi vâ vaṇâṇi vâ vaṇasaṃḍâṇi vâ devakulâṇi vâ selâṇi vâ pavâṇi vâ anna*t*araṃsi etc. ||14||

se bhikkhû vâ 2, se jjaṃ puṇa thaṃḍilaṃ jâṇejjâ: aṭṭâlayâṇi vâ cariyâṇi vâ dârâṇi vâ gopurâṇi vâ anna*t*araṃsi vâ etc. ||15||

se bhikkhû vâ 2, se jjaṃ puṇa thaṃḍilaṃ jâṇejjâ: tiyâṇi vâ caukkâṇi vâ caccarâṇi vâ caummuhâṇi vâ anna*t*araṃsi vâ etc. ||16||

223 se bhikkhû vâ 2, se jjaṃ puṇa thaṃḍilaṃ jâṇejjâ: iṃgâlaḍâhesu vâ khâraḍâhesu vâ maḍayaḍâhesu[12] vâ[12] maḍayathûbhiyâsu vâ maḍayace*t*iyâsu vâ anna*t*araṃsi vâ etc. ||17||

se bhikkhû vâ 2, se jjaṃ puṇa thaṃḍilaṃ jâṇejjâ: nadiyâyayaṇesu[18] vâ paṃkâyayaṇesu vâ ugghâyayaṇesu vâ seyaṇavahaṃsi[20] vâ annayaraṃsi vâ etc. ||18||

se bhikkhû vâ 2, se jjaṃ puṇa thaṃḍilaṃ jâṇejjâ: nadiyâsu vâ maṭṭiyâkhâṇiyâsu naviyâsu goppalehiyâsu[21] gavâṇîsu vâ khâṇîsu vâ anna*t*araṃsi vâ etc. ||19||

se bhikkhû vâ 2, se jjaṃ puṇa thaṃḍilaṃ jâṇejjâ: ḍâga-

[16] B pairaṃti. [17] A kaḍayâṇi. [18] A °âyaṇesu. [19] B oghâ°, cf.[18]. [20] B °paḍhaṃsi. [21] B adds vâ.

vaccaṃsi vâ sâgavaccaṃsi vâ mûlagavaccaṃsi[22] vâ anna-
*t*araṃsi vâ etc. ||20||

se bhikkhû vâ 2, se jjaṃ puṇa thaṃḍilaṃ jâṇejjâ: asaṇa-
vaṇaṃsi vâ saṇavaṇaṃsi vâ dhâyaivaṇaṃsi[23] vâ keyai- 224
vaṇaṃsi vâ ambavaṇaṃsi vâ asogavaṇaṃsi vâ nâgavaṇaṃsi[12]
vâ[12] punnâgavaṇaṃsi vâ cunnagavaṇaṃsi[12] vâ, anna*t*aresu
vâ tahappagâresu vâ pattovaesu va pupphovaesu vâ phalo-
vaesu vâ vîovaesu vâ hari*t*ovaesu vâ no uccârapâsavaṇaṃ
vosirejjâ. ||21||

se bhikkhû vâ 2 sayapâyayaṃ vâ parapâyayaṃ vâ gahâya,
se ttam âyâe egaṃtam avakkamejjâ[24] aṇâvâyaṃsi asaṃloi-
yaṃsi appapâṇaṃsi *jâva* makkaḍâsaṃtâṇayaṃsi ah' ârâmaṃsi
vâ uvassayaṃsi, tato saṃjayâm eva uccârapâsavaṇaṃ vosirejjâ, vosirittâ se ttam â*d*âe egaṃtam avakkamejjâ[25] *jâva*
makkaḍâsaṃtâṇayaṃsi ah' ârâmaṃsi vâ jhâme thaṃḍilaṃsi vâ
anna*t*araṃsi vâ tahappagâraṃsi thaṃḍilaṃsi acittaṃsi tato
saṃjayâm eva uccârapâsavaṇaṃ pariṭṭhavejjâ.[26]

eyaṃ khalu tassa bhikkhussa vâ 2 sâmaggiyaṃ, etc. ||22||

uccârapâsavaṇasattikkayaṃ samattaṃ.

egâdasam ajjhayaṇaṃ.

se bhikkhû vâ 2 muiṃgasaddâṇi vâ naṃdîmuiṃgasaddâṇi 225
vâ jhallarisaddâṇi[1] vâ anna*t*arâṇi vâ tahappagarâṇi[2] virûvarûvâṇi[2] vitatâiṃ saddâiṃ kaṇṇasoyapaḍiyâe no abhisaṃdhâ-
rejjâ gamaṇâe. ||1||

se bhikkhû vâ 2 ahâ v' ega*t*iyâiṃ saddâiṃ suṇeti, taṃ
jahâ: vîṇâsaddâṇi vâ vivaṃcisaddâṇi vâ vavîsagasaddâṇi[3] vâ
tuṇayasaddâṇi vâ paṇayasaddâṇi vâ tumbavîṇiyasaddâṇi vâ
dukuṇasaddâṇi[4] vâ anna*t*arâṇi vâ tahappagârâiṃ virûvarûvâṇi saddâṇi vâ tatâiṃ kaṇṇasoyapaḍiyâe no abhisaṃdhârejjâ 226
gamaṇâe. ||2||

se bhikkhû vâ 2 ahâ v' ega*t*iyâiṃ saddâiṃ suṇeti, taṃ
jahâ: tâlasaddâṇi vâ kaṃsatâlasaddâṇi[5] vâ lattiyasaddâṇi vâ
gohiyasaddâṇi[6] vâ kirikiriyasaddâṇi vâ anna*t*arâṇi vâ

[22] B adds hatthuṃkaravaccaṃsi vâ. [23] A dhoyai, B dhâtai. [24] B avakkame.
[25] A avakamme. [26] B vosirejjâ.

[1] B jhallarî. [2] B °âiṃ. [3] B pappîsa°. [4] B ṇakuṇa°, C dukula°. [5] A om.
[6] B goviya.

tahappaggârâiṃ virûvarûvâiṃ tâlasaddâiṃ kaṇṇasoyapaḍiyâe no abhisaṃdhârejjâ gamaṇâe. ||3||

se bhikkhû vâ 2 . . . taṃ jahâ: saṃkhasaddâṇi vâ veṇusaddâṇi vâ vaṃsasaddâṇi vâ kharamuhisaddâṇi vâ piripiriyasaddâṇi vâ, anna*t*arâṇi vâ tahappagârâiṃ virûvarûvâiṃ saddâiṃ jhusirâiṃ kaṇṇasoyapaḍiyâe no abhisaṃdhârejjâ gamaṇâe. ||4||

se bhikkhû vâ 2 . . ., taṃ jahâ: vappâṇi vâ phalihâṇi[7] vâ *jâva* sarâṇi vâ sarapaṃtiyâṇi vâ sarassarapaṃtiyâṇi vâ anna*t*arâṇi vâ virûvarûvâiṃ saddâiṃ kaṇṇasoyapaḍiyâe no abhisaṃdhârejjâ gamaṇâe. ||5||

227 se bhikkhû vâ 2 . . ., taṃ jahâ: kacchâṇi vâ nûmâṇi vâ gahaṇâṇi vâ vaṇâṇi vâ vaṇaduggâṇi vâ pavvayâṇi vâ pavvayaduggâṇi vâ anna*t*arâṇi vâ etc. ||6||

se bhikkhû vâ 2 . . ., taṃ jahâ: gâmâṇi[2] vâ nagarâṇi vâ nigamâṇi vâ râyahâṇiṃ vâ âsamapayapaṭṭaṇasaṃnivesâṇi vâ anna*t*arâṇi vâ etc. ||7||

se bhikkhû vâ 2 . . ., ârâmâṇi vâ ujjâṇâṇi vâ vaṇâṇi vâ vaṇasaṃḍâṇi vâ devakulâṇi vâ sabhâṇi vâ pavâṇi vâ anna*t*arâṇi vâ etc. ||8||

se bhikkhû vâ 2 . . ., aṭṭâṇi vâ aṭṭâlayâṇi vâ cariyâṇi vâ dârâṇi[5] vâ[5] gopurâṇi vâ anna*t*arâṇi vâ etc. ||9||

228 se bhikkhû vâ 2 . . ., tiyâṇi vâ caukkâṇi vâ caccarâṇi vâ caummuhâṇi vâ anna*t*arâṇi vâ etc. ||10||

se bhikkhû vâ 2 . . ., mahisaṭṭhâṇakaraṇâṇi vâ vasabhaṭṭhâṇakaraṇâṇi vâ assaṭṭhâṇakaraṇâṇi[8] vâ hatthiṭṭhâṇakaraṇâṇi[8] vâ *jâva* kaviṃjalaṭṭhâṇakaraṇâṇi[8] vâ anna*t*arâṇi vâ etc. ||11||

se bhikkhû vâ 2 . . ., mahisajuddhâṇi vâ vasabhajuddhâṇi vâ assajuddhâṇi vâ hatthijuddhâṇi vâ *jâva* kaviṃjalajuddhâṇi vâ anna*t*arâṇi vâ etc. ||12||

229 se bhikkhû vâ 2 . . ., jûhiyaṭṭhâṇâṇi[9] vâ hayajûhiyaṭṭhâṇâṇi vâ gayajûhiyaṭṭhâṇâṇi vâ anna*t*arâṇi vâ etc. ||13||

se bhikkhû vâ 2 . . .,[10] akkhâiyaṭṭhâṇâṇi vâ mâṇummâṇi-

[7] B phalibhâṇi. [8] AB karaṇaṭṭhâṇâṇi. [9] A juddhiya. [10] A jâva suṇeti.

yaṭṭhâṇâṇi vâ mahayâhayanaṭṭagî*t*avâiyataṃtitalatâlatuḍiyapaḍuppavâiyaṭṭhâṇâṇi vâ anna*t*arâṇi vâ etc. ||14||

se bhikkhû vâ 2 . . .,[10] kalahâṇi vâ ḍiṃbâṇi vâ damarâṇi vâ dovajjâṇi vâ verajjâṇi vâ viruddharajjâṇi vâ anna*t*arâṇi vâ etc. ||15|| 230

se bhikkhû vâ 2 . . ., khuḍḍiyaṃ dâriyaṃ parivuyaṃ[11] maṃḍitâlaṃki*t*anittusamâṇiṃ[12] pehâe egapurisaṃ vâ vahâe nîṇijjamâṇaṃ pehâe anna*t*arâṇi vâ etc. ||16||

se bhikkhû vâ 2 annayarâiṃ virûvarûvâiṃ mahâsavâiṃ evaṃ jâṇejjâ, taṃ jahâ: bahusagaḍâṇi vâ bahurahâṇi vâ bahumilakkhûṇi vâ bahupaccaṃtâṇi vâ anna*t*arâṇi vâ tahappagârâiṃ virûvarûvâiṃ mahâsavâiṃ kaṇṇasoyapaḍiyâe no abhisaṃdhârejjâ gamaṇâe. ||17||

se bhikkhû vâ 2 . . . (§ 17) . . ., taṃ jahâ: itthîṇi vâ purisâṇi vâ therâṇi vâ ḍaharâṇi vâ majjhimâṇi vâ âbharaṇavibhûsiyâṇi vâ gâyaṃtâṇi vâ vâyaṃtâni vâ naccaṃtâṇi vâ hasaṃtâṇi vâ namaṃtâṇi vâ mohaṃtâṇi vâ vipulaṃ asaṇapâṇakhâimasâimaṃ[13] paribhuṃjaṃtâṇi[14] vâ paribhâyaṃtâṇi vâ vicchaḍḍamâṇâṇi vâ viggovamâṇâṇi vâ anna*t*arâṇi vâ 231
etc. (cf. § 17). ||18||

se bhikkhû vâ 2 no ihaloiehiṃ saddehiṃ, no paraloiehiṃ saddehiṃ, no su*t*ehiṃ saddehiṃ, no asutehiṃ saddehiṃ, no diṭṭhehiṃ[15] saddehiṃ, no adiṭṭhehiṃ[16] saddehiṃ sajjejjâ, no rajjejjâ, no gijjhejjâ, no ajjhovajjejjâ.

eyaṃ khalu tassa bhikkhussa vâ 2 sâmaggiyaṃ *jâva* jâejjâ si tti bemi. ||19||

saddasattikkayaṃ samattaṃ.

bârasamam ajjhayaṇaṃ.

se bhikkhû vâ 2 ahâ v' ega*t*iyâiṃ rûvâiṃ pâsai, tam jahâ: gaṃthimâṇi vâ veḍhimâṇi vâ pûrimâṇi vâ saṃghâ*t*imâṇi vâ 232
kaṭṭhakammâṇi[1] vâ potthakammâṇi cittakammâṇi vâ maṇikammâṇi vâ daṃtakammâṇi vâ[2] mâlakammâṇi vâ pattachejjakammâṇi vâ vivi*dh*âṇi vâ veḍhimâiṃ anna*t*arâiṃ tahappagârâiṃ virûvarûvâiṃ cakkhûdaṃsaṇa*p*aḍiyae no abhisaṃ-

[11] B pariccittaṃ. [12] AB nivujjhamâṇiyaṃ, Com. nittusamâṇi tti. [12] AC khâimaṃ, B om. khâimasâimaṃ. [14] A °iṃtâṇi. [15] B iṭṭhehiṃ. [16] B kaṃtehiṃ.

[1] B kaṭṭhâṇi. [2] B adds kaṭṭhakammâṇi vâ.

dhârejjâ gamaṇâe. *evaṃ neyavvaṃ jahâ saddapaḍiyâe savvavâittavajjâ rûvapaḍiyâ vi.* ‖ 1 ‖

rûvasattikkayaṃ samattaṃ.

terasamam ajjhayaṇaṃ.

parakiriyaṃ ajjhatthiyaṃ saṃsesiyaṃ [1] no taṃ [2] sâtie, no taṃ niyame. se se [3] paro pâe âmajjejja vâ (pamajjejja vâ); no taṃ sâtie, no taṃ niyame. ‖ 1 ‖

233 se se paro pâ*d*âiṃ saṃvâhĕjja vâ palimaddejja vâ.[4] ‖ 2 ‖

se se paro pâ*d*âiṃ phusejja vâ raejja vâ; no taṃ sâtie, no taṃ niyame. ‖ 3 ‖

s. s. p. p. telleṇa vâ gha*t*eṇa vâ vasâe vâ makkhejja vâ bhiliṃgejja [5] vâ; n. t. s., n. t. n. ‖ 4 ‖

s. s. p. p. loddheṇa [6] vâ kakkeṇa vâ cuṇṇeṇa vâ vaṇṇeṇa vâ ullolejja [7] vâ uvvalejja vâ; n. t. s., n. t. n. ‖ 5 ‖

s. s. p. p. sî*t*odagaviyaḍeṇa vâ usiṇodagaviyaḍeṇa vâ uccho-

234 lejja vâ padhoejja vâ; n. t. s., n. t. n. ‖ 6 ‖

s. s. p. p. anna*t*areṇa vilevaṇajâteṇa âlimpejja vâ vilimpejja vâ; n. t. s., n. t. n. ‖ 7 ‖

s. s. p. p. anna*t*areṇa dhûvaṇajâteṇa dhûvejja vâ padhûvejja vâ; n. t. s., n. t. n. ‖ 8 ‖

s. s. p. pâdâo khâṇuṃ [8] vâ kaṃṭagaṃ vâ nîharejja vâ visohejja vâ; n. t. s., n. t. n. ‖ 9 ‖

s. s. p. pâ*d*âo pûyaṃ vâ soṇiyaṃ vâ nîharejja vâ visohejja vâ; n. t. s., n. t. n. ‖ 10 ‖

235 se se paro kâyaṃ âmajjejja vâ pamajjejja vâ; no taṃ sâtie, no taṃ niyame (*all as in* §§ 2–10; *substitute* kâyaṃ *for* pâ*d*âiṃ). ‖ 11 ‖

se se paro kâyaṃsi vaṇaṃ âmajjejja vâ pamajjejja vâ, no taṃ sâtie, no taṃ niyame (*all as in* §§ 2–6; kâyaṃsi vaṇaṃ *for* pâ*d*âiṃ). ‖ 12 ‖

se se paro kâyaṃsi vaṇaṃ anna*t*areṇaṃ satthajâ*t*eṇaṃ acchiṃdejja vâ vicchiṃdejja vâ, se se paro anna*t*areṇaṃ satthajâ*t*eṇaṃ acchiṃdittâ vâ 2 pûyaṃ vâ soṇiyaṃ

236 vâ nîharejja vâ viso*h*ĕjja vâ, no taṃ sâtie, no taṃ niyame. ‖ 13 ‖

[1] AB saṃsetiyaṃ. [2] A evaṃ, B ttaṃ. [3] B has generally se siyâ or se si. [4] B adds abhiṃgijjejja vâ. [5] B vilaṃgejja vâ. [6] A loddeṇa. [7] B ulloḍejja. [8] B khâṇuyaṃ.

se se paro kâyaṃsi gaṃḍaṃ vâ aratiyaṃ vâ pulayaṃ vâ bhagaṃdalaṃ vâ âmajjejja vâ pamajjejja vâ; no taṃ sâtie, no taṃ niyame (*all as in* §§ 12, 13; *substitute* kâyaṃsi gaṃḍaṃ vâ, etc). ‖14‖

se se paro kâyâo seyaṃ vâ jallaṃ vâ nîharejja vâ visohejja 237
vâ; no taṃ sâtie, no taṃ niyame. ‖15‖

s. s. p. acchimalaṃ vâ kammamalaṃ vâ daṃtamalaṃ vâ nahamalaṃ vâ nîharejja vâ, etc. ‖16‖

s. s. p. dîhâiṃ vâhâiṃ, dîhâiṃ româiṃ, dîhâiṃ bhamuhâiṃ dîhâiṃ kakkharomâiṃ dîhâiṃ vatthiromâiṃ kappejja vâ saṃṭhavejja vâ; n. t. s., n. t. n. ‖17‖

s. s. p. sîsâo likkhaṃ vâ jûyaṃ vâ nîharejja vâ, etc. ‖18‖

s. s. p. aṃkaṃsi vâ paliyaṃkaṃsi vâ tuyaṭṭâvettâ[9] pâdâiṃ[10] âmajjejja vâ pamajjejja vâ; *evaṃ hetthimo gamo pâdâdi*[11] *bhaṇiyavvo.* ‖19‖

s. s. p. aṃkaṃsi vâ paliyaṃkaṃsi vâ tuyaṭṭâvettâ hâraṃ vâ addhahâraṃ vâ urattham vâ geveyaṃ vâ mauḍaṃ vâ pâlaṃbaṃ vâ suvaṇṇasuttaṃ vâ âbiṃdhejja[12] vâ piviṃdhejja[13] vâ; n. t. s., n. t. n. ‖20‖

s. s. p. ârâmaṃsi vâ ujjâṇaṃsi vâ nîharittâ vâ visohittâ[14] vâ pâyâiṃ âmajjejja vâ pamajjejja va; n. t. s., n. t. n. *evaṃ netavvo annamannakiriyâ vi.* ‖21‖

s. s. p. suddheṇaṃ vâ vaibaleṇaṃ teicchaṃ âuṭṭe, s. s. p. asuddheṇaṃ vaibaleṇaṃ teicchaṃ âuṭṭe, s. s. p. gilâṇassa sacittâiṃ[15] kaṃdâni vâ mûlâṇi vâ tayâṇi vâ hariyâṇi vâ khâṇĕttu vâ kaṭṭettu vâ kaṭṭâvettu[16] vâ teicchaṃ âuṭṭejjâ;[17] n. t. s., n. t. n. ‖22‖

kaṭṭuveyaṇâ kaṭṭuveyaṇâ pâṇabhûtajîvasattâ[16] veyaṇaṃ vedeṃti.

eyaṃ khalu tassa bhikkhussa vâ 2 sâmaggiyaṃ, etc. ‖23‖

terasamaṃ sattikkayaṃ samattaṃ.

[9] AC tuyaṭṭâvejjâ. [10] AC pâdâtiṃ. [11] A pâyâc, C pâyâdi. [12] B âviṃhejja. [13] A pâv°, C piṇ°, B viṇihejja. [14] A paribhettâ. [15] B sa vi tâiṃ. [16] A om. [17] B âuṭṭâvejjâ.

[1] AB saṃsetiyaṃ.

caudasamam ajjhayaṇaṃ.

239 se bhikkhû vâ 2 annamannakiriyaṃ ajjhatthiyaṃ saṃsesiyaṃ;[1] n. t. s., n. t. n. se annamanno pâe âmajjejja vâ pamajjejja vâ, n. t. s., n. t. n., *sesaṃ taṃ ceva.*

eyaṃ khalu tassa bhikkhussa vâ 2 sâmaggiyaṃ, etc. ‖ 1 ‖

caudasamaṃ sattikkayaṃ samattaṃ.

sattikkaio samatto.

biiyâ cûlâ.

[1] Á saṃseiyaṃ, B saṃsetiyaṃ.

TAIYÂ CÛLÂ.

PAṂCADASAMAM AJJHAYAṆAṂ.

BHÂVAṆÂ.

teṇaṃ kâleṇaṃ teṇaṃ samaeṇaṃ samaṇe bhagavaṃ Mahâvîre paṃcahatthuttare yâvi hotthâ: hatthuttarâhiṃ cue[1] caittâ gabbhaṃ vakkaṃte; hatthuttarâhiṃ gabbhâo[2] 242
gabbhaṃ sâharie; hatthuttarâhiṃ jâe; hatthuttarâhiṃ savvato[3] savvatâe[3] muṃḍe bhavittâ agârâo aṇagâriyaṃ pavvaie; hatthuttarâhiṃ kasiṇe paḍipuṇṇe avvâghâe nirâvaraṇe aṇaṃte aṇuttare kevalavaranâṇadaṃsaṇe samuppanne; sâ*t*iṇâ bhagavaṃ parinivvue. ||1||

samaṇe bhagavaṃ Mahâvîre imâe osappiṇîe susamasusamâe samâe vîtikkaṃtâe,[1] susamâe samâe vîtikkaṃtâe, susamadûsamâe[2] samâe vîtikkaṃtâe, dûsamasusamâe[3] samâe 243
bahuvîtikkaṃtâe pannattarîe vâsehiṃ mâsehi[4] ya[5] addhanavamasesehiṃ, je se gimhâṇaṃ cautthe mâse aṭṭhame pakkhe âsâḍhasuddhe, tassa ṇaṃ âsâḍhasuddhassa chaṭṭhîpakkheṇaṃ hatthuttarâhiṃ nakkhatteṇaṃ jogovagateṇaṃ[6] mahâvijayasiddhatthapupphuttaravarapuṃ*d*arîyadisâsovatthiyavaddhamâṇâo[7] mahâvimâṇâo vîsaṃ sâgarovamâiṃ âuyaṃ pâlaittâ âukkhaeṇaṃ bhavakkhaeṇaṃ ṭhi*t*ikkhaeṇaṃ cu*t*e caittâ iha khalu Jaṃbuddîve[8] dîve bhârahe vâse dâhiṇaddhabharahe dâhiṇamâhaṇaKuṃḍapurasaṃnivesaṃsi Usabhadattassa mâhaṇassa Koḍâlasagottassa Devâṇaṃdâe mâhaṇîe Jâlaṃdharâyaṇasagottâe[9] sîhabbhavabhû*t*eṇaṃ appâṇeṇaṃ kucchiṃsi vakkaṃte.[10] ||2||

samaṇe bhagavaṃ Mahâvîre tinnâṇovaga*t*e yâvi hotthâ:

1. [1] B cuto. [2] A gabbhâ. [3] A om.

2. [1] B vîti°, vîyi°, vii°, A vîtikaṃt°. [2] A om. dûsamâe. [3] B dus°. [4] A mâsehiṃ. [5] A om. [6] B jogomavâgateṇaṃ. [7] B sovatthiyâ. [8] A Jaṃbûdîve. [9] B Jâlaṃdharâyassagottâe. [10] A vakkaṃto.

caissâmi tti jâṇai, cuemi tti jâṇai, cayamâṇe na jâṇa*t*i. suhume ṇaṃ se kâle pannatte. ‖3‖

tao ṇaṃ samaṇe bhagavaṃ Mahâvîre aṇukaṃpaṃteṇaṃ deveṇaṃ jîyam eyaṃ ti kaṭṭu, je se vâsâṇaṃ tacce mâse
244 paṃcame pakkhe âsoyabahule, tassa ṇaṃ âsoyabahulassa terasîpakkheṇaṃ hatthuttarâhiṃ nakkhatteṇaṃ jogovagateṇaṃ bâsîtîhiṃ[1] râ*t*iṃdiehiṃ vî*t*ikkaṃtehiṃ[2] tesî*t*imassa râ*t*iṃdiyassa pariyâe vaṭṭamâṇe dâhiṇamâhaṇaKuṃḍapurasaṃnivesâo[3] uttarakhattiyaKuṃḍapurasaṃnivesaṃ Nâ*t*âṇaṃ khattiyâṇaṃ Siddhatthassa khattiyassa Tisalâe[4] khattiyâṇîe Vâsiṭṭhasagottâe[5] asubhâṇaṃ poggalâṇaṃ avahâraṃ karettâ subhâṇaṃ poggalâṇaṃ pakkhevaṃ karettâ kucchiṃsi[6] gabbhaṃ sâhara*t*i; je vi ya Tisalâe[4] khattiyâṇîe gabbhe, taṃ pi ya dâhiṇamâhaṇaKuṃḍapurasaṃnivesaṃsi[3] Usabhadattassa mâhaṇassa Koḍâlasagottassa Devâṇaṃdâe mâhaṇîe Jâlaṃdharâyaṇasagottâe[7] kucchiṃsi[6] gabbhaṃ sâhara*t*i. ‖4‖

samaṇe bhagavaṃ Mahâvîre tinnâṇovaga*t*e yâvi hotthâ: sâharijjissâmi tti jâṇa*t*i, sâhariemi tti jâṇai, sâharijjamâṇe vi[1] jâṇa*t*i samaṇâuso. ‖5‖

245 teṇaṃ kâleṇaṃ teṇaṃ samaeṇaṃ Tisalâe[1] khattiyâṇîe aha annayâ ka*d*âi[2] navaṇhaṃ mâsâṇaṃ bahupaḍipuṇṇâṇaṃ addhuṭṭhamâṇaṃ[3] raiṃdiyâṇaṃ vîtikkaṃtâṇaṃ,[4] je se gimhâṇaṃ paḍhame mâse docce pakkhe cettasuddhe, tassa cettasuddhassa[5] terasîpakkheṇaṃ hatthuttarâhiṃ nakkhatteṇaṃ jogovagateṇaṃ samaṇaṃ bhagavaṃ Mahâvîraṃ âroyâ âroyaṃ[6] pasû*t*â. ‖6‖

jaṃ ṇaṃ râtiṃ Tisalâ[1] khattiyâṇî samaṇaṃ bhagavaṃ Mahâvîraṃ âroyâ[2] âroyaṃ[2] pasûtâ, taṃ[3] ṇaṃ râ*t*iṃ[4] bhavaṇava*t*ivâṇamaṃtarajotisiyavimâṇavâsidevehi ya devîhi ya uvayaṃtehi ya uppayaṃtehi ya ege mahaṃ divve devujjo*t*e devasaṃnivâteṇaṃ devakahakkahe uppiṃjalabhû*t*e yâvi hotthâ. ‖7‖

jaṃ rayaṇiṃ ca ṇaṃ Tisalâ[1] khattiyâṇî[1] samaṇaṃ bhaga-

4. [1] B yogamuvagateṇaṃ bâsîhiṃ. [2] A vîtikaṃtehiṃ. [3] A Kuṃḍapuri. [4] A Tisilâe. [5] A °ssa°. [6] B kucchaṃsi. [7] B °ssa°.
5. [1] B adds na.
6. [1] A Tisilâe. [2] B kadâyî. [3] AB addha°. [4] A vîtikaṃtâṇaṃ. [5] A °suddha. [6] B âroggaṃ.
7. [1] A Tisilâ. [2] A aro°. [3] A te. [4] B râtî.
8. [1] A Tisilâ.

vaṃ Mahâvîraṃ âroyâ âroyaṃ pasû*t*â, taṃ rayaṇiṃ ca ṇaṃ bahave devâ ya devîo ya egaṃ mahaṃ amayavâsaṃ ca gaṃdhavâsaṃ ca cuṇṇavâsaṃ ca pupphavâsaṃ[2] ca[2] hiraṇṇavâsaṃ ca rayaṇavâsaṃ ca vâsaṃ vâsiṃsu. ||8||

jaṃ rayaṇiṃ ca ṇaṃ Tisalâ khattiyâṇî samaṇaṃ bhagavaṃ
Mahâvîraṃ âroyâ[1] âroyaṃ[1] pasû*t*â, taṃ ṇaṃ rayaṇiṃ bha- 246
vaṇava*t*ivâṇamaṃtarajotisiyavimâṇavâsiṇo devâ ya devîo ya
samaṇassa bhagavao Mahâvîrassa ko*t*ugabhû*t*ikammâiṃ[2]
tittha*g*arâbhiseyaṃ ca kariṃsu. ||9||

jato ṇaṃ pabhitiṃ bhagavaṃ Mahâvîre Tisalâe[1] khattiyâṇîe kucchiṃsi gabbhaṃ âhue,[2] tato ṇaṃ pabhiti[3] taṃ kulaṃ vipuleṇaṃ hiraṇṇeṇaṃ suvaṇṇeṇaṃ dhaṇeṇaṃ dhanneṇaṃ mâṇikkeṇaṃ mottieṇaṃ saṃkhasilapavâleṇaṃ atîva 2 parivaḍḍhai. ||10||

tato ṇaṃ samaṇassa bhagavao Mahâvîrassa ammâpiyaro
eyam aṭṭhaṃ jâṇittâ[1] nivattadasâhaṃsi vokkaṃtaṃsi sucibhû-
*t*aṃsi vipulaṃ asaṇapâṇakhâimasâimaṃ uvakkhaḍâveṃti,
vipulaṃ asaṇa 4 uvakkhaḍâvettâ mittanâ*t*isayaṇasaṃbaṃ-
dhivaggaṃ uvanimaṃteṃti, 2 ttâ bahave samaṇamâhaṇaki-
vaṇavaṇîmagabhivvuṃḍagapaṃḍaragâîṇa[2] vicchaḍḍeṃti[3]
viggoveṃti[3] visâṇeṃti, dâtâresu ṇaṃ dâyaṃ pajjâbhâeṃti,[3]
vicchaḍḍittâ viggovittâ visâṇittâ[4] dâyaresu ṇaṃ dâyaṃ 247
pajjâbhâěttâ mittanâisayaṇasaṃbaṃdhivaggaṃ bhuṃjâveṃti,[3]
2 ttâ mittanâisayaṇasaṃbaṃdhivaggeṇaṃ im' eyârûvaṃ
nâmadhejjaṃ kareṃti:[5] ||11||

jao[1] ṇaṃ pabhiiṃ ime kumâre Tisalâe[2] khattiyâṇîe kucchiṃsi gabbhe âhue,[3] ta*t*o ṇaṃ pabhiiṃ imaṃ kulaṃ[4] vipuleṇaṃ hiraṇṇeṇaṃ suvaṇṇeṇaṃ dhaṇeṇaṃ[4] dhanneṇaṃ[4] mâṇikkeṇaṃ mottieṇaṃ saṃkhasilappavâleṇaṃ atîva 2 parivaḍḍhai; to[5] hou kumâre Vaḍḍhamâṇe. ||12||

tato ṇaṃ samaṇe bhagavaṃ Mahâvîre paṃcadhâ*t*iparivuḍe, taṃ jahâ: khîradhâîe, majjaṇadhâîe maṃḍâvaṇadhâîe khellâvaṇadhâîe[1] aṃkadhâîe; aṃkâo aṃkaṃ sâharijjamâṇe ramme

8. [2] B om.
9. [1] A ar°, B gg. [2] B bhû*t*.
10. [1] A Tisilâe. [2] A âhûe. [3] B tappabhiti.
11. [1] B jâṇiyâ. [2] B âhiṃcchuṃdaga. [3] A °etî, B °ei. [4] B ss. [5] B kârâveṃti.
12. [1] B adds ya. [2] A Tisilâe. [3] AB âhûe. [4] B om. [5] C taṃ hou ṇaṃ.
13. [1] B kheḍa.

maṇikoṭṭimatale girikaṃdarasamallîṇe va[2] caṃpayapâyave ahâṇupuvvîe saṃvaḍḍhai. ‖ 13 ‖

tao ṇaṃ samaṇe bhagavaṃ Mahâvîre vinnâyapariṇayaviṇiyattabâlabhâve[1] aṇussuyâiṃ[2] orâlâiṃ mâṇussagâiṃ paṃcalakkhaṇâiṃ kâmabhogâiṃ saddapharisarasarûvagaṃdhâiṃ pariyâremâṇe evaṃ câvi viharati. ‖ 14 ‖

samaṇe bhagavaṃ Mahâvîre Kâsavagotte. tassa ṇaṃ ime tinni nâmadhejjâ evam âhijjaṃti: ammâpiusaṃtie Vaddhamâṇe, sahasammudie Samaṇe, bhîmabhayabheravaṃ orâlaṃ[1] acelayaṃ parîsahaṃ[1] sahai tti kaṭṭu devehiṃ se nâmaṃ kayaṃ Samaṇe Bhagavaṃ Mahâvîre. samaṇassa ṇaṃ bhagavao Mahâvîrassa pitâ Kâsavagotte ṇaṃ. tassa ṇaṃ tinni nâmadhejjâ evam âhijjaṃti, taṃ jahâ: Siddhatthe ti vâ, Sejjaṃse, ti vâ Jasaṃse ti vâ, samaṇassa bhagavao
248 Mahâvîrassa ammâ Vâsiṭṭhasagottâ. tîse ṇaṃ tinni nâmadhejjâ evaṃ âhijjaṃti; taṃ jahâ[2]: Tisalâ[3] ti vâ, Videhadinnâ ti vâ Piyakâriṇî ti vâ. samaṇassa bhagavao Mahâvîrassa pittijjae Supâse Kâsavagotte ṇaṃ. samaṇassa bhagavao Mahâvîrassa jeṭṭhe bhâyâ Naṃdivaddhaṇe Kâsavagotte ṇaṃ. samaṇassa bhagavao Mahâvîrassa jeṭṭhâ[4] bhaiṇî Sudaṃsaṇâ Kâsavagotteṇaṃ[5]. samaṇassa bhagavao Mahâvîrassa bhajjâ Jasoyâ Koḍinnagotteṇam[5]. samaṇassa bhagavao Mahâvîrassa dhûtâ Kâsavagotteṇaṃ, tîse ṇaṃ do nâmadhejjâ evam âhijjaṃti: Aṇojjâ ti vâ, Piyadaṃsaṇâ ti vâ. samaṇassa bhagavao Mahâvîrassa nattuî Kosiyagotteṇaṃ, tîse ṇaṃ do nâmadhejjâ evam âhijjaṃti, taṃ[7] jahâ[7]: Sesavatî ti[8] vâ, Jasavatî ti[8] vâ. ‖ 15 ‖

samaṇassa bhagavao Mahâvîrassa ammâpitaro Pâsâvaccijjâ samaṇovâsagâ yâvi hotthâ. te ṇaṃ bahûiṃ vâsâiṃ samaṇo-
249 vâsagapariyâgaṃ pâlaittâ chaṇhaṃ jîvanikâyâṇaṃ saṃrakkhaṇanimittaṃ[1] âloettâ niṃdittâ garahittâ[2] paḍikkamittâ ahârihaṃ uttaraguṇaṃ pâyacchittaṃ paḍivajjittâ kusasaṃthâraṃ duruhittâ bhattaṃ paccakkhâiṃti,[3] bhattaṃ paccakkhâittâ apacchimâe mâraṇaṃtiyâe sarîrasaṃlehaṇâe susi-

13. [2] B vi, A om; B samullîṇe.
14. [1] C pariṇaye, B om; A viṇivitta. [2] B adds appattâiṃ.
15. [1] B °e. [2] A om. [3] A Tisilâ. [4] B kaṇiṭṭhâ. [5] AB correct kâsavî. [6] AC Koḍinnâgotteṇaṃ, B gotteṇaṃ Koḍinnâ. [7] B °om. [8] A °itti.
16. [1] B sarakkh°. [2] B garihettâ. [3] B °aṃti.

yasarîrâ kâlamâse[4] kâlaṃ kiccâ taṃ sarîraṃ[5] vippajahittâ[6] abbhu*t*e kappe devattâe uvavannâ. tao ṇaṃ âukkhaeṇaṃ cutâ[7] ca*r*ittâ Mahâvidehe vâse carimeṇaṃ ûsâseṇaṃ[8] sijjhissaṃti bujjhissaṃti[9] muccissaṃti parinivvâissaṃti savvadukkhâṇaṃ aṃtaṃ karĕssaṃti. ||16||

teṇaṃ kâleṇaṃ teṇaṃ samaeṇaṃ samaṇe bhagavaṃ Mahâvîre nâ*t*e Nâ*t*aputte nâyakulanivvatte[1] videhe Videhadinne videhajacce videhasûmâle tîsaṃ vâsâiṃ videha tti kaṭṭu agâramajjhe[2] vasittâ ammâpi*t*ûhiṃ kâlaga*t*ehiṃ devalogam aṇuppattehiṃ samattapainne ceccâ hiraṇṇaṃ, ceccâ suvaṇṇaṃ, ceccâ balaṃ, ceccâ vâhaṇaṃ, ceccâ dhaṇadha-
nnakaṇa*g*arayaṇasaṃtasârasâvadejjaṃ vicchaḍḍĕttâ viggovittâ 250
vissâṇitta, dâ*t*âresu ṇaṃ dâyaṃ pajjâbhâittâ[3], saṃvaccharaṃ dalaittâ, je se hemaṃtâṇaṃ paḍhame mâse paḍhame pakkhe maggasirabahule, tassa ṇaṃ maggasirabahulassa dasamîpakkheṇaṃ hatthuttarâhiṃ nakkhatteṇaṃ jogovagateṇaṃ abhinikkhamaṇâbhippâe[4] yâvi hotthâ. ||17||

saṃvacchareṇa hohiti
abhinikkhamaṇaṃ tu Jiṇavariṃdâṇaṃ[1] |
to atthasaṃpa*d*âṇaṃ
pavattatî puvvasûrâo ||i||
egâ hiraṇṇakoḍî
aṭṭh' eva aṇûṇagâ sayasahassâ |
sûrodayamâdîyaṃ
dijjai jâ pâyarâso[1] tti ||ii|| 251
tinn' eva ya koḍisayâ
aṭṭhâsîtiṃ ca hoṃti koḍîo |
asiyaṃ ca sa*t*asahassâ
etaṃ saṃvacchare dinnaṃ. ||iii||
Vesamaṇakuṃḍaladharâ
devâ logaṃtiyâ mahiḍḍhîyâ |
bohiṃti ya titthayaraṃ
pannarasasu kammabhûmîsu. ||iv||
baṃbhammi ya kappammi ya

16. [4] Badds ṇaṃ. [5] B sarîriyaṃ. [6] A vipayahittâ. [7] MSS. cute. [8] B uss°. [9] A om.
17. [1] B °viṇivatte, C ṇivatte. [2] A âgâra. [3] B dâyâresu ṇaṃ dâettâ bhâittâ. [4] BC always abhiṇikkh.
v. 1. [1] B °variṃdassa.
v. 2. [1] B pâîrâso.

boddhavvâ Kaṇharâiṇo majjhe |
. loyaṃtiyâ vimâṇâ
aṭṭhasuvatthâ asaṃkhejjâ. || v ||
ete devanikâyâ
bhagavaṃ bohiṃti Jiṇavaraṃ Vîraṃ |
savvajagajjîvahiyaṃ
arahaṃ titthaṃ pavvattehiṃ || vi ||

ta*t*o ṇaṃ samaṇassa bhagavao Mahâvîrassa abhinikkha-
maṇâbhippâyaṃ jâṇittâ bhavaṇavaivâṇamaṃtarajoisiyavi-
mâṇavâsiṇo devâ ya devîo ya saehiṃ 2 rûvehiṃ saehiṃ 2
nevatthehiṃ saehiṃ 2 ciṃdhehiṃ savviḍḍhîe savvajutîe [1]
savvabalasamudaeṇaṃ sayâiṃ 2 jâṇavimâṇâiṃ duruhaṃti,
sayâiṃ 2 jâṇavimâṇâiṃ duruhittâ ahâbâdarâiṃ pŏggalâiṃ
paḍisâḍeṃti,[2] ahâbâdarâiṃ pŏggalâiṃ paḍisâḍittâ [2] ahâsu-
252 humâiṃ poggalâiṃ pariyâiyaṃti, ahâsuhumâiṃ poggalâiṃ
pariyâittâ uḍḍhaṃ uppayaṃti, uḍḍhaṃ uppaittâ tâe ukkiṭṭhâe
sigghâe cavalâe turiyâe divvâe devaga*t*îe ahe ṇaṃ ova*t*a-
mâṇâ 2 tirie ṇaṃ asaṃkhejjâiṃ dîvasamuddâiṃ vîtikkama-
mâṇâ, jeṇ' eva Jaṃbuddîve,[3] teṇ' eva uvâgacchaṃti, ten'
eva uvâgacchittâ, jeṇ' eva uttarakhattiyaKuṃḍapura-
saṃnivese, ten' eva uvâgacchaṃti, ten' eva uvâgacchittâ
jeṇ' eva uttarakhattiyaKuṃḍapurasaṃnivesassa uttarapu-
ratthime disîbhâe, teṇ' eva jhatti vegeṇa uvaṭṭhiyâ. || 18 ||
tao ṇaṃ Sakke deviṃde devarâyâ saṇiyaṃ saṇiyaṃ
jâṇavimâṇaṃ paṭṭhavei 2 ttâ,[4] saṇiyaṃ 2 jâṇavimâṇâo
paccotarati,[5] 2 ttâ [4] egaṃtam avakkamati [6] 2 ttâ [4] maha*t*â
veuvvieṇaṃ samugghâ*t*eṇaṃ samohaṇati,[6] 2 ttâ [4] egaṃ mahaṃ
nâṇâmaṇikaṇa*g*arayaṇabhatticittaṃ subhaṃ cârukaṃtarûvaṃ[7]
253 devachaṃdayaṃ viuvvati,[6] tassa ṇaṃ devachaṃdayassa bahu-
majjhadesabhâge egaṃ mahaṃ sapâyapîḍhaṃ sîhâsaṇaṃ
nâṇâmaṇikaṇa*g*arayaṇabhatticittaṃ subhaṃ cârukaṃtarûvaṃ
viuvvati; [6] || 19 || jen' eva samaṇe bhagavaṃ Mahavîre, teṇ'
eva uvâgacchati,[1] teṇ' eva uvâgacchittâ samaṇaṃ bhagavaṃ
Mahâvîraṃ tikkhutto â*d*âhiṇapa*d*âhiṇaṃ kareti, 2 ttâ samaṇaṃ bhagavaṃ Mahâvîraṃ vaṃdati [2] namaṃsati,[2] vaṃdittâ

18, 19. [1] B om. [2] B pari°. [3] A Jaṃbûdîve. [4] MSS. full phrase. [5] AC paccottar.
[6] A °aṃti. [7] A cârukaṃtaṃ cârurûvaṃ.
20. [1] A °ṃti. [2] AB° aṃti.

namaṃsittâ samaṇaṃ bhagavaṃ Mahâvîraṃ gahâya, jeṇ' eva
devachaṃdae, teṇ' eva uvâgacchati,[1] uvâgacchittâ saṇiyaṃ 2
puratthâbhimuhe sîhâsaṇe nisîyâveti,[1] 2 ttâ sayapâgasahassa-
pâgehiṃ tellehiṃ abbhaṃgeti,[1] 2 ttâ gaṃdhakasâehiṃ ullo-
leti,[1] 2 ttâ suddhodaeṇaṃ majjâveti,[1] 2 ttâ jassa jaṃtapalaṃ [3]
sayasahasseṇaṃ ti paḍolabhittaeṇa pâsâhieṇa [4] sîtaeṇa [5] gosî-'
sarattacaṃdaṇeṇaṃ aṇulimpati [6] îsinîsâsavojjhaṃ varanagara-
paṭṭaṇuggataṃ kusalanarapasaṃsitaṃ[7] assalâlâpelavaṃ cheyâ-
yâriyakaṇagakhaciyaṃtakammaṃ [8] haṃsalâkkhaṇaṃ patta-
juyalaṃ [9] niyaṃsâveti,[1] 2 ttâ hâraṃ addhahâraṃ uratthaṃ
egâvaliṃ pâlaṃbasuttapaṭṭamauḍarayaṇamâlâi âviṃdhâveti,[1]
2 ttâ gaṃthimaveḍhimapûrimasaṃghâtimeṇaṃ malleṇaṃ
kapparukkham iva [10] samâlaṃketi,[1] ||20|| 2 ttâ doccaṃ pi
mahatâ [1] veuvviyasumagghâ*t*eṇaṃ samohaṇa*t*i, egaṃ mahaṃ
caṃdappabhaṃ sibiyaṃ sahassavâhiṇiṃ viuvvai,[2] taṃ jahâ:
îhamiyausabhaturaganaramakaravihagavâṇarakuṃjararurusa- 254
rabhacamarasaddûlasîhavaṇalayavicitta-vijjâharamihuṇajatta-
jogajuttaṃ [3] accîsahassamâliṇîyaṃ [4] suṇirûvi*t*amisimisiṃtarû-
vagasahassakali*t*aṃ îsibhisamîṇaṃ bibbhisamîṇaṃ[5] cakkhullo-
yaṇalĕssaṃ muttâhaḍamuttajâlaṃtaropi*t*aṃ tavaṇîyapavara-
laṃbûsae [6] laṃbaṃtasuttadâmaṃ hâraddhahârabhûsaṇasamo-
ṇa*t*aṃ a*h*iyapecchaṇijjaṃ paumalayabhatticittaṃ [7] nâṇâlaya-
bhattiviraiyaṃ subhaṃ cârukaṃtarûvaṃ[8] nâṇâmaṇipaṃca- 255
vaṇṇaghaṃṭâpaḍâyaparimaṃḍi*t*aggasiharaṃ subhaṃ câru-
kaṃtarûvaṃ pâsâdîyaṃ darisaṇîyaṃ surûvaṃ. ||21||

sîyâ uvaṇîyâ Jiṇa—
varassa jaramaraṇavippamukkassa |
osannamalladâmâ [1]
jalathalayaṃ-divvakusumehiṃ ||vii||
si*b*iyâe majjhayâre
divvaṃ vararayaṇarûvacevatiyaṃ [1] |

20. [3] C ya mullaṃ. [4] A sâhieṇa. [5] B om. [6] B aṇuleppai. [7] B pariammiyaṃ, A corrects parinimmitaṃ. [8] B gaṇagagabhiya°. [9] B bahûjuyalaṃ. [10] A °ru-kkhaṃ va.

21. [1] A mahiyâ. [2] A °eṃti. [3] B om. nara, has jugala for mihuṇa, and cittaṃ for puttaṃ, A sâhala for saddûla. [4] B mâṇiṇîyaṃ. [5] B om. [6] B lattasae. [7] B bhitti, and adds asogalayâbhitticittaṃ kaṃdalayabhitticittaṃ. [8] A subha-kaṃtacâru°.

v. 7. [1] C uvasaṃta.
v. 8. [1] B ciṃcatiyaṃ.

sîhâsaṇaṃ mahariham
sapâdapîḍhaṃ Jiṇavarassa ‖ viii ‖
âlaiyamâlamauḍe[1]
bhâsuraboṃdî varâbharaṇadhârî |
khomayavatthaniyattho
jassa ya mollaṃ sayasahassaṃ ‖ ix ‖
chaṭṭheṇa u bhatteṇaṃ
ajjhavasâṇeṇa sohaṇeṇa[1] Jiṇo |
lesâhi visujjhaṃto
âruhaî uttamaṃ sîyaṃ ‖ x ‖
sîhâsaṇe niviṭṭho
Sakk-Îsâṇâ ya dohi pâsehiṃ |
vîyaṃti câmarâhiṃ
maṇirayaṇavicittadaṃḍâhiṃ ‖ xi ‖
puvviṃ ukkhittâ mâṇusehi
sâhaṭṭharomapulaehiṃ[1] |
pacchâ vahaṃti devâ
suraasurâ garulanâgiṃdâ[2] ‖ xii ‖
purao surâ vahaṃtî
asurâ puṇa dâhiṇammi pâsammi |
avare vahaṃti garulâ
nâgâ puṇa uttare pâse ‖ xiii ‖
vaṇasaṃḍaṃ va kusumiyaṃ
256 paumasaro vâ ja*h*â sarayakâle |
sohai[1] kusumabhareṇaṃ
iya gayaṇa*t*alaṃ[2] suragaṇehiṃ ‖ xiv ‖
siddhatthavaṇaṃ va jahâ
kaṇiyâravaṇaṃ va caṃpagavaṇaṃ vâ |
soha*t*i kusumabbhareṇaṃ
iya gayaṇa*t*alaṃ suragaṇehiṃ ‖ xv ‖
varapaḍahabherijhallari-
saṃkhasa*t*asahassiehi tûrehiṃ |
ga*g*aṇa*t*ale dharaṇi*t*ale
turiyaniṇâ*d*o paramarammo ‖ xvi ‖

v. 9. [1] B mauḍo.
v. 10. [1] B suṃdareṇa.
v. 12. [1] B romakûvehiṃ. [2] B garuḍa.
v. 14. [1] B sobhai. [2] B tale.

tatavita*ṭa*ṃ ghaṇujhusiraṃ [1]
â*ṭ*ojjaṃ cauvihaṃ bahuvihîyaṃ |
vâĕṃti tattha devâ
bahuhiṃ [2] âṇattagasa*ṭ*ehiṃ ||xvii||

teṇaṃ kâleṇaṃ teṇaṃ samaeṇaṃ, je se hemaṃtâṇaṃ, paḍhame mâse, paḍhame pakkhe maggasirabahule, tassa ṇaṃ maggasirabahulassa dasamîpakkheṇaṃ [1] suddhaeṇaṃ [2] divaseṇaṃ vijaeṇaṃ [3] muhutteṇaṃ hatthuttarâhiṃ [4] nakkhatteṇaṃ jogovagateṇaṃ pâîṇagâmiṇîe [5] châyâe viyattâe [6] porisîe chaṭṭheṇaṃ bhatteṇaṃ apâṇaeṇaṃ egaṃ sâḍagaṃ âyâe caṃdappahâe si*b*iyâe sahassavâhiṇîe [7] sadevamaṇuyâsurâe parisâe samannijjamâṇe uttarakhattiyaKuṃḍapurasaṃnivesassa [8] majjheṇaṃ niggaccha*t*i, 2 ttâ jeṇ' eva nâyasaṃḍe ujjâṇe, teṇ' eva uvâgacchati, 2 ttâ îsira*ṭ*aṇappamâṇaṃ 257
acchoppeṇaṃ bhûmîbhâ*g*eṇaṃ saṇiyaṃ 2 caṃdappabhaṃ si*b*iyaṃ sahassavâhiṇiṃ ṭhave*t*i, 2 *jâva* ṭhavettâ saṇiyaṃ 2 caṃdappabhâo siviyâo [9] sahassavâhiṇîo pacco*t*ara*t*i, 2 ttâ saṇiyaṃ 2 puratthâbhimuhe sîhâsaṇe nisî*d*a*t*i saṇiyaṃ [10] âbharaṇâlaṃkâraṃ omuyai. ||22||

Vesamaṇe deve jaṃtuvâyapaḍie [1] samaṇassa bhagavao Mahâvîrassa haṃsalakkhaṇeṇaṃ paḍeṇaṃ âbharaṇâlaṃkâraṃ paḍicchai. [2] tao ṇaṃ se Mahâvîre dâhiṇeṇa dâhiṇaṃ vâmeṇa vâmaṃ paṃcamuṭṭhiyaṃ loyaṃ karei. tao ṇaṃ Sakke deviṃde devarâyâ samaṇassa bhagavao Mahâvîrassa jaṃtuvâyapaḍie vairâmaeṇaṃ thâleṇaṃ kesâiṃ paḍicchai; aṇujâṇesi bhaṃte ti kaṭṭu khîroyasâgaraṃ sâharai. tao ṇaṃ samaṇe bhagavaṃ Mahâvîre dâhiṇeṇa dâhiṇaṃ vâmeṇa vâmaṃ paṃcamuṭṭhiyaṃ loyaṃ karettâ, siddhâṇaṃ namokkâraṃ karei, karettâ savvaṃ akaraṇijjaṃ pâvaṃ ti kaṭṭu sâmâiyaṃ carittaṃ paḍivajjai, sâmâiyaṃ carittaṃ paḍivajjittâ 258
devaparisaṃ ca maṇuyaparisaṃ ca ṭhave*t*i. ||22||

divvo maṇussaghoso
turiyaniṇâo ya Sakkavayaṇeṇaṃ |

v. 16. [1] AC susiraṃ. [2] A bahuyaṃ, B bahûhiṃ.
22. [1] A dasami. [2] B suvvateṇaṃ. [3] B vijaya. [4] A hatthuttara. [5] A pâdîṇa°. [6] A vîtâe. [7] B °ṇîyâe. [8] A °Kuṃḍapuri°. [9] B sîyâo. [10] B om.
23. [1] B tato naṃ Sakke deviṃde devarâyâ. [2] B om. paḍicchai down to sâharai.

khippâm eva nilukko
jâhe[1] paḍivajjai carittaṃ ‖ xviii ‖
paḍivajjittu carittaṃ
ahonisaṃ savvapâṇabhûtahi*t*aṃ |
sâhaṭṭhalomapulayâ
payayâ[1] devâ nisâmeṃti ‖ xix ‖

ta*t*o ṇaṃ samaṇassa bhagavao Mahâvîrassa sâmâiyaṃ khâovasamiyaṃ carittaṃ paḍivannassa maṇapajjavanâṇe nâmaṃ nâṇe samuppanne. aḍḍhâijjehiṃ dîvehiṃ dohi ya samuddehiṃ sannîṇaṃ paṃcĕṃdiyâṇaṃ pajjattâṇaṃ viyattamâṇasâṇaṃ maṇogayâiṃ bhâvâiṃ jâṇei. ta*t*o ṇaṃ samaṇe bhagavaṃ Mahâvîre pavvaite samâṇe mittanâtîsayaṇasaṃbaṃdhivaggaṃ paḍivisajjeti paḍivisajjittâ[1] imaṃ e*t*ârûvaṃ abhiggahaṃ abhigĕṇhai: bârasa vâsâiṃ vosaṭṭhakâe cattadehe je kevi[2] uvasaggâ samuppajjaṃti,[3] taṃ jahâ: divvâ vâ mâṇusâ vâ tericchiyâ[4] vâ, te savve uvasagge samuppanne
259 samâṇe[5] sammaṃ sahissâmi khamissâmi[5] ahiyâissâmi. ‖ 23 ‖

tao ṇaṃ samaṇe bhagavaṃ Mahâvîre im' eyârûvaṃ abhiggahaṃ abhigiṇhittâ[1] vosaṭṭhakâe cattadehe divase muhuttasese Kummâragâmaṃ samaṇupatte.[2] ta*t*o ṇaṃ samaṇe bhagavaṃ Mahâvîre vosaṭṭhakâe cattadehe aṇuttareṇaṃ âlaeṇaṃ aṇuttareṇaṃ vihâreṇaṃ *evaṃ* saṃjameṇaṃ paggaheṇaṃ taveṇaṃ baṃbhaceravâseṇaṃ khaṃtîe mottîe samitîe tuṭṭhîe guttîe ṭhâṇeṇaṃ kammeṇaṃ sucari*t*aphalanĕvvâṇamottimaggeṇaṃ appâṇeṇaṃ bhâvemâṇe viharai. evaṃ vâ[3] viharamâṇassa, je kei uvasaggâ samuppajjiṃsu:[4] divvâ vâ mâṇusâ vâ tericchiyâ[5] vâ, te savve uvasagge samuppanne samâṇe aṇâile avvahite addîṇamâṇase tivihamaṇavayaṇakâyagutte sammaṃ saha*t*i khama*t*i tilikkha*t*i ahiyase*t*i. ‖ 24 ‖

to[1] ṇaṃ samaṇassa bhagavao Mahâvîrassa eteṇaṃ vihâreṇaṃ viharamâṇassa bârasa vâsâ vitikkaṃtâ,[2] terasamassa ya

v. 18. [1] B jâdhi.
v. 19. [1] B savvo.
23. [1] A om. all from pavvaite. [2] B keti. [3] A samuppajjiṃsu. [4] B tiricchâ. [5] A om.
24. [1] B abhiginhei 2 ttâ. [2] B gâmamaṇupatte. [3] B adds te. [4] B °aiṃ. [5] B tiricchiyâ.
25. [1] BC tâ. [2] B vîi°.

vâsassa pariyâe vaṭṭamâṇassa, je se gimhâṇaṃ docce mâse cautthe pakkhe vesâhasuddhe, tassa ṇaṃ vaisâhasuddhassa 260
dasamîpakkheṇaṃ suvvateṇaṃ divaseṇaṃ vijaeṇaṃ muhutteṇaṃ hatthuttarâhiṃ nakkhatteṇaṃ jogovaga*t*eṇaṃ pâîṇagâmiṇîe châyâe viyattâe[3] porisîe Jaṃbhiyagâmassa nagarassa bahiyâ nadîe Ujjuvâliyâe uttare kûle, Sâmâgassa gâhâva*t*issa kaṭṭhakaraṇaṃsi[4] viyâvattassa ceiyassa uttarapuratthime disîbhâe sâlarukkhassa adûrasâmaṃte ukkuḍuyassa godohiyâe âyâvaṇâe âyâvemâṇassa chaṭṭheṇaṃ bhatteṇaṃ apâṇaeṇaṃ uḍḍhaṃ jâṇu aho sirasâ[5] jhâṇakoṭṭhovaga*t*assa sukkajjhâṇaṃtariyâe vaṭṭamâṇassa nivvâṇe kasiṇe paḍipuṇṇe avvâhae nirâvaraṇe aṇaṃte aṇuttare kevalavaraṇâṇadaṃsaṇe samuppanne. ‖25‖

se bhagavaṃ arahâ jiṇe jâe[1] kevalî savvannû savvabhâvadarisî savvadevamaṇuyâsurassa loyassa pajjâe jâṇa*t*î, taṃ jahâ: âgatiṃ[2] gatiṃ[2] ṭhitiṃ[2] cavaṇaṃ uvavâyaṃ bhuttaṃ
pîyaṃ kaḍaṃ paḍisevi*t*aṃ âvîkammaṃ rahokammaṃ laviyaṃ 261
kahiyaṃ[3] maṇomâṇasiyaṃ savvaloe savvajîvâṇaṃ savvabhâvâiṃ jâṇamâṇe pâsamâṇe evaṃ viharai. ‖26‖

jan-naṃ divasaṃ samaṇassa bhagavo Mahârîvassa nevvâṇe[1] kasiṇe *jâva* samuppanne, taṇ-ṇaṃ[2] divasaṃ bhavaṇava*t*ivâṇamaṃtarajo*t*isiyavimâṇavâsidevehi ya devîhi ya ovayaṃtehi ya *jâva* uppiṃjalagabhû*t*e yâvi hotthâ. ‖27‖

ta*t*o ṇaṃ samaṇe bhagavaṃ Mahâvîre uppannaṇâṇadaṃsaṇadhare appâṇaṃ ca logaṃ ca abhisamĕkkha puvvaṃ[1] devâṇaṃ dhammam âikkhatî, ta*t*o pacchâ maṇussâṇaṃ. ‖28‖

ta*t*o ṇaṃ samaṇe bhagavaṃ Mahâvîre uppannaṇâṇadaṃsaṇadhare Goyamâ*d*îṇaṃ samaṇâṇaṃ niggaṃthâṇaṃ paṃca mahavvayâiṃ sabhâvaṇâiṃ chajjîvanikâyâiṃ âikkhati bhâsati parûve*t*i, taṃ jahâ: puḍhavikâe *jâva* tasakâe. ‖29‖

paḍhamaṃ bhaṃte mahavvayaṃ:

paccakkhâmi savvaṃ pâṇâivâyaṃ, se suhumaṃ vâ bâyaraṃ vâ tasaṃ vâ thâvaraṃ vâ, n'eva sayaṃ pâṇâ*t*ivâyaṃ karejjâ

[3] B vîittâe. [4] A adds uḍḍhaṃ jâṇu aho sirasâ jhâṇakoṭṭhovagae. [5] B adds dhammajjhâṇovagatassa.
26. [1] B jûṇae. [2] A °tîṃ, B °tî. [3] B kaṃvetaṃ.
27. [1] B nivvâghâe. [2] A taṃ ṇaṃ.
28. [1] B puvvâ ṇaṃ.

3, jâvajjîvâe tivihaṃ tiviheṇaṃ maṇasâ vayasâ kâyasâ tassa bhaṃte paḍikkamâmi niṃdâmi garahâmi appâṇaṃ vosirâmi.
262 tass' imâo paṃca bhâvaṇâo bhavaṃti.

tatth' imâ paḍhamâ bhâvaṇâ: iriyâsami*t*e se niggaṃthe, no aṇairiyâsami*t*e [1] tti. kevalî bûyâ: aṇairiyâsami*t*e [2] se niggaṃthe pâṇâiṃ 4 abhihaṇejja vâ pariyâvejja vâ uddavejja vâ: iriyâsami*t*e se niggaṃthe, no aṇairiyâsami*t*e [3] tti paḍhamâ bhâvaṇâ. ‖1‖

ahâ' varâ doccâ bhâvaṇâ: maṇaṃ parijâṇai se niggaṃthe; je ya maṇe [1] pâvae sâvajje sakirie aṇhayakare che*d*akare
263 bhe*d*akare adhikaraṇie pâ*d*osie pari*t*âvi*t*e pâṇâivâdite [2] bhûtovaghâtie, tahappagâraṃ maṇaṃ no pa*dh*ârejjâ; [3] maṇaṃ parijâṇati se niggaṃthe, je ya maṇe apâvae tti doccâ bhâvaṇâ. ‖2‖

ahâ' varâ taccâ bhâvaṇâ: vaiṃ parijâṇati se niggaṃthe *jâva* vaî pâviyâ sâvajjâ *jâva* bhûtovaghâ*t*iyâ, tahappagâraṃ vaiṃ no uccârejjâ [1]; vaiṃ parijâṇai se niggaṃthe *jâva* vaî [2] apâviya tti. taccâ bhavaṇâ. ‖3‖
264 ahâ 'varâ cautthâ bhâvaṇâ: âyâṇabhaṃḍanikkhevaṇâsami*t*e [1] se niggaṃthe, no aṇâyâṇabhaṃḍanikkhevaṇâsami*t*e. kevalî bûyâ: âyâṇabhaṃḍanikkhevaṇâasami*t*e se niggaṃthe pâṇâiṃ bhûyâiṃ jîvâiṃ sattâiṃ abhihaṇejja vâ *jâva* uddavejja vâ. tamhâ [2] âyâṇabhaṃḍanikkhevaṇâsami*t*e se niggaṃthe, no aṇâyâṇabhaṃḍanikkhavaṇâsami*t*e [3] tti cautthâ bhâvaṇâ. ‖4‖

ahâ 'varâ paṃcamâ bhâvaṇâ: âloiyapâṇabhoyaṇabhoî se niggaṃthe, no aṇâloiyapâṇabhoyaṇabhoî. kevalî bûyâ: aṇâloiyapâṇabhoyaṇabhoî se niggaṃthe pâṇâṇi [1] vâ bhûtâṇi vâ jîvâṇi vâ sattâṇi vâ abhihaṇejja vâ *jâva* uddavejja vâ. tamhâ âloiyapâṇabhoyaṇabhoî se niggaṃthe, no aṇâloiyapâṇabhoyaṇabhoi tti paṃcamâ bhâvaṇâ. ‖5‖

ettâvayâva [2] mahavvayaṃ sammaṃ kâeṇa phâsie pâlie tîrie kiṭṭie avaṭṭhite âṇâe ârâhie yâvi bhavati.

paḍhame bhaṃte mahavvae [3] pâṇâivâ*t*âo veramaṇaṃ. ‖I‖

I. 1. [1] A uṇa°, B airiyâ°. [2] B iriyaasamite. [3] AB iriyâsamite
2. [1] B om. je ya maṇe. [2] B pâṇâivâta. [3] B om. maṇaṃ no padhârejjâ.
3. [1] A saṃpahârejjâ. [2] A vaiṃ.
4. [1] B adds matta after bhaṃḍa. [2] A om. [3] A âyâṇa . . . asamie.
5. [1] A pàṇûti. the rest i. marg. by 2. hd. [2] B ettâvattâva. [3] B °yaṃ.

ahâ 'varaṃ doccaṃ mahavvayaṃ: paccakkhâmi savvaṃ
musâvâyaṃ[1] vaidosaṃ,[2] se kohâ vâ lohâ vâ bhayâ vâ hâsâ 265
vâ; n' eva sayaṃ musaṃ bhâsejjâ, n' ev' annehiṃ musaṃ
bhâsâvejjâ, annaṃ pi musaṃ bhâsaṃtaṃ na samaṇujâṇejjâ.
tivihaṃ tiviheṇaṃ maṇasâ vayasâ kâyasâ tassa bhaṃte
paḍikkamâmi *jâva* vosirâmi.

tass' imâo paṃca bhâvaṇâo bhavaṃti.

tatth' imâ paḍhamâ bhâvaṇâ: aṇuvîi bhâsî se niggaṃthe,
no aṇaṇuvîibhâsî.[1] kevalî bûyâ: aṇaṇuvîibhâsî[1] se
niggaṃthe samâvadejjâ[2] mosaṃ vayaṇâe. aṇuvîibhâsî[1] se
niggaṃthe, no aṇaṇuvîibhâsi[3] tti paḍhamâ bhâvaṇâ. ||1||

ahâ 'varâ doccâ bhâvaṇâ: kohaṃ parijâṇa*t*i se niggaṃthe, 266
no kohaṇâe[1] siyâ. kevalî bûyâ: kohappatte[2] kohî samâvadejjâ mosaṃ vayaṇâe. kohaṃ parijâṇati se niggaṃthe, na
ya kohaṇâe[3] siya[4] tti doccâ bhâvaṇâ. ||2||

a*h*â 'varâ taccâ bhâvaṇâ: lobhaṃ parijâṇa*t*i se niggaṃthe,
no ya lobhaṇâe siyâ. kevalî bûyâ: lobhapatte lobhî samâvadejjâ mosaṃ vayaṇâe. lobhaṃ parijâṇati se niggaṃthe, no
ya lobhaṇâe siya[4] tti taccâ bhâvaṇâ. ||3||

ahâ 'varâ cautthâ bhâvaṇâ: bhayaṃ parijâṇati se niggaṃthe,
no ya bhayabhîrue siyâ. kevalî bûyâ: bhayappatte[2] bhîrû
samâvadejjâ mosaṃ vayaṇâe. bhayaṃ parijâṇa*t*i se niggaṃthe,
no bhayabhîrue siyâ. cautthâ bhâvaṇâ. ||4||

ahâ 'varâ paṃcamâ bhâvaṇâ: hâsaṃ parijâṇa*t*i se
niggaṃthe, no ya[5] hâsaṇâe[6] siyâ. kevalî bûyâ: hâsa-
ppatte[2] hâsî samâvadejjâ mosaṃ vayaṇâe. hâsaṃ parijâṇa*t*i
se niggaṃthe, no ya[5] hâsaṇâe[7] siya tti paṃcamâ bhâvaṇâ. ||5||

ettâvatâva[8] mahavvae sammaṃ kâeṇa phâsie *jâva* âṇâe
ârâhite yâvi bhavati. 267

doccaṃ bhaṃte mahavvayaṃ.[9] ||II||

ahâ 'varaṃ taccaṃ mahavvayaṃ: paccakkhâmi savvaṃ
adinnâdâṇaṃ, se gâme vâ nagare vâ araṇṇe vâ, appaṃ vâ
bahuṃ vâ aṇuṃ vâ thûlaṃ vâ cittamaṃtaṃ vâ acittaṃ[1] vâ;

II. [1] A °vâya. [2] A vati.
1. [1] A aṇuvîyi, B aṇuvíyî. [2] B samâvajejjâ. [3] A °bhâse.
2-5. [1] AB kohaṇe. [2] B patte. [3] A °ṇae. [4] AB si. [5] A om. [6] B bhâsaṇâe. [7] B bhayahâsaṇâe. [8] B etâ°, A ettâvatâ; A adds i. marg. vîe. [9] B mahavvae.
III. [1] B cittamaṃtamacittaṃ.

n' eva sayaṃ adinnaṃ giṇhejjâ, n' ev' annehiṃ geṇhâvejjâ, annaṃ pi gĕṇhaṃtaṃ na samaṇujâṇejjâ; jâvajjîvâe *jâva* vosirâmi.

tass' imâo paṃca bhâvaṇâo.

tatth' imâ paḍhamâ bhâvaṇâ: aṇuvîi[2] mioggahajâî[3] se niggaṃthe, no aṇaṇuvîi[3] mioggahajâî[4] se niggaṃthe. kevalî bûyâ: aṇaṇuvîi[2] mioggahajâî[3] se niggaṃthe adinnaṃ giṇhejjâ. aṇuvîi[2] mittoggahajâî[4] se niggaṃthe, no aṇaṇuvîi[2] mioggahajâi[4] tti paḍhamâ bhâvaṇâ. ||1||

ahâ 'varâ doccâ bhâvaṇâ: aṇunnaviya pâṇabhoyaṇabhoî se niggaṃthe, no aṇaṇunnaviya pâṇabhoyaṇabhoî. kevalî bûyâ aṇaṇunnaviya pâṇabhoyaṇabhoî[5] se niggaṃthe adinnaṃ bhuṃjejjâ.[6] tamhâ aṇunnaviya pâṇabhoyaṇabhoî se
268 niggaṃthe, no aṇaṇunnaviya pâṇabhoyaṇabhoî ti doccâ bhâvaṇâ. ||2||

ahâ 'varâ taccâ bhâvaṇâ: niggaṃthe ṇaṃ ôggahaṃsi oggahiyaṃsi ettâvatâva[7] oggahaṇasîlae siyâ. kevalî bûyâ: niggaṃthe ṇaṃ oggahaṃsi oggahi*t*aṃsi ettâvatâva[7] aṇoggahaṇasîle adinnaṃ giṇhejjâ. ettâvatâva oggahaṇasîlae siya[8] tti taccâ bhâvaṇâ. ||3||

ahâ 'varâ cautthâ bhâvaṇâ: niggaṃthe ṇaṃ oggahaṃsi oggahiyaṃsi abhikkhaṇaṃ 2 oggahaṇasîlae siyâ. kevalî bûyâ: niggaṃthe ṇaṃ oggahaṃsi oggahi*t*aṃsi abhikkhaṇaṃ 2 aṇoggahaṇasîle adinnaṃ giṇhejjâ. niggaṃthe oggahaṃsi oggahiyaṃsi abhikkhaṇaṃ 2 oggahaṇasîlae ti cautthâ bhâvaṇâ. ||4||

ahâ 'varâ paṃcamâ bhâvaṇâ: aṇuvîi[2] mi*t*oggahajâ*t*î se niggaṃthe sâhammiesu, no aṇaṇuvîi[2] mi*t*oggahajâtî. kevalî bûyâ: aṇaṇuvîi mitoggahajâî sâhammiesu adinnaṃ ogiṇ-
269 hejjâ. se aṇuvîi mioggahajâî[4] se niggaṃthe sâhammiesu no aṇaṇuvîi mioghahaṃ. paṃcamâ bhâvaṇâ. ||5||

ettâvatâva mahavvae *savvaṃ jâva* âṇâe ârâdhite yâvi bhavati.

taccaṃ bhaṃte mahavvayaṃ. ||III||

ahâ 'varaṃ cautthaṃ mahavvayaṃ: paccakkhâmi[1] savvaṃ

III. [2] B aṇuvîyi. [3] AB jâtî; B mitto°. [4] B mittoggahajâtî. [5] B pâṇabhoyaṇaṃ. [6] A bhuṃje. [7] B etâ°. [8] ABC si.
IV. [1] B paccâikkhâmi.

mehuṇaṃ, se divvaṃ vâ mâṇusaṃ vâ tirikkhajoṇiyaṃ vâ, n' eva sayaṃ mehuṇaṃ gacche, *taṃ ceva adinnâdâṇavattavvayâ bhâṇiyavvâ jâva* vosirâmi.

tass' imâo paṃca bhâvaṇâo bhavaṃti.

tatth' imâ paḍhamâ bhâvaṇâ: no niggaṃthe abhikkhaṇaṃ 2 itthîṇaṃ kahaṃkahaittae siyâ. kevalî bûyâ: niggaṃthe ṇaṃ itthîṇaṃ kahaṃ kahamâṇe saṃti bhedâ saṃti vibhaṃgâ saṃti kevalipannattâo dhammâo bhaṃsejjâ. no niggaṃthe itthîṇaṃ kahaṃkahei siya tti[2] paḍhamâ bhâvaṇâ. ||1||

ahâ 'varâ doccâ bhâvaṇâ: no niggaṃthe itthîṇaṃ maṇoharâiṃ iṃdiyâiṃ âloettae nijjhâettae[3] siyâ. kevalî bûyâ: 270
nigghaṃthe ṇaṃ itthîṇaṃ maṇoharâiṃ iṃdiyâiṃ âloemâṇe nijjhâemâṇe saṃti bhe*d*â saṃti vibhaṃga *jâva* dhammâo bhaṃsejjâ. no niggaṃthe itthîṇaṃ maṇoharâiṃ iṃdiyâiṃ âloëttae nijjhâettae siya tti doccâ bhâvaṇâ. ||2||

ahâ 'varâ taccâ bhâvaṇâ: no niggaṃthe itthîṇaṃ maṇoharâiṃ puvvarayâiṃ puvvakîliyâiṃ sumarittae siyâ. kevalî bûyâ: niggaṃthe ṇaṃ itthîṇaṃ puvvarayâiṃ puvvakîliyâiṃ saramâṇe saṃti bhe*d*â *jâva* dhammâo bhaṃsejjâ. no niggaṃthe puvvarayâiṃ puvvakîliyâiṃ sarittae siya tti taccâ bhâvaṇâ. ||3||

ahâ 'varâ cautthâ bhâvaṇâ: nâ 'timattapâṇabhoyaṇabhoî[4] se niggaṃthe, no[5] pâṇîyarasabhoyaṇabhoî. kevalî bûyâ: atimattapâṇabhoyaṇabhoî se niggaṃthe pâṇîyarasabhoyaṇabhoî ya[6] tti bhedâ *jâva* bhaṃsejjâ. nâ 'timattapâṇabhoyaṇabhoî se niggaṃthe, no pâṇîyarasabhoyaṇabhoi tti cautthâ bhâvaṇâ. ||4||

ahâ 'varâ paṃcamâ bhâvaṇâ: no niggaṃthe itthîpasupaṃḍagasaṃsattâiṃ sayaṇâsaṇâiṃ sevittae siyâ. kevalî bûyâ: niggaṃthe ṇaṃ itthîpasupaṃḍagasaṃsattâiṃ sayaṇâ- 271
saṇâiṃ sevamâṇe saṃti bhedâ *jâva* bhaṃsejjâ. no niggaṃthe itthîpasupaṃḍagasaṃsattâiṃ sayaṇâsaṇâiṃ sevittae siya tti paṃcamâ bhâvaṇâ. ||5||

ettâvatâva mahavvae sammaṃ kâeṇa *jâva* ârâ*h*ite yâvi bhavati.

cautthaṃ bhaṃte mahavvayaṃ. ||IV||

IV. [2] B adds bemi. [3] A om. [4] B bhotî. [5] A na. [6] B om.

ahâ 'varaṃ paṃcamaṃ bhaṃte mahavvayaṃ: savvaṃ pariggahaṃ paccâikkhâmi, se appaṃ vâ bahuṃ vâ aṇuṃ vâ thûlaṃ vâ cittamantaṃ vâ acittaṃ[1] vâ, n' eva sayaṃ pariggahaṃ gĕṇhejjâ, n' ev' anneṇaṃ pariggahaṃ gĕṇhâvejjâ, n' ev' aṇṇaṃ pariggahaṃ geṇhaṃtaṃ samaṇujâṇejjâ *jâva* vosirâmi.

tass' imâo paṃca bhâvaṇâo.

tatth' imâ paḍhamâ bhavaṇâ: so*t*aeṇaṃ jîve maṇunnâmaṇunnâiṃ saddâiṃ suṇei, maṇunnâmaṇunnehiṃ saddehiṃ no sejjejjâ, no rajjejjâ, no gijjhejjâ, no mujjhejjâ, no ajjhovajjejjâ,[2] no viṇigghâyam âvajjejjâ.[2] kevalî bûyâ: niggaṃthe ṇaṃ maṇunnâmaṇunnehiṃ saddehiṃ sajjamâṇe *jâva* viṇigghâyam âvajjamâṇe saṃti bhe*d*â saṃti vibhaṃgâ[3] saṃti kevali-
272 pannattâo dhammâo bhaṃsejjâ.

na sakkâ na souṃ saddâ soyavisayam âga*t*â |
râgadosâ u je tattha taṃ bhikkhû parivajjae ||

sotao jîvo maṇunnâmaṇunnâiṃ saddâiṃ suṇeti. paḍhamâ bhâvaṇâ. ||1||

ahâ 'varâ doccâ bhâvaṇâ: cakkhûo jîvo maṇunnâmaṇunnâiṃ rûvâiṃ pâsa*t*i. maṇunnâmaṇunnehiṃ rûvehiṃ sajjamâṇe rajjamâṇe *jâva* saṃghâyam âvajjamâṇe saṃti bhe*d*â saṃti vibhaṃgâ[3] *jâva* bhaṃsejjâ.

na sakkâ rûvam adaṭṭhuṃ cakkhuvisayam âga*t*aṃ |
râgadosâ u je tattha taṃ bhikkhû parivajjae ||

cakkhûo jîvo maṇunnâmaṇunnâiṃ rûvâiṃ pâsa*t*i tti[1] doccâ bhâvaṇâ. ||2||

ahâ 'varâ taccâ bhâvaṇâ: ghâṇao jîvo maṇunnâmaṇunnâiṃ gaṃdhâiṃ agghâyai. maṇunnâmaṇunnehiṃ gaṃdhehiṃ no sajjejjâ[4] *jâva* viṇigghâyam âvajjejjâ. kevalî bûyâ: maṇunnâmaṇunnehiṃ gaṃdhehiṃ sajjamâṇe *jâva* viṇigghâyam âvajjamâṇe saṃti bhedâ saṃti vibhaṃgâ *jâva* bhaṃsejjâ.

273 na sakkâ[5] gaṃdham agghâum nâsâvisayam âgayaṃ |
râgadosâ u je tattha te bhikkhû parivajjae ||

ghâṇao jîvo maṇunnâmaṇunnâiṃ gaṃdhâiṃ agghâyati tti taccâ bhâvaṇâ. ||3||

V. [1] B om. [2] A °vadejjâ. [3] A vi*h*aṃgâ. [4] A harejjâ. [5] B adds ṇaṃ.

ahâ 'varâ cautthâ bhâvaṇâ: jibbhâo[6] jîvo maṇunnâmaṇunnâiṃ rasâiṃ assâdeti. maṇunnâmaṇunnehiṃ rasehiṃ no sajjejja, no rajjejjâ *jâva* no viṇigghâ*t*am âvajjejjâ. kevalî bûyâ: niggaṃthe ṇaṃ maṇunnâmaṇunnehiṃ rasehiṃ sajjamâṇe *jâva* viṇigghâyam âvajjamâṇe saṃti bhedâ *jâva* bhaṃsejjâ.

na sakkâ rasam aṇâsâtuṃ[7] jîhâvisayam âgataṃ |
râgadosâ[8] u je tatttha te[9] bhikkhû parivajjae ||

jîhâo jîvo maṇunnâmaṇunnâiṃ rasâiṃ assâdeti cautthâ bhâvaṇâ. || 4 ||

ahâ 'varâ paṃcamâ bhâvaṇâ: phâsao jîvo[10] maṇunnâmaṇunnâiṃ phâsâiṃ paḍisaṃvedetî; maṇunnâmaṇunnehiṃ phâsehiṃ no sajjejja, no rajjejjâ, no gijjhejjâ, no mujjhejjâ, no ajjhovajjejjâ, no viṇigghâ*t*am âvajjejjâ. kevalî bûyâ: niggaṃthe ṇaṃ maṇunnâmaṇunnehiṃ phâsehiṃ sajjamâṇe *jâva* viṇigghâ*t*aṃ âvajjamâṇe saṃti bhedâ saṃti vibhaṃgâ 274
saṃti kevalipannattâo dhammâo bhaṃsejjâ.

na[11] sakkâ na saṃveditum phâsaṃ visayam âgayaṃ |
râgâdosâ[12] u je tattha te[13] bhikkhû parivajjae ||

phâsao jîvo maṇunnâmaṇunnâiṃ phâsâiṃ paḍisaṃvedeti.[14] paṃcamâ bhâvaṇâ. || 5 ||

ettâvatâva mahavvae sammaṃ kâeṇaṃ phasi*t*e pâlie tîrie kiṭṭie[15] âṇâe ârâ*dh*i*t*e yâvi bhavati.

paṃcamaṃ bhaṃte mahavvayaṃ. || V ||

icc etehiṃ mahavvaehiṃ paṇuvîsâhi ya[16] bhâvaṇâhiṃ sampanne aṇagâre ahâsuyaṃ ahâkappaṃ ahâmaggaṃ sammaṃ kâeṇa phâsittâ pâlittâ tîrittâ kiṭṭittâ âṇâe ârâhiyâ vi bhavati.

bhâvaṇâ samattâ.

paṃcadasamam ajjhayaṇaṃ.

taiyâ cûlâ.

V. [6] B jîmûto, C jîhâo. [7] B âeteorasaṃ. [8] A °se, B °so. [9] A se, B taṃ. [10] ABC om. [11] A no. [12] B °so. [13] B taṃ. [14] B veyayitti. [15] B adds avatthite. [16] A sâihiṃ.

CAUTTHÂ CÛLA.

VIMUTTÎ.

aṇiccam âvâsam uveṃti jaṃtuṇo
paloyae sŏccam idaṃ aṇuttaraṃ |
viosire vinnu agârabaṃdhaṇaṃ
abhîru ârambhapariggahaṃ cae[1] ||1||
tahâgayaṃ bhikkhum aṇaṃtasaṃjayaṃ
aṇelisaṃ vinnu caraṃtam esaṇaṃ |
tudaṃti vâyâhi[2] abhiddavaṃ narâ
sarehi[2] saṃgâmagayaṃ[3] va kuṃjaraṃ ||2||
tahappagârehi[2] jaṇehi[2] hîlie
276 sasaddaphâsâ pharusâ udîri*t*â |
titikkhae nâṇi aduṭṭhacetasâ
giri vva vâteṇa na saṃpavevae[4] ||3||
uvehamâṇe kusalehi[2] saṃvase
akaṃtadukkhî[5] tasathâvarâduhî |
alûsae savvasahe mahâmuṇî
tahâ hi se sussamaṇe samâhi*t*e ||4||
vidû nate dhammapayaṃ aṇuttaraṃ
viṇîyataṇhassa muṇissa jhâyao[6] |
samâhiyass' aggisihâ va teyasâ
tavo ya pannâ ya jaso ya vaḍḍhatî ||5||
diso disaṃ[7] 'ṇaṃtajiṇeṇa nâtiṇâ
mahavvayâ khemapadâ pave*dit*â |
mahâgurû nissayarâ udîritâ
278 tamaṃ va tejo tidisaṃ pagâsa*g*â ||6||
sitehi[8] bhikkhû asito parivvae
asajjam itthîsu caejja pûyaṇaṃ |
aṇissio[6] logam iṇaṃ tahâ paraṃ

[1] B caye. [2] AB ṃ. [3] B °vayaṃ. [4] B °veyae. [5] B aṃk°, C akkaṃtadukkhaṃ. [6] B °e. [7] A disiṃ. [8] B ṃ.

na nijjatî [6] kâmaguṇehi [2] paṇḍi*t*e ‖7‖
tahâ vimukkassa parinnacâriṇo
dhi*t*îmato dukkhakhamassa bhikkhuṇo |
visujjha*t*î jaṃsi malaṃ pure kaḍaṃ
samîriyaṃ ruppamalaṃ va jo*t*iṇâ ‖8‖
se hu pparinnâsamayaṃmi [9] vaṭṭa*t*î
nirâsase uvarayamehuṇe care |
bhujaṃgame juṇṇatayaṃ jahâ jahe [10]
vimuccatî [11] se duhasejja mâhaṇe ‖9‖
jaṃ âhu ohaṃ salilaṃ apâragaṃ
mahâsamuddaṃ va bhuyâhi duttaraṃ | 279
a*h*' eva [12] ṇaṃ parijâṇâhi paṃḍie [13]
se hu muṇî aṃtakaḍe tti vuccatî ‖10‖
jahâ hi baddhaṃ iha mâṇavehi ya [14]
jahâ ya tesiṃ tu [15] vimokkha âhite |
ahâ tahâ baṃdhavimokkha je vi*d*û
se hu muṇî aṃtakaḍe tti vucca*t*i ‖11‖
imaṃmi [16] loe parato [17] ya ḍosu vi
na vijja*t*î baṃdhaṇăṃ jassa [18] kiṃci vi |
se hu nirâlaṃbaṇe appatiṭṭhite
kalaṃkalîbhâvapahaṃ vimuccai ‖12‖

tti bemi.

vimuttî samattâ.

solasamam ajjhayaṇaṃ.

cautthâ cûlâ.

[9] B pari°. [10] B vae. [11] B visujjhatî. [12] B eya. [13] The metre will be correct if we read ah' evam eṇaṃ parijâṇa paṃḍie. [14] AC °hiṃ om. ya, B yâ. [15] B bhu. [16] B ime ya. [17] B paraye. [18] B tassa.

Lightning Source UK Ltd.
Milton Keynes UK
UKHW041025040822
406842UK00002B/327

9 783348 014687